Stories about Stories

Stories about Stories

FANTASY AND THE REMAKING OF MYTH

Brian Attebery

OXFORD
UNIVERSITY PRESS

OXFORD

UNIVERSITY PRESS

Oxford University Press is a department of the University of Oxford.
It furthers the University's objective of excellence in research, scholarship,
and education by publishing worldwide.

Oxford   New York
Auckland   Cape Town   Dar es Salaam   Hong Kong   Karachi
Kuala Lumpur   Madrid   Melbourne   Mexico City   Nairobi
New Delhi   Shanghai   Taipei   Toronto

With offices in
Argentina   Austria   Brazil   Chile   Czech Republic   France   Greece
Guatemala   Hungary   Italy   Japan   Poland   Portugal   Singapore
South Korea   Switzerland   Thailand   Turkey   Ukraine   Vietnam

Oxford is a registered trade mark of Oxford University Press
in the UK and certain other countries.

Published in the United States of America by
Oxford University Press
198 Madison Avenue, New York, NY 10016

© Brian Attebery 2014

Library of Congress Cataloging-in-Publication Data
Attebery, Brian, 1951–
Stories about stories : fantasy and the remaking of myth / Brian Attebery.
    p.   cm.
Includes bibliographical references and index.
ISBN 978–0–19–931606–9 (hardcover : acid-free paper) — ISBN 978–0–19–931607–6
(pbk. : acid-free paper) 1. Fantasy literature—History and criticism—Theory, etc.
2. Literature and myth. 3. Myth in literature. I. Title.
PN56.F34A88 2014
809.3'8766—dc23
                                                                    2013023205
9780199316069
9780199316076 (pbk.)

1   3   5   7   9   8   6   4   2

Printed in the United States of America on acid-free paper

{ CONTENTS }

{ ACKNOWLEDGMENTS }

This book is the product of many conversations over the past dozen years, some of them with people I have yet to meet in person. I have benefitted greatly from the ideas and encouragement of Gary Wolfe, Farah Mendlesohn, Marek Oziewicz, Ursula K. Le Guin, Nalo Hopkinson, Michael Swanwick, John Clute, Tom Shippey, Greg Bechtel, Monty Vierra, Tiffany Martin, Delia Sherman, Kim Selling, Ellen Kushner, Grace Dillon, Chip Sullivan, Karen Joy Fowler, Jennifer Eastman Attebery, and all my colleagues at the *Journal of the Fantastic in the Arts* and Idaho State University. My thanks also to Idaho State University for sponsoring two sabbaticals, Uppsala University for hosting me as a visiting researcher, and many helpful librarians, including those at Sydney University and the Merril Collection.

Some chapters incorporate material from the following:

"Stories Linked to Stories: Fantasy as a Route to Myth." *Relevant across Cultures: Visions of Connectedness in Modern Fantasy Literature for Young Readers.* Ed. Justyna Deszcz-Tryhubczak, Marek Oziewicz, and Agata Zarzycka. Wrocław: Oficyna ydawnicza, 2009. 19–31.

"Exploding the Monomyth: Myth and Fantasy in a Postmodern World." *Considering Fantasy: Ethical, Didactic, and Therapeutic Aspects of Fantasy in Literature and Film.* Ed. Justyna Deszcz-Tryhubczak and Marek Oziewicz. Wrocław: Oficyna Wydawnicza, 2007. 209–20.

"Aboriginality in Science Fiction." *Science Fiction Studies* 32 (2005): 385–404.

"Patricia Wrightson and Aboriginal Myth." *Extrapolation* 46 (2005): 329–39.

"High Church versus Broad Church: Christian Myth in George MacDonald and C. S. Lewis." *The New York Review of Science Fiction* 207 (Nov. 2005): 14–17.

"Myth and History: Molly Gloss's *Wild Life* and Alan Garner's *Strandloper*." *The New York Review of Science Fiction* 154 (June 2001): 1, 4–6.

"Make It Old: The Other Mythic Method." Proceedings of the International Conference "In the Mirror of the Past: Journeys from History to HISTORY."

My thanks to the original publishers for permission to reprint.

Stories about Stories

Introduction

Fantasy can be tiny picture books or sprawling epics, formulaic adventures or intricate metafictions. The category includes some of the most popular imaginative creations of all time—J. K. Rowling's Harry Potter, Terry Pratchett's Discworld, J. R. R. Tolkien's Middle-earth—and some of the most obscure. Like any literary mode, it may be employed by great artists or hacks. It flatters readers by making them over into heroes, yet it also flattens their pretensions and challenges their deepest beliefs. Fantasy means fairy tales by Thackeray and Wilde and Dinesen, beast fables from Beatrix Potter to Franz Kafka, the nonsense of Lewis Carroll, the profound sense of Ursula K. Le Guin, the cosmic paranoia of H. P. Lovecraft, and the philosophical playfulness of Italo Calvino. *The* book of the twentieth century, according to a number of readers' polls, was a fantasy, *The Lord of the Rings*. Other fantasies are as trivial and ephemeral as mayflies: Tolkien knockoffs and movie spinoffs.

Before any serious discussion of fantasy literature can take place, a number of obstacles must be cleared away. One is the problem of terminology: the same word gets bandied about in psychiatric sessions and literary discussions, not to mention titles of erotic romps on late-night cable TV. Another is the interchangeability of a lot of what is labeled "fantasy" on the supermarket book rack, much of it the unimpressive formula fiction that discerning fans call "extruded fantasy product."[1] One of the greatest obstacles is the fact that those who don't or can't read fantasy consider themselves superior to it and to the rest of us—as if color-blind people were to declare the use of red and green to be an aesthetic defect.[2] The tremendous popularity of particular fantasy texts only tends to make those color-blind people even more resentful. And we cannot forget the book burners: people who consider fantasy of any stripe to be suspect on religious grounds, either because they believe it encourages witchcraft and devil worship or simply because it isn't true and therefore denies Creation.

This last situation, the push to ban fantasy, is the least problematic of the bunch. Book burners at least take fantasy seriously. They recognize that fantasy employs the mechanisms of the sacred: prophecy, miracle, revelation, transformation. According to J. R. R. Tolkien, the defining characteristic of all "fairy-stories," by which he meant both traditional and literary fantasies, is their final breathtaking turn toward redemption, or "eucatastrophe." He saw each individual tale as a lesser stand-in for the greater narrative of salvation. In other words, his model for the structure of fantasy was Christian myth. I have corralled most of my definitions into the Taxonomic Interlude that follows chapter 1, but I should note that here and throughout this book, *myth* is used to designate any collective story that encapsulates a world view and authorizes belief. Thus Christian myth includes the Creation accounts and flood story from Genesis; the cycle of incarnation, atonement, and resurrection from the Gospels; the Apocalypse; and various medieval embroideries on those, such as the story of Adam's first wife Lilith. The problem for literalists is not that fantasy denies Christian myths but that it rearranges, reframes, and reinterprets them. Fantasy is fundamentally playful—which does not mean that it is not serious. Its way of playing with symbols encourages the reader to see meaning as something unstable and elusive, rather than single and self-evident.

Furthermore, not all fantasy derives from biblical narratives or Christian symbols. This is either a problem or a redeeming virtue, depending on one's religious orientation. Modern fantasy draws on a number of traditional narrative genres—sacred and secular legends, Märchen, epics, and ballads—and a wide array of cultural strands, including pre-Christian European, Native American, indigenous Australian, and Asian religious traditions. For my purposes, and taking a cue from Jacob Grimm, I also use *myth* as an umbrella term over these various traditional forms, although I do not subscribe to his belief that peasant tales were the diminished remnants of a Teutonic mythology. Rather, magical tales and supernatural ballads share with hero legends and stories of creation a sense of mystery and meaning that can be exploited by modern storytellers. Since the time of the Grimms, fantasy writers have treated all those oral genres as part of a single resource: different veins in the same mother lode of symbolic narrative. A motif from a saint's legend can be incorporated into an imitation of a wonder tale. Tolkien's English epic, *The Lord of the Rings*, was concocted from bits of Celtic myth and Norse saga and Finnish balladry, along with images from *Beowulf* and *Sir Gawain and the Green Knight*. Ursula K. Le Guin's American fantasy cycle, the story of Earthsea, mingles Asian dragon lore, European tales of wizardry, North American shamanism, and ethnologic concepts of *mana* and naming magic. Lesser fantasists copy the greater, so their indebtedness to oral tradition is as great, though secondhand.

I do not want merely to claim that one can find myth *in* fantasy, though that is certainly the case. Rather, I am looking at the way writers use fantasy to reframe myth: to construct new ways of looking at traditional stories and beliefs. A useful comparison is with influence studies: literary investigations into the impact of one writer on another. Noting that Shakespeare borrowed plots from Ovid, for instance, is mildly interesting. It gives us a glimpse into the playwright's methods and tells us which earlier texts had some currency in the late sixteenth century. But the more important questions all have to do with what Shakespeare did with his borrowings. How did they allow him to comment on current events, challenge his contemporaries, create what amounts to a new model of the mind? Writing about similar approaches to art history, Michael Baxandall pointed out that

> "Influence" is a curse on art criticism primarily because of its wrong-headed grammatical prejudice about who is the agent and who the patient: it seems to reverse the active/passive relation which the historical actor experiences and the inferential beholder will wish to take into account. If one says that X influenced Y it does seem that one is saying that X did something to Y rather than Y did something to X. But in the consideration of good pictures and painters the second is always the more lively reality[. . .]. If we think of Y rather than X as the agent, the vocabulary is much richer and more attractively diversified: draw on, resort to, avail oneself of, appropriate from, have recourse to, adapt, misunderstand, refer to, pick up, take on, engage with, react to, quote, differentiate oneself from, assimilate oneself to, assimilate, align oneself with, copy, address, paraphrase, absorb, make a variation on, revive, continue, remodel, ape, emulate, travesty, parody, extract from, distort, attend to, resist, simplify, reconstitute, elaborate on, develop, face up to, master, subvert, perpetuate, reduce, promote, respond to, transform, tackle . . . —everyone will be able to think of others. Most of these relations just cannot be stated the other way round—in terms of X acting on Y rather than Y acting on X. To think in terms of influence blunts thought by impoverishing the means of differentiation. (*Patterns* 58–59)

Accordingly, instead of spending much time simply identifying a particular Celtic myth in a work of modern fantasy, we should look at how the fantasist appropriates from, engages with, travesties, and reconstitutes the myth. The modern reuse will never be the same as the original performance. Most myths come down to us stripped of context. The voices, gestures, rituals, and social interactions that once guided interpretation are gone. Fantasy provides new contexts, and thus inevitably new meanings, for myth. Fantasy spins stories about the stories. That is the cultural work it performs, to borrow Jane Tompkins's term. Every fantastic narrative "is engaged in solving a problem or a set of problems specific to the time in which it was written" (Tompkins 38). For other kinds of narrative, those problems may have to do with justice, gender, race, identity, and so on. Fantasy can deal with any of these, but every fantasy also proposes a different way of bringing the strange, the magical, the numinous into modern life. Each distortion, each elaboration on mythic motifs offers a new way to relate to ancient beliefs and seemingly timeless mysteries. Furthermore, the most powerful and provocative fantasies recontextualize myths, placing them back into history and reminding us of their social and political power. By telling stories about, around, and upon mythic stories, we put ourselves onto the same stage with the gods and heroes and monsters and thus are forced to confront our godlike, heroic, and monstrous selves.

As mentioned earlier, exploring myth is not the only thing fantasy does. In the hands of a Terry Pratchett or a James Morrow, the fantastic is a glorious vehicle for satire on contemporary mores and institutions. Fantasy can be a way of meditating on history, as in John Crowley's Ægypt quartet (1987–2007), Delia Sherman's *The Porcelain Dove* (1993), or Susanna Clarke's *Jonathan Strange & Mr. Norrell* (2004). Fairy tales offer scenarios for maturation and self-discovery; and modern literary variants of those tales, such as two novels, both titled *Beauty*, by Sheri S. Tepper (1991) and Robin McKinley (1978), respectively, revise the scripts by which readers make sense of gender and authority. Magic and symbolism are inextricably linked (Frazer's magical Laws of Contagion and Similarity match up neatly with C. S. Peirce's semiotic categories of index and icon and roughly with Freud's operations of displacement and condensation), and thus fantasy proves to be an inexhaustible generator of fresh symbols for death and desire. And fantasy is fun. For those attuned to its charms, fantasy can be a game with endlessly varied outcomes and a vacation for the weary soul—and neither amusement nor escape is anything to condemn or undervalue.

But fantasy's main claim to cultural importance resides, I believe, in the work of redefining the relationship between contemporary readers and mythic texts. It shares that work with such enterprises as depth psychology, religion, and popular media. Unlike those institutions, fantasy claims no authority nor exerts hegemony. It denies its own validity; the one characteristic shared by all fantasy narratives is their nonfactuality. The fundamental premise of fantasy is that the things it tells not only did not happen but *could* not have happened. In that literal untruth is freedom to tell many symbolic truths without forcing a choice among them.

In the following chapters, I outline the history of fantasy as a history of mythopoiesis, modern myth-making—though fantasy "makes" myth only in the sense that a traditional oral performer makes the story she tells: not inventing but recreating that which has always existed only in performance, in the present. This term entered critical discourse about fantasy when J. R. R. Tolkien used "Mythopoiea" as the title of a poem based on a conversation with C. S. Lewis, in which Lewis described myths as "lies breathed through silver" (Carpenter 147). Tolkien's view was that the myth-making imagination always tends toward truth, rather than lies; that fantastic stories lead toward a genuine understanding of the conditions of existence. The poem is itself a story about stories and is now part of the larger conversation between fantasy and myth, along with Tolkien's and Lewis's various stories and essays; works by their friends and acquaintances; earlier writers who influenced them; later writers who, as Baxandall says, differentiate themselves from, align themselves with, or remodel them; and scholars like me whose job it is to moderate the discussion and make the connections more apparent.

I begin, in chapter 1, by exploring the intertwined early histories of myth and fantasy. The story of the emergence of fantasy as a literary mode is also the story of the scholarly discovery of myth. The same people were involved in both efforts, and both had the same goal: to make ancient and powerful symbolic structures available to modern readers. From the Brothers Grimm at the beginning of the nineteenth century to Andrew Lang at the end, the scholars and writers who paid closest attention to oral narrative and their written offshoots were also involved in retelling, imitating, and popularizing myth in the form of fantasy. Some of these writers, such as Hans Christian Andersen, George MacDonald, Nathaniel Hawthorne (with his *Wonder Book for Boys and Girls*), and Lang, are closely associated with the fairy tale and with children's literature. Others, such as William Morris, H. Rider Haggard, and MacDonald in his Germanic *Kunstmärchen* mode (*Phantastes* and *Lilith*) wrote romances for adults with a more deliberately mythic resonance.

Following chapter 1 is a shorter Taxonomic Interlude, a break from the historical sequence in which I take up some of the issues arising from the concept of genre. Literary studies and folklore share the assumption that it is instructive to sort individual texts into categories, which can then be examined together for shared features and effects. This section looks at the way genres such as fantasy and myth are normally defined and how both category and definition can be misused, especially when taxonomies turn into hierarchies. Drawing on the logicians' idea of fuzzy sets, I offer my own definition of literary genres such as fantasy and science fiction. I also look at the way such genres as tale, legend, and myth blur and reconfigure themselves in cultural context. Those three folk genres are generally acknowledged as primary sources for literary fantasy, but I suggest adding one other: Carl von Sydow's concept of the memorate, which is an eyewitness account of an encounter with extraordinary or numinous forces. In later chapters, I look at literary narratives that I believe function much as memorates do: bringing together the world of concrete personal experience and that of the sacred or supernatural. Memorates are realistic narratives about magical narratives; so too are many works of modern fantasy.

Subsequent chapters examine different aspects of fantasy's ongoing interaction with the mythic. Chapter 2 looks at the generation that grew up on MacDonald and Morris, including the most famous and influential group of writers and defenders of the fantastic: the Inklings. In addition to Lewis and Tolkien, this generation (defined as those born between 1880 and 1899) included

E. R. Eddison, Lord Dunsany, P. L. Travers, James Branch Cabell, and a number of other major fantasists. It was also the generation that invented Modernism: James Joyce, Virginia Woolf, T. S. Eliot, Ezra Pound. In this chapter, I compare what Eliot called the "mythical method" with the other significant mythic method represented by modern fantasy. As demonstrated in the work of Hope Mirrlees and Charles Williams, the two early-twentieth-century movements turn out to be more similar than might appear, and more closely in touch.

Chapter 3 takes up Christian mythopoeisis, looking especially at the relationship between C. S. Lewis and his acknowledged master George MacDonald. Lewis's way of dealing with that influence illustrates most of Baxandall's verbs of use: he emulates and assimilates MacDonald's fairy tale method but also willfully misunderstands or misrepresents many of the earlier writer's ideas on salvation and belief. Both fantasists constructed narratives that work through traditional symbols and push concepts of the sacred to their logical conclusions. Though Judeo-Christian myth became essentially unalterable once it passed from oral to written form, by inserting scriptural motifs into narrative structures derived from classical myth and Märchen, both MacDonald and Lewis found ways to reconfigure and thus reinterpret biblical narratives of creation, fall, and salvation. Their results differ, but both helped to demonstrate the power of the fantastic as a vehicle of religious thought.

As Tolkienian fantasy became a major publishing category, other writers responded either by imitating *The Lord of the Rings* or by finding alternative ways to combine mythic motifs with a variety of realist fictional techniques and the various formulas of popular romance. Those techniques and formulas fill in for the full cultural context that has been stripped from most myths—but they also thereby mark its absence. Drawing again on folkloristics in chapter 4, I develop the idea that the traditional genre of memorate, a personal experience story attached to a supernatural or sacred legend, can, by analogy, illuminate the way writers such as Alan Garner and Ursula K. Le Guin incorporate the experiences and consciousness of Moderns into the world of myth.

Chapter 5 looks at the cosmopolitanization of fantasy. After the first flush of Tolkien imitation, writers began to expand their territory to include—or to colonize—mythic traditions from the entire world, rather than just from Europe's northwest corner. Authorized by mythographers such as Carl Jung, Mircea Eliade, and especially Joseph Campbell, fantasy writers in the 1970s and 1980s looked far and wide for new material, seeking both to avoid imitating Tolkien and to emulate his success in bringing traditional materials into the Modern world. Eventually, their efforts came up against a barrier: the issue of ownership of living traditions. My central example is Patricia Wrightson, who was first hailed as a sympathetic translator of Aboriginal myth into modern fantasy and later condemned as an exploiter and cultural appropriator and whose work warrants a new and more nuanced reading.

One way to avoid the charge of appropriation is to stick to one's own traditions. Chapter 6 is about angels. Of all figures from Judeo-Christian lore, angels most readily lend themselves to creative mythopoiesis, because they are neither natural nor divine. They mediate between heaven and earth; they can be talked to, wrestled with, desired, coerced. In the 1980s and 1990s, angels were everywhere: in books, on television, in theater and the movies, and in merchandising. Though it might seem that this boom represented an American turn toward Christian orthodoxy, a closer look at the actual depiction of angels reveals a surprising lack of agreement about which scriptural or folkloric version of angels should be drawn on and how literally they should be taken. Differing levels of belief in angels and different conceptions of their nature challenge writers to find appropriate narrative frameworks for dealing with something seen as literal truth by some readers and as metaphor or outright falsehood by others. Angel stories illustrate the way fantastic fiction debates myth: such stories allow various cognitive minorities (in Peter Berger's terminology) to challenge the majority and perhaps even to reveal hidden fissures within what seems to be consensus.

Pausing again in the evolutionary narrative, I examine recent attempts to discredit or ban fantasy on religious grounds. Enough examples exist to fill a full-sized chapter (or book), but there is a certain sameness to the complaints. A brief interlude will suffice to demonstrate that fundamentalist responses to fantasy are based not only on a particular theological stance toward magic and the supernatural but also on a particular reading strategy. Fundamentalist readers of biblical narratives seek similarly to restrict the use and interpretation of sacred symbols in fantasy. This reading strategy also reflects a specific social position. Only those who see themselves as speaking not just for a cognitive majority but for an entire like-minded community can offer absolute judgment on an entire body of literature and its meaning.

The writers I look at in chapter 7 do not consider themselves to be writing from such uniformity of belief. Their own journeys across cultures and conceptual systems lead them to see meaning as always multiple and contradictory. This chapter returns to the global context of chapter 5, but this time from the perspective of the formerly colonized rather than the colonizers. For writers such as Nalo Hopkinson, Amitav Ghosh, and Leslie Marmon Silko, the fantastic becomes a way to represent the inevitable double vision of those who are both inside and outside Western and Modern culture. Mary Louise Pratt has analyzed historical texts written by colonized peoples, calling them examples of the "arts of the contact zone." Such texts mimic European modes while subverting their assumptions, offering one message to the stranger and another to the insider. Postcolonial fantasies mark the existence of many such meeting places; one could even say that their multiple encodings and generic ambiguities transform the fantastic itself into a contact zone.

Similar sorts of doubleness and self-awareness are hallmarks of postmodernity. In chapter 8, I look at writers who have used the fantastic to challenge the binaries of modern/primitive and self/other. Reflecting postmodernism's self-consciousness about storytelling and employing its typical disruptions of genre and violations of textual boundaries, writers such as Alan Garner, Jeanne Larsen, Molly Gloss, and Ursula K. Le Guin bring history into myth and let the cultural outsider critique the Modern. Such disruptions predate the current era, of course, and will continue to be important after postmodernism starts to seem quaintly historical. Accordingly, I classify this development not as postmodern fantasy but as the situated fantastic, adapting my term from Donna Haraway's discussion of "situated knowledges." All knowledge is local: we understand the universe through metaphoric extensions of our bodies and, because sign systems are collective, we are all immersed in the symbolic languages of our own communities. Fantasy writers increasingly take this immersion as something to be examined, questioned, and revised. Many twenty-first-century fantasies not only represent contradictory worldviews and incommensurable mythologies within their imagined universes but also use those contradictions to generate new patterns of storytelling.

Each of these chapters illustrates a significant moment in the long history of interaction between written fantasy and traditional oral narratives of magic and the sacred. It may not be evident from these summaries whether this is primarily a literary study or a cultural history. Am I investigating the genre of fantasy or tracing the repurposing of myth in modern culture? As I hope to make clear, these are not either-or questions. The nature and power of fantastic literature can hardly be understood without reference to the close collaboration between fantasy writers and myth scholars and popularizers. Conversely, fantasy offers a glimpse into the process by which mythic patterns transmit cognitive structures even without the sanction of official belief. To study myth in the modern world is to study the fantastic imagination, and vice versa. Fantasy's enduring appeal—despite occasional countermoves of censure or critical disdain—indicates its adaptability to changing intellectual currents and its applicability to a host of social needs. The range and intensity of recent responses to fantasy, from book burning to Pottermania, testifies to its current cultural importance. I hope to show that one reason for that importance is fantasy's capacity for mythopoeiesis: the making of narratives that reshape the world.

{ 1 }

Fantasy as a Route to Myth

The relationship between myth and fantasy is a particularly convoluted one. To begin with, both words have so many meanings and applications that they can be synonyms or direct contraries. Either can be spoken with anything from hushed reverence to lip-curling scorn, the latter especially by those whose usage always implies mereness: "just a myth," "only fantasy." Both words have wandered far from their Greek origins, and yet both are called back periodically to their original meanings of story (*mythos*) and vision (*phantasia*).[1]

Accordingly, I must take some time to recapitulate the histories of both terms before I can get to my main claim: that fantasy, as a literary form, is a way of reconnecting to traditional myths and the worlds they generate. It is not the only way, of course. Schoolchildren study Greek and Roman myths. Opera lovers watch heroically scaled Wotans and Brünnhildes reenact the Germanic end times. Mythological sculptures hold up cornices on courthouses and banks. Self-help books teach us to invoke our inner goddesses. Religious institutions frame selected *mythoi* as sacred scripture and surround them with ceremony and doctrine. Critics invoking Freud or Jung find echoes of ancient myth in modern novels. Picasso painted myths; Martha Graham choreographed them; Hitler invoked them. Everyday language hides old gods: martial arts, hermetically sealed bottles, venereal disease. New Age therapists offer vision quests by appointment.

Myth is all around us, and yet we are not sure what it is or how to touch it or let it touch us. Fantasy is an arena—I believe the primary arena—in which competing claims about myth can be contested and different relationships with myth tried out. The reasons have to do with the development of our modern understanding of myth, on the one hand, and the invention of the fantasy genre, on the other—and with the fact that these are not two different stories but two aspects of the same historical narrative.

Myth and Modernity

The closest I have ever come to experiencing living myth was listening to Kath Walker, a poet and storyteller, beside a campfire on an island in Moreton Bay in Queensland, Australia. Walker, who later reassumed her Aboriginal name of Oodgeroo, was an experienced negotiator between worlds. At school and then at work as a secretary and telephone operator, she had acquired a transplanted English culture much of which we, her American listeners, shared. At home she had learned the history, the language, and the narrative traditions of her clan, the Noonuccal. When she talked to us of the creation of the world by Rainbow Serpent or the battle between the hero Biyami and his brother-enemy Bunyip, she was adapting narratives that had already moved from their original context. Once community performance, then family lore, the stories now became part of a cross-cultural exchange. Knowing that, she selected and reshaped, translated and explained, and made the stories serve an entirely new purpose: to entertain and educate visitors who might then spread the word that her people had neither vanished nor lost their way in the modern world. Yet in spite of the reconfiguring and repurposing, the myths maintained a startling power. Four decades later, I still remember their effect: how the world came alive around us as she spoke. The stories seemed like visitors from another world—powerful, enigmatic beings that observed and tested us as we puzzled over them.

Even as I describe this sensation, it seems a bit over the top. My anecdote makes me sound like a tribal wannabe, a pseudo-mystic sitting at the foot of a colorful native guru, taking notes for my next anthro-pop bestseller. But I have no claim to Kath Walker's stories, though I can go back and read versions of them in her book *Stradbroke Dreamtime* (1972). My own tribal lore consists mostly of a few anecdotes, some family recipes (sourdough biscuits, rhubarb pie), and a goodly number of jokes. Like most contemporary North Americans, European Australians, and Western Europeans, I know myths primarily through printed literature. I generally refer questions about the world and my role in it to science and to history, rather than to oral narrative and traditional practice.

Rather than keep the spotlight on myself, then, I will take my experience as more or less typical (an assumption that will come into question later) and henceforth refer to people like me as Moderns. The capital letter is intended to inflect the term with a degree of irony. We Moderns are up to date, rational, well armed, technologically savvy: the very model of a modern major/general consciousness. We have defined ourselves, since the period historians now call the Early Modern era, against others who are seen as backward, savage, primitive. We, in contrast, are the enlightened heirs of Bacon, Drake, Shakespeare, and Newton (in that Early Modern period); Darwin, Watt, and Marx (in the industrial age); Freud, Ford, Einstein, and Picasso (in the twentieth century).

From a Modern point of view, space is also time, in that the farther from cultural centers we travel, the farther we venture into our own past. We see myth as something from an earlier age and those who maintain mythic traditions as survivals: living cultural fossils. We admire their vivid imaginations and regret the loss of such primitive faith, but we would not trade our central heating, automobiles, and Internet for their masks and miracles.

One problem with these categories is that they define someone like Oodgeroo as not Modern. The Kath Walker I met was thoroughly immersed in late-twentieth-century culture and, more pointedly, politics. There was a reason she was camped on the spot of land she called Moongalba, or the Sitting Down Place; a reason she was willing to talk about her history and traditions to young American visitors; and a reason she made sure we understood that even as simple an act as squatting gracefully on the ground was an assertion of identity and homage to the past. She did not have clear title to her family's Sitting Down Place, which she wanted to turn into an Aboriginal cultural center. The Queensland government was fighting her efforts and contesting her claims. Walker was a keen observer of racial struggles elsewhere; she had been watching American activists, both African American and Native American, and was looking for ways to adapt their strategies of resistance, pride, and power into the nascent Aboriginal Power movement. She saw myth as a source of all three. It encouraged her to resist a dominant culture that defined her as nonexistent (a legal principle called Terra Nullius decreed that the Australian continent was legally unoccupied before the arrival of Europeans). It gave her pride in the hidden wealth of a people who kept few material possessions. It authorized her to rename herself and her place and, in that renaming, to assert power to redefine the nation, reclaim the past, and reconnect with the natural world.

It is no wonder that many white Australians at that time saw Walker as dangerous. It wasn't just that she was an activist, and an articulate one. She was also a myth bearer. Myths are dangerous, though one would not get that impression from coming across a collection of Greek myths retold for children, such as Nathaniel Hawthorne's *A Wonder Book for Boys and Girls* (1852). In that volume and its sequel, *Tanglewood Tales*, Hawthorne did for Ovid what Charles and Mary Lamb did for Shakespeare: not completely falsifying the originals but making them accessible to children and acceptable to parents and teachers. Hawthorne's versions of the stories of Persephone and Midas recast them as fairy tales: giving them child protagonists, bowdlerizing sexual content, and making the gods into fairy godparents. Hawthorne's myths would never lead to sit-ins or court challenges. They do not offer to remake the universe. Yet in their own cultural setting as living traditions, the Greek myths were probably not unlike Walker's. The story of how these powerfully strange narratives were domesticated into children's entertainments is a long and convoluted one.

Hawthorne's tales were probably my first exposure to classical myths; they certainly have been for many Moderns of the past century and a half. For those who missed Hawthorne or were ready to move on from him, there was Thomas Bulfinch. Bulfinch is to mythology as Henry Gray is to human anatomy or Noah Webster to the dictionary: eponymous, ubiquitous, ever in print. Bulfinch's *Mythology* (1881) was originally Bulfinch's *The Age of Fable* (1855). The earlier book became the first and most important portion of the compendium edition, the part containing the Greek and Roman tales for which he is best remembered. The difference in titles is significant. Andrew Von Hendy (2002), in *The Modern Construction of Myth*, points out that the word *myth* came into common English use rather late:

> While words such as "mythologist" and "mythology" appear early in the vernaculars (they are recorded even in English by 1425, and by the early seventeenth century most of the forms of this word in use now, including "mythic," "mythographer," and "mythologize" have been launched on their careers), we discover one striking exception: the word "myth," common enough in Latin, is nowhere to be found. In its stead, to signify the relevant kind of tale, the vernaculars resort to the Latin word for "story," *fabula,* and thus develop analogues of the English "fable." The key to this puzzling split in linguistic behavior lies in observing the meaning attached to "mythology" and its grammatical variants. They always refer to the hermeneutical activity of reading the stories allegorically. "Mythology" is not a body of stories, but the scholarly science of allegorical reading; "to mythologize" means not to invent or relay a mythos, but to engage in that kind of interpretative practice. (2)

Thus Bulfinch was retelling fables, not myths. The difference is that fables are literature of a particular sort: a way of making moral points through amusing narratives that cannot be taken literally. Myths, however, are not literature but sacred narrative, and they mean what they say, however difficult that meaning might be to grasp. At least that is the distinction that began to be drawn by the Romantics. One of the markers of the shift toward Romantic thinking was that in their usage, "the word 'myth' [came] into use perhaps above all to connote a religious dimension to story, a dimension allegorized 'fable' had forfeited and to which unallegorized 'fable' had never aspired" (Von Hendy 3).

Bulfinch reflects earlier usage in his title and his 1855 preface, which never does employ the word *myth* but rather refers to "the stories of mythology" (4). His goal is not to explore sacred beliefs but to introduce readers to those stories as sources of literary convention and allusion and to "mythology" as a way of reading: "Thus we hope to teach mythology not as a study, but as a relaxation from study; to give our work the charm of a story-book, yet by means of it to impart a knowledge of an important branch of education" (4–5).

His intended readers are those who cannot read the original Greek or Latin texts or cannot be bothered to do so:

> To devote study to a species of learning which relates wholly to false marvels and obsolete faiths is not to be expected of the general reader in a practical age like this. The time even of the young is claimed by so many sciences of facts and things that little can be spared for set treatises on a science of mere fancy. (4)

In other words, he is retelling a charming set of untruths for the young, for the lower classes, and for women: the work is addressed to "the reader of English literature, of either sex, who wishes to comprehend the allusions so frequently made by public speakers, lecturers, essayists, and poets" (5). Gentlemen, who of course studied Latin, could continue to read Ovid and Virgil and get the unexpurgated versions, the gods in all their randy coupling, petty spite, and deep mystery. For the rest of us Moderns, the problematic "false marvels and obsolete faiths" could be dealt with by learning to read mythologically; that is, allegorically.

Bulfinch's title makes one other important distinction. Not only are these stories to be read as fables, but they also reflect another "age." Fables are archaic: the time for creating or believing in them is over. For Bulfinch's intended readers, fact reigns supreme, whereas fancy, as represented in the gods and monsters of the ancient world, is a source of amusement and poetic figuration. One can compare *The Age of Fable* with another volume published four years later: Darwin's *The Origin of Species*. Though one presents putative falsehoods and the other meticulous observations, both are products of the Victorian mania for collecting. Each holds out an array of specimens as evidence of where we came from and how the world has evolved. Bulfinch even demonstrates some of Darwin's keenness for comparison: at the end of the volume, he offers a couple of alternatives to the classical tradition that has been synonymous with mythology. The final sections of the book touch on Norse, Egyptian, and "Oriental" mythology, though increasingly sketchily, as the scholar's knowledge and interest diminish. These parts are like a museum annex—there for the sake of completeness but not part of the main tour.

As fable turned into myth, though, traditions other than those of Greece and Rome became the primary focus of scholarship, and the comparative method replaced Bulfinch's mostly aesthetic perspective. Whereas Bulfinch could say of Norse, Egyptian, and Near Eastern mythology that "these topics have not usually been presented in the same volume with the classical fables" (5), by the end of the nineteenth century it was the norm to group Homer's epics with Germanic or South Asian texts. In this respect, Bulfinch, like most popularizers, was behind the academic curve. Such comparisons had begun to arise in the eighteenth century, as explorers and archivists discovered texts new to or long forgotten by the European literary world, starting with the book that was Bulfinch's source for Scandinavian fables: Paul Henri Mallet's *Northern Antiquities* (1756). The strange world of Nordic gods and giants revealed in Mallet's collection posed the first significant challenge to Homer and Ovid and led other scholars to seek further afield for more alternatives to classical myth. The effort resulted in:

> a whole string of texts unearthed by the diligence of scholars, and seized on by eager nationalists (often the same people): the *Nibelungenlied* for the Germans, republished in many editions from 1807; *Beowulf* for the English (first edition 1815, though claimed as a Danish work by its Icelandic editor); the *Mabinogion* for the Welsh (first edition, with translation into English, in parts 1838–1845). (Shippey 307)

To these European examples one can add texts brought to Europe as part of a larger colonial enterprise: the Egyptian *Book of the Dead*, named and translated into German by Karl Richard Lepsius in 1842; the Sanskrit epic *Ramayana*, translated into English by Ralph T. H. Griffith in 1870–1874; the Sumerian/Akkadian *Epic of Gilgamesh*, translated into English by George Smith in 1872; the *Mahabharata*, translated by Kisari Mohan Ganguli between 1883 and 1896; the Persian *Shahnameh*, rendered as *The Epic of Kings* by Helen Zimmern in 1883. The discovery of *Gilgamesh*, with its strangely familiar flood story, encouraged the reading of Genesis as another set of Middle Eastern myths.

In the New World, the Meso-American *Popul Vuh* was transcribed and translated into Spanish by Francisco Ximénez in the early eighteenth century. More directly influenced by the Romantic quest for myth, Henry Schoolcraft collaborated with his half-Ojibwa wife Jane Johnston Schoolcraft to produce a set of *Indian Tales and Legends* in two volumes (1839), which became the source for Longfellow's 1855 poem *The Song of Hiawatha*. In notes published with the poem, Longfellow called it "this Indian *Edda*" (299).

Everybody, it seemed, had a mythology. If no epic could be found in manuscript form, one could be cobbled together from scattered songs and legends, detected in disguise as a set of peasant tales, recorded or reconstructed from oral performances, or even manufactured as an outright forgery, like James MacPherson's songs of Ossian. The line between forgery and creative reconstruction is not easy to draw. Whereas MacPherson is mostly on one side of that line, the Finnish scholar Elias Lönnrot is a neighbor on the other. Hypothesizing that the many local Finnish ballads of heroes and magicians must once have been part of a single grand narrative, he set out to construct one, which we now know as the *Kalevala* (1835). The interrelatedness of these national projects is shown by the fact that the *Kalevala* was one of Longfellow's models for "Hiawatha" and the source of its hypnotic meter. Unlike MacPherson, Lönnrot used authentically traditional materials, and he kept careful notes on both his sources and his additions (Shippey 325). In a sense, he became the Finnish Homer, except that the Homeric singers who combined historical events, cosmogonic myths, and folktales into the *Iliad* and the *Odyssey* did so in performance, as participants in, rather than observers of, an oral poetic tradition.

The second option, to offer a collection of peasant tales in lieu of a national epic, was the one elected by Jacob and Wilhelm Grimm. Though we now usually classify fairy tales and myths as separate branches of oral literature (see the "Taxonomic Interlude" that follows this chapter), the Grimms' collection of *Kinder- und Haus-Märchen* (1812) was originally offered to scholars as an exercise in myth reconstruction. It was part of the same project that produced Jacob Grimm's *Deutsche Mythologie* (1835), in which he strove to reconstruct a vanished German mythos out of various remnants and analogues: Roman records, medieval romances, local legends, Märchen, folk beliefs, dialect words, and the more fully recorded religious traditions of the Scandinavians. In view of this last, the English translator of Grimm's great work chose to translate its title as *Teutonic Mythology*, rather than *German Mythology*, though he admitted that Jacob Grimm intended to distinguish German from Scandinavian myth, because the latter's "fulness would have thrown the more meagre remains of the Deutsch into the shade" (Stallybrass viii). The English title more accurately reflects Grimm's sources but misrepresents his nationalistic aims: "Having observed that her Language, Laws, and Antiquities were greatly underrated, I was wishful to exalt my native land" (Grimm lv). To restore a nation's lore was to recapture its spirit.

As philologists, as well as folklorists, the Grimms were interested generally in tracing the spread and evolution of Indo-European languages, together with the mythic worldview they believed underlay those languages. Comparative philology pointed, for instance, toward a widespread belief in a pantheon of Sky Father, Earth Mother, and their kin, now reduced mostly to place names and days of the week. If the gods could lurk in the atlas and the calendar, they could also be lying forgotten in other cultural commonplaces. After the spread of Christianity, the old myths were no longer declaimed at court or performed in temples, but perhaps they might still linger around woodcutters' fires and beside peasant hearths. Like a hero in one of their tales, the myth sought by the Brothers Grimm was hiding in plain sight, clad in homespun cloth and animal skins. All it needed was a pair of fairy godfathers to spot its true value and restore it to a place of honor. The reward was, of course, a kingdom—the German nation that had never existed and yet could be imaginatively reconstructed once its mythology was reclaimed. Jacob Grimm, especially, strove to create "the illusion that religious and geographical divisions within Germany masked an underlying unity that only an historian could see. Further, he transfigured the image of Germany's popular cultures, infusing the ordinary with a religious resonance" (Williamson 134).

With the success of the Grimms' collection, other bodies of *Märchen* were assembled around Europe, always with the larger goal of recovering a national myth. What began as a Romantic nationalist project, however, gradually became something else: scientific study of folk narrative and folkways. The Grimms themselves started the transformation. They kept careful field notes and, despite their fudging of sources and a heavy editorial hand in published versions, their interest in language meant that they listened to the voices of storytellers and made an effort to reproduce an oral style on the page. Indeed, sometimes they altered sources (including tales extant only in Latin in medieval manuscripts) to make them sound like their generalized notion of a peasant storyteller. As the Grimms' influence spread, more and more students of folktale, such as Peter Christen Asbjørnsen and Jørgen Moe in Norway and Aleksander Afanasiev in Russia, followed their example, and eventually the more scientific process represented by their notes replaced the model of their published volumes. The task of locating bodies of myth passed from literary scholars and philologists to the new disciplines of folklore and ethnology. By the early twentieth century, the academic study of folk narrative came to emphasize verbatim transcription of texts and systematic comparison of variants. By mid-century, as recording technology improved and folklorists became more aware of the importance of context, collectors learned to record not only the words of the text but also performance style, audience response, and eventually the storyteller's own perspective on the narrative and its meanings.

There is an enormous difference between a bare text in a book and myth wrapped in its full cultural context. Much of the significance of a traditional story is implied rather than stated outright, many of the meanings depend on cultural knowledge external to the text itself, and the intentions behind any performance will vary according to the audience and the situation. Contemporary folklorist Barre Toelken, who has spent decades working with Navajo storytellers, confesses that he will never know their myths as his friends within the group know them. Each time he comes back to the stories of Coyote or Changing Woman, he finds new layers of meaning; each time further aspects of their significance elude him ("Beauty" 443).

In order to reach this degree of awareness, Toelken had to give up the superior position of the Modern observer. In an introduction to a volume assembled by Toelken and Larry Evers, the editors discuss the power dynamics of ethnological studies. The typical situation since the time of the Brothers Grimm has been that of the outsider-scholar who collects texts from the insider-informant but then publishes those texts with full editorial and interpretive control. The storyteller gives up all rights to the shape and meaning of the stories, which thereby become timeless and anonymous, rather than personal and purposeful. They can become whatever the interpreter wants them to be: metaphors of the growth and death of vegetation (according to James Frazer's *The Golden Bough*), parables about the sky and the setting sun (to Max Müller), evidence of lost national greatness and unity (to Richard Wagner), symbolic representations of psychic trauma (to Freud), or signposts toward psychic integration (to Jung). Stripped of their original contexts, myths are easily turned into propaganda or self-help manuals—the popularity of Joseph Campbell's monomyth testifies to the ease of the latter transformation.

It is no wonder that individuals who willingly or unwittingly subject their own mythic traditions to such abuse are referred to by such loaded words as "informant" or "collaborator." As Evers and Toelken point out, "the verb 'collaborate' has a special resonance in the context of any Native American community, which the second meaning in the following entry captures well: '1. to work together, especially in a join intellectual effort; 2. to cooperate treasonably, as with an enemy occupying one's country'" ("Collaboration" 1). Theorizing about myth is not the worst thing that has ever been done to indigenous peoples, but it does have the effect of stealing one of their most valuable resources.

Most theories of myth are based on printed texts, whose narrators are effectively erased. As Toelken (1979) points out, even a conscientious collector such as Franz Boas left much of the meaning out of his recorded versions of Kathlamet and other Northwest myths:

> Without ethnographic evidence of the fullest sort (so we can approximate the cultural meanings of these items on the idea, word, and phrase levels and hence the people's likely response to them), without an appreciation of the mechanics of oral tradition, the prose narratives left to us by scholars like Boas must remain stark skeletons. [. . .] Most of the real meaning in these myths seems to take shape "between the lines," in the dramatic tension set up between congruent layers of narrative. (*Dynamics* 220).

Hence folklorists and ethnopoeticists, those who know something of oral performance, tend to resist totalizing theories of myth. Some of those totalizing theories show up in the 1955 volume called *Myth: A Symposium*, edited by Thomas Sebeok. Within that collection, in which Claude Lévi-Strauss articulated his structural theory of myth and others pronounced on myth's significance to literature, religious experience, and psychology, one voice stands out for its modest skepticism. Stith Thompson, the great cataloguer of folk motifs, pointed out that we rarely have adequate information about the intentions of the storyteller who invented a particular mythic narrative. Even if folklorists decide a particular story fits the definition of a myth, they are left with the problem of deciding what it might mean:

> On the whole, however, a quest for meanings outside the tale or myth itself is doomed to failure, because we simply do not know the frame of mind of the unknown person in the unknown place and the unknown time and the unknown culture who first contrived the story. The search for the original meaning of any folk story is quite as impossible as the search for the origin of that story. For both quests adequate data are missing. We are left with a choice of making a guess according to our own predilections or of saying that we do not know. It is by all means preferable to say that we do not know. (Thompson 178)

But Thompson was working with written records rather than live performances. Where traditions are still active, it is possible to gather information about the way the story reflects the beliefs, values, and situation of a present-day performer—not its original meaning, but its meaning here and now—if a collector simply bothers to ask. Barre Toelken has spent decades learning how and what and whom to ask and learning to listen to the answers. As mentioned earlier, his understanding of particular stories has changed many times throughout his career, along with his understanding of his and any outsiders' responsibility toward the community whose property the stories remain. Coming back to a Coyote story he was first told in 1956, wrote about in 1969, returned to with more complex interpretations in 1981 and again in 1987, and discovered therein an entirely new gendered dimension in 2000, Toelken makes himself into the butt of a teaching story. He suggests that twenty-first-century folklorists learn from his mistakes and consider the following guidelines:

1. Men and women hold different but complementary details; collect from all members, starting with the women in a matriarchal culture.
2. Coauthor articles on other cultures. This would have made me ask questions about everything; as it was, I simply did not ask. Besides, "author" carries some distinction in function, not just a matter of politeness. It is meaning of a different sort (not right versus wrong).
3. More important, my long-range view is substantially different from the short range.

This was a simple tale (1956), a complex double-level tale (1981), a reference to medicine (1987), and finally a depiction of witchcraft (current [2000]). The four are connected, but you can see how my concerns have shifted: from tales that do not hurt anybody to tales that do (and what happens when they do?). ("Beauty" 444)

Toelken's approach to myth is in many ways the opposite of Bulfinch's museum-style display of fixed and anonymous texts. Deriving ultimately from the Grimms' collecting practices but informed by ideas from such academic and Native scholars as Franz Boas, Linda Dégh, Dell Hymes, Dennis Tedlock, Elaine Lawless, George Hunt, George Wasson, and Yellowman, Toelken's method is thickly descriptive and interactive. "Thick description" is Clifford Geertz's phrase for an ethnography that seeks out every possible contextual association and symbol system within the culture, so that a single event such as a Balinese cockfight becomes a key to a whole worldview. Unlike Geertz, though, Toelken insists that the best person to identify these connections and their significance is not the outside observer but the insider participant. If the myths are not ours, then neither is full understanding of their meanings.

This was pretty much the perspective I brought to my meeting with Kath Walker. Though I was just a beginning folklore student in 1973 and had not read Barre Toelken's work, I had absorbed many of his ideas. Toelken is a family friend; he often dropped by our house on his way from Oregon, where he taught, to Utah, where his adopted Navajo family lived. I listened in on many conversations in which he talked with other folklorists (including my father) about his work with native colleagues and his struggles to understand and to represent their traditions fairly. By the time I was a college student encountering Aboriginal stories, I had been through an informal ten-year seminar on folk narrative. I was ready to recognize that the myths I had always loved in their print versions were only the remnants of traditions like those that informed the lives of Oodgeroo and her people. They had once been spoken or sung by performers who meant something by them, something not entirely contained within the words of the story but dependent on the occasion, the ritual frame, the audience, and the obligations that such stories carry.

The hardest lesson for a Modern to learn is that others are Modern, too. The moment of storytelling is always Now, not some primordial past or dusty historical display. Hearing Barre Toelken tell Coyote stories secondhand and listening as Kath Walker adapted her family traditions, I experienced something that changed the way I read Homer and the Norse Eddas. There are ghosts on the page now. I detect a phantom performer, adjusting the telling to situation and audience. The audience is there, guiding the performance with their responses. All around are patterns of kinship and enmity and injustice and obligation, which are coded into the narrative if one knows to look for them. There are indoor and outdoor spaces of performance, each with culturally defined patterns of meaning. In the audience are both true believers and skeptics, as well as some whose belief is partial and parabolic—each of these stances being an attempt to understand what the story says about the gods, the universe, and human society.

The model of myth proposed by folklorists differs considerably from those invoked by psychologists and philosophers and literary critics. The psychoanalytic view of myth, for instance, is that its meanings are unavailable to those who recite them: they are hidden, coded, unconscious. Many folklorists, though, suggest that storytellers are not only aware of the symbolic dimensions (including sexual) to their tales but also better able to explicate the codes than Freudian or Jungian commentators who always and only find what the psychoanalytic model tells them to expect. Myth scholars who follow Sir James Frazer think of myth either as an attempt to explain natural processes—failed science—or as an attempt to force the universe to do humans' bidding—magical thinking. Toelken's view is that myth's primary purpose is neither to explain nor to coerce but to *enact* the universe, or some important aspect of it.

> A good story is like an affective ritual: it puts you there, makes you experience or reexperience something. And that something is an otherwise-abstract but real idea from your culture, made concrete and experiential

through the imagination and knowledge which you bring to the story performance, enhanced by the power of the performer. (*Anguish* 112).

As noted earlier, myths vary considerably in content, setting, and form. Though
they usually involve gods or godlike beings, those beings might be as hapless
as Coyote or as humanly fallible as Pandora. A myth might take place in the
heavens or at an ordinary hearthside. The trajectory of the story might be high
tragedy or low comedy, and the same events might be found in stories we
would ordinarily call fairy tales or legends, just as many of Bulfinch's "fables"
are probably best categorized as magical tales or hero legends. Any of these
sorts of stories become mythic when they establish the realm of the "abstract
but real," which others call the sacred or *kairos* or the Dreamtime—and allow
us to enter into it. Stories that do so come with obligations: the sacred must be
paid for. That is true whether one belongs to the myth-bearing culture or
comes to it from outside.

The payment for outsiders is an acknowledgment of our own complicity in
history. Myths are not timeless; like the individuals who perform them, they
reflect historical processes, and they change over time as the cultures that
maintain them change. They are not universal, for the full significance of a
myth depends on a web of associations and social interactions shared by storyteller and listeners. It is not true that, as Lévi-Strauss asserts, "Myth is the
part of language where the formula traduttore, traditore [translator, traitor]
reaches its lowest truth value" ("Structural" 85). Once the myth has been translated into print, it has already been betrayed; it is only that further translation
across linguistic boundaries does relatively little additional harm.

For Moderns, there are two categories of myth: those that have already lost
their cultural contexts, such as the Greek or Norse myths retold in Bulfinch,
and those that belong to groups who have been wronged by Modern civilization. Living mythic traditions are the ones that still exist in spite of the Western
world's attempts to displace, disrupt, convert, and/or kill the groups that maintain them. Any fair use of those traditions in scholarship or in literature demands an acknowledgment of the history of mistreatment and a chance for the
other to speak, rather than being interpreted and analyzed and spoken for. It
also involves an emphatic "thank you" for the generosity of such storytellers as
Kath Walker who choose, despite past and ongoing injustices, to lend their
myths to outsiders: to instruct us in the sacred and give us a glimpse of the
numinous.

My journey toward an understanding of myth more or less reflects the historical sequence by which the scholarly world came to know it. "Myth" started
out as a smallish set of classical fables but grew to include a host of world mythologies. Those were later revealed to be selections from larger traditional
oral narrative traditions embedded in specific ways of life. The idea of myth as
something timeless and universal gave way to an understanding of particular

myths as dynamic and culturally specific. As different models of myth emerged and were in turn replaced, each left a mark on a generation of poets and fiction writers, so that the entire history of the science of myth can be found reproduced in literary form. Nowhere is this more true than in fantasy literature.

The History of Fantasy as the History of the Myth Concept

Fantasy is a form of literary narrative that is one degree more fictional than fiction. Fiction differs from nonfiction in that its central assertions are untrue. If a novel starts out "Once there was a man called Fred," we are to understand that there was actually no such man and that, despite what we are told of his actions and thoughts, he never did or thought any of it. Other people, though, did and do similar things: fiction works metonymically, by naming and describing representative, rather than actual, individuals. One might say that part of the fiction is the premise that these imaginary people have real neighbors, whom they resemble in various ways. The metonymic function extends to setting: even if the locale is invented, the presumption is that one could get there from places in the real world. Fantasy, by contrast, takes place in a setting that cannot be reached by any nonmagical means. (The case of "real world" or "low" fantasy is more complicated, but the rule still holds.) In fantasy, our "Fred" not only *does* not exist, but *could* not exist—at least not as described, experiencing what he is said to experience. Fantasy-Fred might transform into a wolf, live a thousand years, or have his soul cut out by an evil magician. If realistic fiction is primarily metonymic, fantasy is inescapably metaphoric; because the presence of the impossible blocks a literal reading, we are invited to look at Fred and his world as some sort of iconic stand-in for everyday life, rather than as an extension from it.

By renouncing claims to report directly on reality, fantasy acquires the potential (not always realized) to generate powerful symbols. Like dream or myth, it uses symbols to tell the truths that the conscious mind cannot grasp or fears to face. Yet unlike myth, fantasy speaks with no cultural authority. It pretends to be a mere game, a simple amusement for children or a pastime for an idle hour. Like a jester in a Shakespeare play, it is free to speak forbidden truths because no one pays it any mind. And, like the Elizabethan theater, the genre of fantasy has become a space for cultural negotiation, to borrow Stephen Greenblatt's term, in part because of its seeming inconsequentiality. Whereas Marlowe and Shakespeare dramatized contesting models of gender, knowledge, and authority, fantasy pits different myths and responses to myth against one another. Those responses include different levels of belief, from literal through figurative and secondary to complete rejection. They also include different kinds of engagement—moral, social, liturgical, psychological—and different kinds of obligation. Fantasy can be used to weigh the claims of

myth against those of its Modern rivals, history and science. The latter is especially prominent in fantasy's sister genre, science fiction, and in the blended
genre of science fantasy, which is examined in more detail later.

Scholars have offered many accounts of fantasy, historical and descriptive,
and, as mentioned before, common usage gives the term many contradictory
meanings. My own understanding of fantasy as a literary practice (rather than
a state of consciousness) derives from a long line of writers: George MacDonald, William Morris, J. R. R. Tolkien, C. S. Lewis, Ursula K. Le Guin, Diana
Wynne Jones, Jane Yolen, and many others. Their works and stated intentions
indicate that fantasy cannot be understood in isolation; rather, the story of its
emergence as a modern genre is best told as a counterpoint to the history of
myth. Once it did emerge, modern fantasy changed that history retroactively,
made it seem to be heading toward an inevitable culmination, and turned a set
of disparate literary responses into stages of an evolution.

Long before there was a genre that could be called fantasy, some versions of
the fantastic mode were available. Richard Mathews claims that the first written
fantasies "are magical tales from Egypt recorded on papyrus that has been
dated from about 2000 B.C.E." ("Fantasy" 6). It is possible, though difficult to
prove, that those Egyptian tales were indeed, as Mathews states, intended to
be read as imaginative fictions rather than as accounts of actual encounters
with the divine. Leaving that question unanswered, we are probably better off
considering them, along with the *Odyssey*, the *Epic of Gilgamesh*, and other
ancient narratives, as what John Clute calls "taproot texts": narratives that
document mythic elements without clearly revealing, as Clute indicates fantasies began to do during the Age of Reason, their "author's consciousness that
he is transforming a traditional story containing supernatural elements into a
work mediated through—and in a telling sense defined by—those elements"
("Taproot Texts," 921).

However, even before Clute's eighteenth-century dividing line, back in the
Age of Fable, as Bulfinch calls it, when gods and magic were part of lived
reality for most people, there were a few writers whose response to myth—
casting doubts, taking liberties, reinventing—more closely resembles that of
the self-conscious modern fantasist than the devout worshipper of Zeus or
Demeter. Two works from the first and second centuries C.E. might be considered at least precursors of modern fantasy. The earlier is Ovid's *Metamorphoses*, which compiles a number of Greek and Roman stories of interactions with
the gods and retells them with wit and what appears to be irreverence. Robert
A. Segal contrasts Ovid's version of the story of Adonis with that of his Greek
predecessor Apollodorus:

> Where Apollodorus presents the story as true, Ovid presents it as fictional.
> Where Apollodorus tells it as straight, Ovid twists it to fit larger themes—
> notably, that of transformation, as in Myrrha's becoming a tree and Adonis'

becoming a flower. Where Apollodorus intends his story to be taken literally, Ovid intends his to be read metaphorically. Where Apollodorus is serious, Ovid is playful. ("Myth," 10)

The second writer of proto-fantasy is Apuleius, whose work is also titled *Metamorphoses*, or, more commonly, *The Golden Ass*. Apuleius adapts a traditional plot about a magical mixup that transforms his protagonist into an ass. Amid the bawdy comedy and social satire that ensues, Apuleius touches on higher mythic themes twice, once in the embedded narrative of Cupid and Psyche and again in the final conversion of his antihero to the cult of Isis, who not only provides the cure to his transformation but also calls him to be her priest. The delicate allegory of the former segment and the devout tone of the latter are both rather startling in the context of what is mostly an amoral romp.

Both works titled *Metamorphoses* function as fantasy to the degree that they are not authorized or reverent retellings of myth. As Segal says, they play with the material: inventing details, rearranging incidents, and inviting a response of amusement rather than awe. Yet both generate moments of poignancy and glimpses of the numinous. We cannot go back and ask Ovid whether he believed any of the stories or test Apuleius's degree of commitment to his goddess (into whose mysteries he was eventually initiated), but we can perceive in their texts a balance between complete skepticism and unquestioning faith—a state of temporary or compartmentalized commitment that corresponds to what J. R. R. Tolkien was to call Secondary Belief. The power of their stories depends partly on the fact that they know others believe, whatever their own doubts. They know the stories work, whether or not they are literally true.

From the later parts of Bulfinch's Age of Fable, medieval treatments of myth and legend, including *Beowulf*, the *Nibelungenlied*, Snorri Sturluson's prose *Edda*, the Welsh *Mabinogion*, and the entire Arthurian cycle, are marked by a similar state of suspension. In each of these texts, pagan motifs are revisited by the writers with an overlay of Christian judgment—of necessity, as written literature and the Roman alphabet accompanied Christianity to the north of Europe. Such texts document the overlap between indigenous oral traditions and imported literary and religious practices. In Snorri's case, the overlap was a close one, as some of his thirteenth-century Icelandic neighbors still privately worshipped the old gods, despite the country's official conversion in 1000. (A Swedish gravesite from the same era contained both Christian crosses and Thor's hammers—someone was hedging his bets.) Farther south and later on, there was little or no overlap between Christian literacy and pagan orality. By the time Marie de France wrote her *lais* in the late twelfth century, the Celtic gods of her native Brittany were long gone, first replaced by Roman deities and then banished by the Church. Even in Brittany, however, local legends and tales lived on. Marie's stories often combine legend motifs such as the werewolf of "Bisclavret" with the literary form of the romance; that literary tradition in turn draws from an older oral tradition of heroic ballad and epic. Marie's contemporary Chrétien de Troyes freely mingled pagan figures with Christian themes. The former include the Lady of the Fountain (something between a local goddess and a mortal votary of the same) who marries the knight Yvain. Among the latter is Perceval's encounter with the grail. The grail (not yet holy) is Chrétien's addition to the Arthurian mythos and is itself probably a conflation of magical cauldrons from Celtic tradition with the Communion chalice. Chrétien's successors further connect the grail with that chalice's prototype, the cup from the Last Supper.

By the end of the medieval era, writers such as Chaucer were constructing highly sophisticated blends of pagan and Christian myth. One of the most intricate is the anonymous fourteenth-century romance *Sir Gawain and the Green Knight*. From its Christmas—or is it Yuletide?—setting to the wilderness "chapel" where the title characters confront one another, this poem works on both levels simultaneously. Poised between Gawain's faith and the Green Knight's magical invulnerability and vegetation-god hue, the story invokes two mythic traditions without wholly rejecting either. In this willingness to be two things at once, both Christian and pagan, devout and playful, *Sir Gawain* is probably the closest analogue in the medieval world to J. R. R. Tolkien's version of modern fantasy. Not surprisingly, Tolkien was one of the poem's most passionate advocates and sympathetic interpreters.

Writers in the Early Modern period often depicted a lower mythology of witches, magicians, and fairy folk coexisting with the higher deities of Greece and Rome, as well as with Christian angels and demons. Shakespeare's plays invoke Jove and Diana, and the latter makes an appearance as the *dea ex machina* who brings about the impossible happy ending of his Greek-style romance *Pericles*. Robin Goodfellow and other sprites of the English countryside are recast as sylvan demigods in *A Midsummer Night's Dream*. Their fairy superiors, Titania and Oberon, report in turn to the Olympians. In *The Tempest*, the magician Prospero dabbles with Paracelsian spirits of earth and air. The former, Caliban, swears allegiance to the witch-god Setebos, while the latter, Ariel, refers to Jove and Saturn. Prospero himself calls on a trio of pagan goddesses, Iris, Ceres, and Juno, to bless his daughter's engagement and yet looks to heaven (presumably a Christian one) and asks the audience for their prayers to serve as his "indulgence," lest his ending be "despair." The implication is that his magic leaves him vulnerable to damnation, like his magical predecessor on the Elizabethan stage, Marlowe's Doctor Faustus.

Marlowe's play also mixes pagan and Christian myth when the demonic Mephistophilis tempts Faustus with a vision of Trojan Helen. In *Doctor Faustus*, though, the more significant rivalry is not between Christian and pagan myth but between the older mythologies and a newer cultural narrative, science. Basing the character and his fate on German oral tradition, Marlowe adds to the legendary magician a new motivation: to know the world scientifically and to control it through his knowledge. *Doctor Faustus* is an ancestor of modern science fantasy, and Faustus is the first mad scientist—the progenitor of Mary Shelley's Victor Frankenstein. Faustus's madness is simply curiosity untempered by faith or human sympathy. He acquires great power through his infernal bargain, but he uses it in a peculiarly childlike manner, to spy on the great and to play pranks. With no mythic narrative to govern his appetites and shape his aspirations, he falls away from his original nobility and works out his own damnation with little prodding from Mephistophilis. Shakespeare's Prospero shows some of the same arrogance. His fate differs from Faustus's partly because his concern for his daughter and, ironically, his love for his familiar spirit Ariel help him retain his humanity.

Whereas Marlowe privileges Christian myth over pagan in his version of the magician tale, so that Faustus's magic is necessarily black and its source demonic, Shakespeare uses classical tradition to keep Prospero's magic on the white side. Prospero's final speech renouncing his powers is borrowed from Ovid: a speech by the enchantress Medea with the more sinister elements edited out. Later commentators were uneasy with this blurring of the lines between male mage and female witch, white magic and black, pagan sprites and Christian devils. They hastened to rewrite Prospero/Medea into versions of the damned Faust. George Sandys's commentary on Medea in his 1632 edition of Ovid suggests that as a witch, Medea was a mere thrall to demonic forces:

> These wonders were not effected by the vertue of words, or skill of *Medea*; but rather by wicked Angels, who seem to subject themselves, the better to delude, to the art of the Inchantresse. (Lamb 546–47)

Another way Shakespeare keeps Prospero's magic more or less untainted is by juxtaposing English fairy lore with the pagan supernatural. The elves that sour the grass and make fairy rings grow are too homelike, too familiar, to seem evil. By identifying Prospero's Ariel with such beings, Shakespeare keeps Christianity at bay: its black-and-white morality is not allowed fully to encompass and evaluate other mythic systems. As in *Sir Gawain*, balancing two traditions allows for more leeway, more play, in the fantasy.

The century after Shakespeare's death is better known for political strife and Puritan austerity than for imaginative play, and John Milton is not usually thought of as a fantasist. Yet *Paradise Lost* is a foundational text for a number of later fantasies, including C. S. Lewis's space trilogy (pro-Milton) and Philip Pullman's His Dark Materials trilogy (anti-), and the work itself has been described within science fiction and fantasy fandom as Bible fan fiction or "fanfic" (see, e.g., "Fan Fiction and Academia"). Milton originally considered writing on King Arthur, as had proto-fantasists Thomas Malory in the fifteenth century and Edmund Spenser in the sixteenth century, rather than the biblical Fall. His ultimate choice to retell Genesis meant that, unlike his masque *Comus*, his epic stays within a single mythic tradition and avoids some of the anxieties—and pleasures—that come from yoking two incompatible systems of belief. Yet the choice of epic as a form meant that traces of classical myth remain. An epic is not just a long story with a vast setting. Epics have heroes, and in the absence of any other figure of comparable stature, Satan tends to grab the spotlight. He is, in essence, both Mephistophilis and Faustus, anguished tempter and fallen hero. In filling in the setting and back-story of the Fall, Milton provides a wealth of fantastic detail reminiscent of the imaginative grotesqueries of Hieronymus Bosch's paintings. In addition, Milton borrows techniques from the theater, such as Satan's soliloquies, that complicate his characters and give them an inner life that mythic figures from oral tradition do not have. It is no wonder that William Blake, among others, considered Satan the real hero of the piece.

Like Milton, Blake, writing in the late eighteenth century, continues to exert an influence on contemporary fantasy not only because of the startlingly fresh imagery of his poems and drawings but also because of his role in the reconfiguration of myth leading up to the Romantic movement. Like his German contemporaries Friedrich Schelling, Friedrich Schiller, and Novalis, Blake felt the lack of a compelling mythic system on which to ground a new poetry and a new philosophy. Neither classical nor biblical mythology filled the bill. Schiller's poem "Die Götter Griechenlands" or "The Greek Gods" (1788) expresses nostalgic longing for an unalienated consciousness before science, before the natural world emptied itself out, before language and truth parted ways (Von Hendy 21). Such a golden age was the Age of Fable. Schlegel, in his *Dialogue on Poetry* (1800), complains that "Our poetry lacks a focal point such as mythology was for the ancients; and one could summarize all the essentials in which modern poetry is inferior to the ancients in these words: 'We have no mythology'" (Schlegel 1968, 81; quoted in Von Hendy 31).

This is the break that distinguishes Clute's taproot texts from modern fantasy. The difference is not the ability to apply skeptical reason to magical motifs and supernatural beliefs; rather, it is the new awareness of myth as something belonging to others, to the past, to unfallen primitives. The advent of the scholarly study of myth marked the loss of myth. In response to this lack a number of writers attempted not merely to retell old fables but to invent new mythologies. One of the first such invented myths is Mozart's *The Magic Flute* (1791), in which Mozart and his librettist Emanuel Schikaneder combined Masonic ritual and fairy tale to produce a fable of (masculine) enlightenment. Following their example, Novalis and others created the *Kunstmärchen*, or literary fairy tale. Their tales usually do not much resemble oral tales but instead construct eerie dreamscapes and wandering narratives of loss and transformation, such as Ludwig Tieck's "Der blonde Eckbert" (1797), the embedded fairy tale in Novalis's novel *Heinrich von Ofterdingen* (1800), and E. T. A. Hoffmann's "The Sand-Man" (1816). Perhaps because the dissociation of modern life is not so easily banished, the mood of most *Kunstmärchen* is not consolatory but uncanny–indeed, Freud's theory of the *unheimlich* is based primarily on Hoffman's tale.

Influenced by Milton and Dante (both of whose works he illustrated), Blake eschewed fairy tale for poetic epic. He wrote several, including one titled *Milton a Poem* (1804–10). In them, he developed an elaborate invented mythology, based on Greek, Gnostic, and biblical motifs but drastically reconfigured, so that the creator figure becomes a repressive demiurge and the feminine principle a potential source of emancipation rather than, like Milton's Eve, of sin and exile. Blake remakes Milton into a spokesman for his own unorthodox religious philosophy. (The same tactic was later used, in reverse, by C. S. Lewis in his Blakean fantasy *The Great Divorce*, in which a fictionalized George MacDonald renounces his own universalism and proclaims Lewis's more orthodox Christian views.) Blake's Milton announces that he comes

> [. . .] in Self-annihilation & the grandeur of Inspiration
> To cast off Rational Demonstration by Faith in the Saviour
> To cast off the rotten rags of Memory by Inspiration
> To cast off Bacon, Locke & Newton from Albions covering
> To take off his filthy garments, & clothe him with Imagination
> To cast aside from Poetry, all that is not Inspiration
> That it no longer shall dare to mock with the aspersion of Madness
> Cast on the Inspired, by the tame high finisher of paltry Blots,
> Indefinite, or paltry Rhymes; or paltry Harmonies. (Object 43,
>   lines 2–10)

The problem with Blake's invented mythology is that the reader does not share it. Whereas Homer's audience already knew the Olympic pantheon and the whole story of the Trojan War and Milton's reader knew the Hebrew Genesis and Christian interpretations of it, no one except Blake knows who Albion and Los and Urizen might be. Indeed, Blake's meanings are obscure enough that his etching "The Ancient of Days," representing Urizen the compass-wielding demiurge, is frequently reproduced as a devout image of God creating the world. One would hardly guess from the picture alone that Urizen is allied with the Modern icons "Bacon, Locke & Newton" and thus is the enemy of poetic vision and spiritual renewal. Blake's longer poems are dense with abstractions and rife with obscure titanic characters performing even more obscure actions. Invented myth needs some other form than the verse epic to communicate its symbolism. Blake's nineteenth-century successors found two more workable forms: fairy tale and prose romance.

One of the greatest of these successors, George MacDonald, was strongly influenced by German Romanticism, and his first major work, *Phantastes* (1858), is a response to Novalis, reproducing *Kunstmärchen*'s dreamlike randomness and blurry symbolism. After an epigraph from Novalis that claims,

"*Ein Mahrchen ist wie ein Traumbild ohne Zusammenhang*" ("a fairy tale is like a dream vision without coherence"), the story is structured less like a Märchen than like an Arthurian romance, with a quest, knights, damsels, giants, and an evil enchantress. It is a Spenserian romance, moralized and elaborately allegorical (Docherty 39), but the allegory and indeed the plot are incoherent. The many sources and models remain separate and undigested. We do not know what brings the hero Anodos to Fairy Land (though the transformation of his earthly bedroom into an enchanted glade is one of the great set pieces of the book). We do not know what his purpose is, who he is fighting, why his erotic object is split into multiple figures, such as the virtuous wife of a knight and the duplicitous Alder Maiden. The "Traumbilder," or dream visions, are vivid and compelling, but the personal mythology MacDonald is working out remains almost elusive as Blake's.

It was only when MacDonald moved away from the Romantic *Kunstmärchen* and began to imitate folk Märchen that his stories became effective tools for exploring the mysteries of life, death, morality, creativity, and the unconscious—the stuff of myth. The tales published by the Brothers Grimm are efficient, logical, and pragmatic. Their characters rarely wander without purpose; they are occupied with maintaining households, escaping abusive parents, getting enough to eat. The objects in traditional Märchen are solid and substantial, even if they have magical properties. MacDonald, who would have heard similar tales in the Scottish highlands as he was growing up, learned how to incorporate that hardheadedness in his tales for children. In *At the Back of the North Wind* (1871), *The Princess and the Goblin* (1872), and *The Princess and Curdie* (1883), MacDonald found a form that allowed him to explore mythic motifs (taking Jacob Grimm's view that Märchen are submerged myth) within essentially realistic contexts: dream visions in daylight. Thus fantasy as a modern fictional genre and a conscious practice can be said to have begun with MacDonald. He became a model, and not merely a source, for later fantasists such as Lewis and Tolkien.

In his final major work, *Lilith* (1896), MacDonald returned to the plot of *Phantastes* but cut much of the Romantic excess and replaced the eclecticism with a single mythos. The title character of Lilith is the demoness of Jewish folklore: Adam's first wife, who refused to bow down to her mortal husband and was replaced by the more compliant Eve. Both Adam and Eve show up in the book, and so does Lucifer, referred to as the Shadow. This roster makes *Lilith* sound like another piece of Bible fanfic, except that Lilith does not appear in the Bible as a character but only as a term for some sort of night spirit—a lilith, rather than *the* Lilith—and the working out of her relationships and fate in the novel is far from conventionally Christian. *Lilith* is a complex and peculiar work, and MacDonald's relation to Christian myth is equally complex and surprising. I return to those topics later in this volume, but for now it is sufficient to let MacDonald stand for a new and mostly successful strategy for combining mythic materials with fairy tale structures and the kind of closely observed detail that marks his non-fantastic regional fiction.

MacDonald's 1883 essay "The Fantastic Imagination" further cements his position as a major bridge between German Romanticism and modern fantasy. He starts the essay by defining fairy tale in terms very similar to those used by Tolkien in his essay "On Fairy-Stories": "That we have in English no word corresponding to the German Mährchen [sic], drives us to use the word Fairytale, regardless of the fact that the tale may have nothing to do with any sort of fairy" (MacDonald 23). He describes the setting of the fairy tale as "another world, but one to which we feel a tie" and insisted on the logical consistency (no more of Novalis's "*ohne Zusammenhang*") of the imagined world:

> His world once invented, the highest law that comes next into play is, that there shall be harmony between the laws by which the new world has begun to exist; and in the process of his creation, the inventor must hold by those laws. The moment he forgets one of them, he makes the story, by its own postulates, incredible. To be able to live a moment in an imagined world, we must see the laws of its existence obeyed. Those broken, we fall out of it. (24)

Other important parts of his definition include the responsibility of the writer to hold fast to moral truths, however fanciful the narrative context, and the irreducibility of fantastic symbols. Fantasy, like myth, is meaningful, but the significance cannot be translated into other terms than its own:

> It cannot help having some meaning; if it have proportion and harmony it has vitality, and vitality is truth. The beauty may be plainer in it than the truth, but without the truth the beauty could not be, and the fairytale would give no delight. Everyone, however, who feels the story, will read its meaning after his own nature and development: one man will read one meaning in it, another will read another. (25)

Other Victorian writers copied the fairy tale with greater or lesser success. Many of those writers were MacDonald's friends, including John Ruskin, whose *The King of the Golden River* (published in 1851 but composed ten years earlier) is one of the first English literary fairy tales. MacDonald encouraged Charles Dodgson to publish *Alice in Wonderland* (1865) after testing it out on the MacDonald children. Others in MacDonald's literary circle wrote their own fantasies for children—most notably Charles Kingsley (*The Water Babies* 1863) and Jean Ingelow (*Mopsa the Fairy* 1869).

If George MacDonald is one major node in the network that created modern fantasy—what is often called mythopoeic fantasy—Andrew Lang is another. Lang's own literary fairy tale, *Prince Prigio* (1889), is less successful than those mentioned in the previous paragraph, partly because it is too arch, too much aware of its place within a literary tradition. But Lang connects with two other strands of mythic thought that developed from Romanticism: scientific folklore and what we might call atavistic romance. Lang is now probably best known as the editor of a series of fairy tale anthologies, starting with *The Blue Fairy Book* (1889), but he also played a major part in the scholarly debate over the nature and origins of myth in such works as *Myth, Ritual and Religion* (1887). In opposition to Max Müller and his philological approach, Lang argued for the interpretation of myth in the context of ethnographic data and especially evidence of ritual practices. He saw in mythic narratives—including fairy tales—survivals of "savage" beliefs in shamanistic magic, totemic animals, and animism: "the stage of culture when men did not sharply distinguish between the human and the natural world" (Dorson 34). The idea of the savage is always tinged with envy and nostalgia: those who consider themselves civilized also tend to think of themselves as less forceful and free, less "virile" (to use a favorite Victorian epithet) than their primitive counterparts. A form of popular fiction that arose in the mid-nineteenth century was the male romance: a story of adventure that involved a well-born Modern man journeying into an exotic and primitive civilization and therein finding his own savage masculinity. The best known of these "colonial adventures," as Robert Dixon calls them, were the novels of H. Rider Haggard, such as *She* (1887), *The World's Desire* (1890), *Montezuma's Daughter* (1893), and *Stella Fregelius: A Tale of Three Destinies* (1903). Those last three were all cowritten by Andrew Lang, who brought his knowledge of myth and the ancient world to add to Haggard's narrative urgency and murky eroticism.

The same impulse that led Haggard and Lang to seek out survivals of the primitive in exotic locales spurred the interest of Tennyson, Robert Browning, and William Morris in England's own more colorful and less civilized past. All three participated in the Victorian revival of things Arthurian, and Morris revived the prose romance in such stories as "Gertha's Lovers" and "The Hollow Land" (both 1856). Colin Manlove suggests that these stories encouraged Mac-Donald to set *Phantastes* in an imaginary medieval world; however, Morris differs from MacDonald in being interested in the past for its own sake, "because he has a passion for the middle ages and wants to bring them to life, and also to give a sense of the utterly past" (Manlove 67). This interest led Morris to study not only Malory and the English romance tradition but also its wilder cousin, the Scandinavian saga. Working with the Icelandic scholar Eiríkr Magnússon, he translated *Gretissaga* in 1869, and he published a retold version of the story of the Nibelungs as *Sigurd the Volsung* (1877). Andrew Wawn emphasizes the importance of Morris's study of saga and Norse myth in the creation of his late romances, starting with *The House of the Wolfings* (1889):

> Old Icelandic texts had certainly provided Morris with a set of narrative molds into which he could pour his molten narrative material–journeys, famous weapons, non human foes, ancient traditions, threatened communities, and the like. (4)

According to Farah Mendlesohn and Edward James, it was Morris, in works such as *The Wood Beyond the World* (1894), who invented the technique of setting fantasies in a wholly other world. Rather than using a dream vision or other framing device, "Morris constructs a world as if it is the only world that exists" (Mendlesohn and James 22; emphasis in original). Though the location of MacDonald's *The Princess and the Goblin* is uncertain and possibly otherworldly, it is difficult to think of any other exceptions to this claim, and Morris is a major figure in the development of fantasy as a genre, strongly influencing William Butler Yeats, Lord Dunsany, E. R. Eddison, J. R. R. Tolkien, and many later writers. His turn away from classical and biblical myth led successors such as Tolkien to look even further afield: to pre-Arthurian versions of Celtic myth, to the *Kalevala*, to the Arabian Nights and Persian myth, and eventually, with the fantasy boom of the 1960s, outward to the rest of the world.

The full story of that broadening vision is the subject of this book. In incorporating various myths, including non-European ones, into fantasy, writers found themselves confronting radically different visions of society, the natural world, and the self. They also came up against communicative barriers and ethical issues, such as the right of outsiders to transform sacred texts into popular entertainments. As they explored different myth traditions, they found themselves dealing with history in unexpected and disturbing ways and having to reinvent the forms of fantasy and even fiction itself. The nature of belief begins to alter when one makes the imaginative leap from a Modern sensibility to some other worldview. Truth changes, and thus so does fictionality. In the twentieth and twenty-first centuries, fantasy has continued to offer modes of storytelling that challenge not only the norms of novelistic, bourgeois realism (as endorsed by critics such as Ian Watt and Q. D. Leavis) but also religious and scientific attempts to constrain or usurp the power of myth.

Taxonomic Interlude: A Note on Genres

Both literary studies and folklore are built on the idea of genres, rather as biology is built on categories, from kingdom to species, reflecting morphological similarity and common descent. However, unlike, say, raptors and perching birds, different genres do not exist until someone imagines them. Genre terms are both descriptive and constitutive. Once a particular type of text is called a *ballad* or a *sonnet*, then ballads and sonnets exist, and they have whatever properties we perceive in the examples. But which examples? There is where the process gets complicated.

No one disputes the use of the term *sonnet* for Shakespeare's verse arguments, but there are many problematic or borderline cases. Can a poem with fifteen lines instead of fourteen be a sonnet? What if a poet calls something a sonnet but violates all conventions of rhyming and meter? What about a passage from a play or a novel that falls into sonnet form? If a form as strictly conventional as a sonnet can pose problems, the situation for something like a novel is nearly hopeless. When is a novel really a romance? Is a novel in verse part of the genre? How about a nonfiction novel? Is the novel really a supergenre, with subcategories that deserve genre status? Furthermore, when applied to fiction, "genre" can become a negative term: a way of sorting out the formulaic chaff from the literary wheat. Book reviewers often distinguish genres—mysteries, Westerns, science fiction, and the like—from nongeneric or "literary" fiction. Though this usage does not reflect a real difference so much as indicate blindness to the conventionality of their favored forms, it does complicate any discussion of fictional genres, including fantasy.

The fantastic—that is, creative and disruptive play with representations of the real world—can be found in many genres of oral and written storytelling. Most of the fantastic fiction in a bookstore can be found in a single section that is sometimes labeled "science fiction" and sometimes "fantasy." That section, however, rarely includes works older than the late nineteenth century (for example, *Gulliver's Travels*), works in verse or dramatic form (*The Tempest*), or translations (*The Master and Margarita, One Hundred Years of Solitude*), even when such works incorporate significant elements of the fantastic. And the two rival labels signal another definitional problem. Fantasy and science fiction are shelved together or near one another because the same writers often write both and have overlapping audiences of fans. However, among those fans, some claim that science fiction is a subcategory of fantasy, others that fantasy is simply a specialized (or even defective) branch of science fiction. There have been innumerable arguments about where to put particular writers such as Ray Bradbury and about whether certain works belong in either one.

To avoid this sort of border war, I proposed in an earlier book that all genres are what logicians call fuzzy sets: categories defined not by a clear boundary or any defining characteristic but by resemblance to a single core example or group of examples (*strategies*). This way of thinking about categories is similar to Ludwig Wittgenstein's idea of family resemblances; in both cases, the qualities of the category depend on the prototypes one chooses. One difference between these two ways of thinking about genres is that fuzzy sets involve not only resemblances but also degrees of membership. Instead of asking whether or not a story is science fiction (SF), one can say it is *mostly* SF, or *marginally* SF, or *like* SF in some respects. Allowing for partial membership in genre categories helps explain how genres can hybridize. A book such as Bradbury's *The Martian Chronicles*, for instance, demands to be read as both (mostly) fantasy and (mostly) science fiction. There are enough similar examples that it is worth positing a new genre—science fantasy—which will have its own core examples and distant relatives.

I still like this way of cutting through the Gordian knot of genre classification, but it does not account for all the historical and social dimensions of genre. For instance, the term "science fiction" has an identifiable origin in pulp magazines of the 1920s through 1950s; we think of earlier stories by Poe, Verne, and Wells as SF partly because of their being republished and discussed in those magazines. Editors of the magazines, especially Hugo Gernsback, had a particular technophilic agenda that was taken up by social organizations of fans. A parallel, noncommercial publishing industry arose within fandom: first in letter columns in the magazines, then in mimeographed or photocopied fanzines, and later on the Internet. Much of the critical terminology for describing SF arose within such fan publications, which have also often served as an entry for fledgling writers. Fantasy has a longer and more complicated history, and no single defining moment. However, certain key developments can be identified within the history of the fantastic: the Romantic and Gothic passion for the supernatural; the Victorian and Edwardian fairy tale revival; such magazines as *Weird Tales* and *Unknown*; the unexpected best-sellerdom of Tolkien's *The Lord of the Rings* and the paperback book industry's response.

Each of these concentrations of activity reflected a unique historical situation; each reached out to—and helped construct—a particular audience; each was a response to specific social pressures and intellectual issues. Fuzzy set theory does not say much about history, audience, or purpose, but it does not conflict with those perspectives, either, so long as we remember to ask not only "To what extent is this story a fantasy?" but also "How does this story relate to prior and subsequent instances of the fantastic?" "Who is this story addressed to?" and "What cultural work does this story undertake by being part of the fantasy category?"

Genres of folk narrative present some of the same definitional problems as genres of written literature, but they also involve a very different cultural situation. In literary discussions, producers, consumers, and definers are usually part of the same group, using the same language to describe the material (SF fandom, with its in-house critical tradition, is a rare exception). Since the time of Wilhelm and Jacob Grimm, however, folklorists have attempted to study their subject scientifically, which means, among other things, creating categories that folk narrators and audiences would not recognize. The three major categories of prose narrative described by the Grimms—myth, tale, and legend—are *etic*, or analytic, categories: distinctions based on formal differences as perceived by outside observers. The *emic* categories of storytelling within a particular culture might be quite different. There might be only two categories, or half a dozen, and their defining features might be differences unperceived by outsiders. What the folklorist calls a Märchen, a storyteller might call a Jack tale, or just an old-timey story.

Though the Grimms' categories have been periodically rethought and the distinctions among them refined and revised, most systematically by William Bascom, the basic division remains useful as an analytical and pedagogical tool. The common definition of folktale, the Grimms' *Märchen*, is a highly structured folk fiction, sometimes magical but often bawdy and comically realistic. Their legend, or *Sage*, was a more loosely structured and localized narrative illustrating sacred or secular beliefs. A legend is any story told as truth—though Bill Ellis points out that, in practice, that means "any story believed by an informant and disbelieved by a folklorist" (5). A less ethnocentric definition allows for more shadings of belief but retains the core idea that the narrated events might indeed have happened:

> Thus, even the most hardened skeptic who relates an alleged encounter with a ghost, only to refute and ridicule it, nevertheless concedes by so doing that this is a narrative that requires disproof. He also enables listeners of the opposite party to pick it up and repeat it as evidence for their own belief. (Ellis 6)

As this example shows, questions of belief are especially complex when the legend is a supernatural one. Supernatural legends are not always easy to distinguish from myths. Both embody beliefs. Both can invoke a sense of mystery and the sacred. But whereas legends take place locally and in historical time—the search for the Holy Grail, for instance—myths take place outside of ordinary time. Bascom specifies a setting in the remote past (4), but myths may take place either at the beginning of the world or its ending, Genesis or the Revelation, or they may occur in some eternal Now—what Mircea Eliade called the Eternal Return. When exactly does Demeter go searching for her lost daughter? Every winter, when the earth goes cold and barren. When is Osiris reborn? Whenever the Nile floods. Both myths and legends can be explanatory, but whereas legends might explain the origins of local land features and place names, myths establish the fundamental orders of nature and society. Bascom explains that myths "are the embodiment of dogma; they are usually sacred; and they are often associated with theology and ritual" (4).

In his entry in *Myth: A Symposium*, Stith Thompson warned that no one definition of myth, especially one based on European models, will fit all traditions: "With such a group as the North American Indians, then, it is often possible to speak of certain tales as essentially mythological because they deal with origins and with higher powers. But in the study of a particular tale, as it spreads over the continent, it is often impossible to know whether the native teller thinks of it as myth or ordinary story" (174). Significantly, Thompson seems to be suggesting that myths *are* tales, at least formally, though they are treated differently from ordinary tales.

Barre Toelken shares Thompson's earlier skepticism about categories or genres of folklore. He describes a set of Coyote stories shared by a family of Coos Indian background. The stories are comical, risqué, and told primarily for entertainment, like European folktales, but they are also subject to the restrictions placed on many religious narratives: told only in winter, preferably out of doors on camping or hunting trips, and only once a season by any one narrator (169). Are they myths or folktales? The question is not exactly meaningless, but any answer may say more about the observer than about the story itself.

To further complicate things, mythic ideas are not necessarily communicated in the form of individual prose narratives. A story can be sung or chanted instead of spoken, taking the form of a ballad or epic. Mythic motifs might be invoked in hymns or healing ceremonies. The central action of a myth might be enacted or danced or depicted graphically instead of recited. Legends, too, are often communicated indirectly, their core beliefs being alluded to rather than fully narrated. The Swedish folklorist Carl von Sydow identified one of the ways legend can be passed along and its truth-value reinforced: through a type of narrative that he called *memorate* (87). A memorate is a firsthand account of an experience, usually a supernatural or paranormal one, that links the teller to a traditional belief or legend. The experience often hinges on some strange physical sensation such as bright lights, eerie sounds, pictures falling off a wall, or the feeling of waking up with a weight pressing on one's chest.

The sensations are individual, but the explanation is found among the teller's culturally determined, collectively held categories: it was a poltergeist, or the Holy Spirit; a ghost; the Nightmare. Lauri Honko explains that memorates bridge the gap between personal experience and traditional belief:

> during the experience itself a person often does not yet know what the creature he sees is. He might already be convinced of the supernormal nature of the vision, but the interpretation does not yet occur. This kind of supernatural being, which as yet has no exact image attached, can be called a *numen*. (16)

Only afterward, when the experience is recounted, does it become assimilated to traditional legend and belief with the aid of listeners who might include "spirit belief specialists, influential authorities, whose opinion, by virtue of their social prestige, becomes decisive" (Honko 18). Memorates belong mostly to the individual, but legends are group property. Both are formulaic, but in a memorate, formularization is an attempt to give structure and sense to an otherwise inexplicable personal experience.

A number of such memorates were collected several years ago by a student of mine in a folklore class. The town I live in adjoins the Fort Hall Indian Reservation. Like most reservations, Fort Hall is a patchwork of properties held by tribal members—Shoshone and Bannock—and various outsiders. My student, who is Anglo-American, had lived and worked on the reservation. She learned from her coworkers, both Native and white, that the area known locally as the Portneuf Bottoms, a tangle of willow-lined streams and sagebrush meadow, is haunted by spirits known as Water Babies. These are sacred beings, part of the traditional worldview of the Great Basin tribes. My student did not try to collect any of the sacred stories about Water Babies, or Pā´ōna; instead, what she found was that the Native belief had crossed over into non-Indian culture and had taken the form of various folk genres other than sacred legend.

When Anglo-Americans talk about Water Babies, the emphasis is not on the mythic status of the creatures but rather on the emotions and experiences of the tellers. The emotional import ranges from a sort of relishing of the eerie to skepticism and dismissive humor, sometimes with a racist tinge. For instance, in many retellings, the river bottoms become a version of a haunted house, and the story becomes one of teenagers daring one another to confront the scary presence—usually in hopes of setting up a romantic situation. When the Water Babies legend is transformed into such a dating story, the sacred context is reduced to a vague acknowledgment of past beliefs, and the numinous experience is conveyed in terms of a few sense impressions: a sound like an electrical surge, a ripple in the water, glowing eyes in the darkness (Crook). Such memorates intersect with a related category of narrative, the urban legend. Some of the personal experience stories of Water Babies incorporate motifs from "parked teenager" legends, in which the dating couple is threatened by a ghost, a wild animal, or a madman. In memorates connected to such legends, the actual threat is deferred or manifested indirectly: cars fail to start; people act under compulsion or have trouble breathing.

It is almost impossible to extricate elements of legend (for von Sydow, *fabulate*) from the memorate's remembered details filtered through traditional formulas. The two genres are frequently associated, and the same events can occur in both. Group storytelling sessions alternate between recounted legends and personal memories triggered by the legend motifs. After someone tells a legend, it is often followed up or tagged with a related memorate. If the teller wasn't actually there on the scene, he heard it from a friend of a friend, who was. The usual explanation given by folklorists for attaching personal anecdotes to legends is that the memorate validates the legend. Linda Dégh gives the alternative name "witness-legend" to memorates, especially those retold by someone other than the original experiencer (61). The word "witness," like other language connected to memorates, such as "corroborate," "vouch," "authentic," and "testimony," demonstrates their perceived function as shoring up the otherwise hard-to-swallow aspects of the legend. In the case of the Water Babies stories, though, the point seems to be not so much establishing the story's truthfulness as demonstrating that the teller has genuinely, if briefly, entered into the realm of the numinous.

Memorates show up on just about every occasion that includes telling or alluding to supernatural legends. These include ghost story sessions, performances of fairy lore in places such as the Scottish Hebrides where the fairy faith is active, and personal testimony in religious meetings, especially, in the United States, among Mormons and Pentecostal Christians. In each case, the purpose is to link the traditional and sacred with the personal. It is true that we attach memorates to legends as validation of supernatural narratives, myths as well as legends. It is hard to deny an eyewitness report, even of seeming impossibilities. As Elliott Oring says, "the closer the connection of a narrator to his or her source, the more credible the account is likely to be" (3). But there is another purpose, one which these stories share with written fantasy. Not only does the personal experience story "authenticate" the legend, but it also, in a sense, "legendizes" the teller by establishing a connection between personal history and the world of myth. This is the same point made by J. R. R. Tolkien in his Andrew Lang lecture "On Fairy-stories." He mentions that a widely distributed tale "resembling the one known as the Goosegirl (*Die Gänsemagd* in Grimm) is told about Charlemagne's mother Bertha (52). Historians explain that "the Goosegirl Märchen became attached to Bertha," but it would be more accurate to say that "Bertha was turned into the Goosegirl" (53)—in other words, that she became attached to folk tradition. Like other historical figures, she was thrown into the "Cauldron of Story" (52). Memorates throw us into the pot as well. They attach the teller and, indirectly, the listener to the world of legend, as well as reestablishing the legend's supernatural elements as part of the world of experience.

Written literature can draw on any and all of these oral genres. A short story can imitate a tall tale or supernatural legend. A poem can imitate an oral ballad. A novel can be a veritable compendium of other text forms, from bawdy tales to sacred songs. Mimetic fiction often depicts scenes of storytelling, which can produce startling shifts in genre. Different levels of embedding allow the same novel to be both fantastic and realistic, a have-one's-cake-and-eat-it technique already familiar by the time Homer had Odysseus narrate his fantastic adventures in the *Odyssey*, either fooling the credulous listeners or providing them with his true history.

One lesson we can take from all these generic puzzles is that no single answer will do: the question of what genre a particular text belongs to will never be resolved, nor need it be. The interesting question about any given story is not whether or not it is fantasy or science fiction or realistic novel, but rather what happens when we read it as one of those things. What happens when we read *Frankenstein* as an instance of the philosophical Gothic? How does that reading differ from one that looks for the markers of science fiction, or horror? Depending on the generic perspective one favors, certain details of plot and motivation will stand out, while others will recede into the background. The central questions will shift. Different reading contexts will suggest themselves, including groupings of related works. Like individual performers within the same storytelling tradition, individual readers will perform the same texts with very dissimilar results: sometimes more effectively, sometimes less.

Throughout this study, I propose a number of groupings of and ways to read fantastic texts, and some of those ways of reading are derived from folklore scholarship rather than literary criticism. Folklorists have rarely assumed, as have many literary scholars, that the primary purpose of narrative is to report on the world as it is. Nor do they privilege the individual creator over received tradition (although folklorists have come around to honoring the skilled performer's role in giving voice, shape, and intentionality to traditional materials). Insights derived from the study of oral genres are often more useful in reading modern fantasy than are critical standards developed for reading the bourgeois novel—one obvious instance is Vladimir Propp's folktale morphology. Though my title refers to myth, I draw on many of the folk genres within which mythic motifs and structures are found, including epic, legend, and folktale. In this I am following the venerable tradition of Jacob Grimm, not to mention slews of comparative mythologists, psychoanalysts, and structuralists, all of whom roam freely among narrative modes, although I try to maintain genre distinctions in talking about individual folk texts. Of the folk genres mentioned here, the least familiar is probably the memorate, and yet the core of my argument is that oral memorate and written fantasy are analogous in function. Both bridge the gap between narrative, the natural habitat of gods and heroes, and ordinary experience. Both allow us to imagine our way into the realms of wonder and mystery and to account for incursions of the numinous into our daily lives. As I claimed earlier, the important question for any genre is what happens when we read something as an instance of that genre. By sampling different periods and formulations of fantasy throughout this book, I hope to suggest not only the breadth and artistic potential of fantasy as a genre but also some of the less obvious and more intriguing ways that we, as readers, can perform it.

Make It Old: The Other Mythic Method

The second decade of the twentieth century was a time of tremendous change. Those who lived through it—and, between the Great War and the subsequent influenza epidemic, millions did not—came out on the other end as different people in a different world. War is always a source of social upheaval, and this was a war beyond any previous in geographical scope and human cost. However, many other changes were already in the works before the war broke out. The legacy from previous decades included the women's movement; socialism and anarchism; labor unrest; tottering colonial empires; population shifts and deliberate exterminations of minority peoples; new media, including wireless radio and moving pictures; transportation breakthroughs, such as the automobile and the airplane; Einstein's theory of special relativity; Freud's model of the unconscious; and Pavlov's experiments with behavioral control. The war compounded the effects of these already disruptive ideas and trends.

The transformation can be summed up by four well-known quotations (three of them a bit well worn, too, as descriptors of the period). The first is Virginia Woolf's comment that "On or about December, 1910, human character changed" ("Mr. Bennett" 4). Woolf (always quick to pick up subtle signals) pinpointed an unusually early date, but she was right about a dramatic break in consciousness. Despite many cultural continuities (there are always continuities, no matter how great the cataclysm), the world was different because the lenses people looked through were different. Her sort of people—European, well educated, well off—were Modern in a way that even the most sophisticated Victorians were not: disillusioned, cut loose from the past, open to social experimentation, literally or figuratively shell shocked. "You're all," said Gertrude Stein to her younger colleagues in my second catchphrase, "a lost generation" (Hemingway 29).

An altered consciousness calls for an inventive artistic response. The response of many artists was to embrace the new, the startling, the Modern.

Every art found its own way to be Modern. Stravinsky shocked the musical world with dissonance and jazzy, asymmetrical rhythms. Dancers Nijinsky and Duncan brought primitive rituals and open sexuality onto the stage. Braque and Picasso broke up solid objects and superimposed perspectives to create cubism. The new art of the cinema played with camera angles and montages to reeducate viewers in the art of seeing. Designers and architects of the 1920s and 1930s embraced the machine: everything from radios to restaurants pretended to be steamships and airplanes. And in poetry, the byword was Ezra Pound's dictum (and my third catchphrase): "Make it new" ("Make It New" 1934).

Fantasy seems out of place in this garish Modern world. The Inklings—Tolkien and Lewis and their tweedy friends—look like a holdover from an earlier era, a besieged remnant fighting a rearguard action in the pubs and studies of Oxford. Yet the Lost Generation was also a generation of fantasists. Most of the influential Modernists were born between 1880 and 1899; the oldest were young men and women in 1910, and the youngest came of age during the war. The same is true of the writers who created the best-known fantasies of the twentieth century. James Joyce and Virginia Woolf were born in 1882; so was E. R. Eddison. Ezra Pound was born in 1885, a year before Charles Williams. Hope Mirrlees, born in 1887, was a year older than T. S. Eliot; Tolkien was four years younger. The era that embraced Freud and Ford, that shocked and shattered and declared its independence from the past, also produced its share of fables and fairy tales.

One way to make sense of these seemingly incompatible trends is to apply Raymond Williams's concepts of dominant, residual, and emergent culture. Any historical moment, says Williams, can be defined by its dominant pattern: feudalism, bourgeois culture, and so on. However, the hegemony of the dominant culture is challenged from two directions: from the past and its not-yet-vanished ways of living and seeing and from the future, the cultural alternative that will eventually take over. It would be easy to identify fantasy as an aspect of residual culture in the early twentieth century, especially from a Marxist perspective such as Williams's. Williams cites three examples of contemporary (i.e., 1970s) residual culture: organized religion, rural community, and monarchy (R. Williams 122). Each of these cultural residues is associated with some or all of the Inklings, who were, for instance, not just religious but publicly so. Charles Williams and C. S. Lewis wrote books on Christianity, and Tolkien considered *The Lord of the Rings* an essentially Catholic book (*Letters* 172). Tolkien's Shire is an idealized version of an English rural community, as are the gatherings of talking animals and nature spirits in Lewis's Narnia. The "return of the king" is not just the title of one of the three volumes of Tolkien's epic; monarchy is a central metaphor for order regained and justice restored. The same is true in Lewis's *Prince Caspian*. The Inklings generally shared a reverence for tradition and (except perhaps Williams, the Londoner) a love of nature both pastoral and wild. Tolkien and Lewis were not particularly interested in the innovations of their contemporaries in the literary world, preferring instead to harken back to such models as MacDonald and Morris, who were themselves looking over their shoulders at Milton, Blake, and beyond to the Middle Ages. In place of Pound's "make it new," they might well have adopted as a rallying cry, "Make it old!"

Yet the residual is not necessarily retrograde intellectually, nor socially conservative. It can also, according to Williams, be oppositional. It expresses "certain experiences, meanings, and values which cannot be expressed or substantially verified in terms of the dominant culture" (122) and thus serves as a check on the dominant consensus. This ability to oppose the hegemonic is lost, though, when residual culture is appropriated as mere decoration or entertainment. Williams might have been thinking of genre fiction when he describes the process of being "incorporated, as idealization or fantasy, or as an exotic—residential or escape—function of the dominant order itself" (122).

If residual culture is that which used to be dominant, emergent culture is that which is going to be important. Thus identifying it is always a matter of hindsight. Williams identifies the truly emergent with the arising of a new economic class, whose interests and practices simply do not register within the dominant order. Like the residual, the aspiring emergent can either serve as an oppositional or merely an alternative form of culture. In the latter role, its potential disruptions are domesticated and brought into the larger social order. Williams might identify the popular version of science fiction—*Star Wars*, for example—as such an alternative: falsely emergent because the dominant class has already figured out how to make sense of it (for instance, in 1980s political rhetoric) and how to use it as idealization and escape.

The usual narrative of twentieth-century literary history treats the Modernists as examples of emergent culture breaking free of forms that no longer expressed people's sense of themselves and their lives. Fantasy, if considered at all within the historical narrative, is treated as an eddy in the time stream, a nostalgic swing into an imaginary past. Its kings, countryside, and spirituality are seen as inconsequential archaisms, temporary fads, just as the Tolkien boom of the 1960s was expected to be a temporary phenomenon.

That last prediction should give historians pause. *The Lord of the Rings* did not go away, and the fantasy fad threatens to take over not only as entertainment but as a serious challenge to realistic models of fiction, just as other manifestations of myth confront secular rationality in political and social spheres. Hindsight may have to revise itself. The residual might turn out to be the emergent, or at least another face of the emergent.

I propose looking at early-twentieth-century fantasy as not an anachronistic alternative to Modernism but as one of its important manifestations. It may at times be best analyzed as a residual component, at others as emergent, but in both cases as part and parcel of the era, partaking fully in its cultural convulsions. The Inklings and their fellow fantasists may not have identified themselves as Modernists, but they were inescapably part of the Modern era. They lived through the same events, confronted the same horrors, made in their daily lives the same adjustments to new ideas and devices. If we define Modernism not as a style but as a condition, everyone living through the 1910s and 1920s shared that condition, just as everyone who lived through the turn of the millennium shares a set of experiences that define postmodernity. We are all postmodern, whether or not we consider ourselves postmodernists. Fredric Jameson, drawing on Williams's work, defines postmodernism as a "conception which allows for the presence and coexistence of a range of very different, yet subordinate features" (*Postmodernism* 4). Modernism similarly includes a range of features, including two alternative versions of the return to myth.

The idea that links Pound's era with Tolkien's, the Lost Generation with the Inklings, can be found in my fourth quotation. In a 1923 review of *Ulysses*, T. S. Eliot identified something in Joyce's practice—or in his own, projected onto Joyce—that he called "the mythical method." (Note: Eliot's phrasing seems to me to suggest that the method itself is a myth; I prefer to shorten the first word to "mythic," as I have done throughout this chapter when not quoting him.) Here is the longer passage in which the phrase occurs:

> In using the myth, in manipulating a continuous parallel between contemporaneity and antiquity, Mr. Joyce is pursuing a method which others must pursue after him. They will not be imitators, any more than the scientist who uses the discoveries of an Einstein in pursuing his own, independent, further investigations. It is simply a way of controlling, or ordering, of giving a shape and a significance to the immense panorama of futility and anarchy which is contemporary history. It is a method already adumbrated by Mr. Yeats, and of the need for which I believe Mr. Yeats to have been the first contemporary to be conscious. It is a method for which the horoscope is auspicious. Psychology (such as it is, and whether our reaction to it be comic or serious), ethnology, and *The Golden Bough* have concurred to make possible what was impossible even a few years ago. Instead of narrative method, we may now use the mythical method. It is, I seriously believe, a step toward making the modern world possible for art [. . .]. (177–178)

This paragraph has been rightly used to open up modernist texts such as *Ulysses* and Pound's *Cantos*. It has not been employed with *The Lord of the Rings* (though Tom Shippey mentions it briefly in *J. R. R. Tolkien: Author of the Century*, 313) or that work's predecessors: Eddison's *The Worm Ouroboros*, Hope Mirrlees's *Lud-in-the-Mist*, or Charles Williams's *War in Heaven*. And yet everything Eliot says in his description of *Ulysses* applies as well or better to those texts. Everything, that is, except for the phrase "instead of narrative method." The principal difference between the Modernists' mythic method and that of fantasy is that the latter constructs apparently seamless narratives that put the mythic on the same diegetic plane as the modern, or at least modern sensibility.

Any characterization of Modernism will depend on which texts we take as core examples, of course. Even within the subcategory of Modernist reworkings of myth, we find a bewildering array of examples, each leading toward different definitions and conclusions. One form of modernism might be defined by Hilda Doolittle's lyric tributes to Sappho in *Sea Garden* (1916); another could be based on Francis Poulenc's Dadaist opera *Les Mamelles de Tirésias* (1947). Each, in its own way, follows the method Eliot describes as "manipulating a continuous parallel between contemporaneity and antiquity," though the forms of manipulation differ wildly. However, since Eliot named the method, I will examine his own practice, especially in "The Waste Land" (1922).

The poem's title and overt instructions in Eliot's footnotes point toward a specific mythic source: Arthurian romance, and especially the Grail Quest that leads knights toward the ruined castle and wasted kingdom of the Fisher King. Eliot cites the once-standard work of Jessie Weston to support the idea that the Grail story *is* mythic. For Weston, the Grail story is primarily pagan, deriving from rituals of sacrifice and fertility. Associations with Christian belief and biblical narrative are later add-ons. Eliot uses both the pagan and Christian aspects of the story to construct a guide through and a commentary on a set of scenes from contemporary life. To represent the latter, Eliot combines pastiche and parody with imagistic detail and wistful lyricism (deliberately roughened up by Ezra Pound's editing). The myth appears mostly in the form of oblique allusions (reinforced by the notes) and Janus-faced characters: modern types who are also degraded versions of gods, magicians, and heroes. Two such characters are "Madame Sosostris, famous clairvoyante" with a "wicked pack" of Tarot cards (lines 43 and 46) and "Mr Eugenides, the Smyrna merchant/ Unshaven, with a pocket full of currants" (lines 208–209). Madame Sosostris's card readings are an ironic reference to prophets such as the Cumaean Sibyl, whose words from Petronius's *Satyricon* are quoted at the beginning of the poem. As glossed in Eliot's note, the epigraph says, "I have seen with my own eyes the Sibyl hanging in a jar, and when the boys asked her 'What do you want?' she answered, 'I want to die.'" Though the Sibyl is, in Petronius and in Ovid, a pathetic shriveled figure who forgot to ask for eternal youth to go with her gift of immortality, she nevertheless represents divine prophecy, the voice of Apollo speaking through his priestess. Madame Sosostris is a corrupted version of the Sibyl, giving trivial advice to society ladies. The powerful symbols of life and death on her cards—the Hanged Man, the Wheel—mean nothing to her or her customers, other than as a sort of horoscope suggesting ways to avoid daily hazards.

Mr. Eugenides is introduced briefly as a sinister and seductive outsider who invites the poem's speaker "To luncheon at the Cannon Street Hotel/Followed by a weekend at the Metropole" (lines 212–213). Marjorie Perloff points out that the merchant is obviously propositioning the narrator with the offer of a stay at a prominent Brighton hotel, although his invitation is only a "travesty of the Fisher King's invitation to the quester outside the Grail Castle" (12). The currants in his pocket are a shriveled (and thus Sibylline) remnant of the grapes of mystery cults and biblical feasts. As always in the poem, emotional engagement is either mocked or diverted into mythic references. Eliot's note tells us to read Mr. Eugenides not as a real object of desire and alarm but as an echo of other figures—perhaps *all* the other figures—in the poem: "Just as the one-eyed merchant, seller of currants, melts into the Phoenician Sailor, and the latter is not wholly distinct from Ferdinand Prince of Naples, so all the women are one woman, and the two sexes meet in Tiresias" (note to line 218).

There is a lot of slippage here, reflecting Freud's notions of condensation and displacement, the ways dream and myth evade conscious censorship. Though Eliot disparages psychology, "such as it is, and whether our reaction to it be comic or serious," he has clearly absorbed Freud's ideas and found them poetically useful. Smyrna is indistinguishable from Phoenicia and from the isle of *The Tempest*. A homosexual assignation with a foreigner segues into the tawdry tale of a London typist waiting for her boyfriend. The masculine seer becomes indistinguishable from the feminine Sybil. The modern world metamorphoses into the mythic realm of Shakespeare and Ovid, the biographical self disappears, and suddenly Eliot the poet is off the hook. None of this is personal, not the anxiety, desire, or disappointment; instead it is the ailing soul of the age revealed in the mirror of myth.

Two other elements are only hinted at here but are more fully developed in other Eliot poems. One is the choice of Christian myth above all others. This choice becomes more explicit in the later Eliot, but it is signaled in "The Waste Land" by the unseen and androgynous companion in the desert:

> Who is the third who walks always beside you?
> When I count, there are only you and I together
> But when I look ahead up the white road
> There is always another one walking beside you
> Gliding wrapt in a brown mantle, hooded
> I do not know whether a man or a woman
> —But who is that on the other side of you? (lines 359–367)

Eliot's footnote identifies Shackleton's experiences in the Antarctic as the source of this eerie image, but it also calls to mind the Apostles finding themselves accompanied by the risen Christ on the road to Emmaus.

The second theme is the anti-Semitism that blames Jews for the downfall of Western civilization. This is a central component of medieval Christianity, and anyone making reference to mythic materials from medieval tradition can divorce himself from that attitude only by deliberate effort. Eliot makes no such effort. Eliot's anti-Semitism, for instance in "Burbank with a Baedeker,

Bleistein with a Cigar" (1920), hardly compares with that of his Modernist colleagues Wyndham Lewis and Ezra Pound; nevertheless, it represents a darker aspect of his turn toward religion. The more strongly he associates the good with Christianity, the more he must dissociate himself from such figures as Mr. Eugenides, who, though not called a Jew, is a merchant, is ethnically marked and associated with the Orient and "stands as a symbol of the decay of Europe" (Roessel 171). Another sort of slippage allows Eliot to bring in Jews in lines that link Mr. Eugenides to the drowned Phlebas: "Gentile or Jew/O you who turn the wheel and look windward,/Consider Phlebas, who was once tall and handsome as you" (lines 317–320). A suppressed section called "Dirge" makes the link explicit, parodying Ariel's song "Full fathom five" to describe the decaying body of the drowned Jew Bleistein (Julius 141).

Phlebas/Eugenides has to be drowned, because he is the outsider, the mage, and the object of unacceptable desire. All of those things must be thrown out, abjected, in Julia Kristeva's terms, in order to reconstruct the self as pure Christian spirit. The entire poem enacts the ritual sacrifice of a symbolic king, a pattern justified by references to Weston and Frazer, but the ritual also has a more personal significance, hinted at but perpetually withheld. Eliot's brilliant lyricism and elaborate mystification pull off his trick, but only if the reader is willing to read hypertextually, to reassemble "these fragments I have shored against my ruins" (line 430), to fill in the mythic context following Eliot's guidance, and to avoid looking too closely at things such as the author's biography and politics. Not all readers are willing or able to invest so much in reading a single text, mythic or not. For many, the poem is mostly "immense panorama of futility and anarchy" and not enough shape or significance.

But what if "The Waste Land" were not a densely allusive and cryptically fragmented poem but a novel? Such a novel would juxtapose the Holy Grail and sterile urban life; there would be charlatans masquerading as real prophets and vice versa; characters would undergo spiritual crises and transformations; there would be sinister Easterners and scenes of sexual degradation; visions of hell would be counterpointed with moments of redemption; the desired and forbidden other would be expelled. Novelistic discourse could fill in the gaps left in Eliot's poem, or at least seem to, with realistic settings, dramatic scenes, internal monologues, and a plot. It would not matter too much what sort of plot: the function would be to carry readers along and perhaps distract our attention while the symbols did their work. The novel could be a romance, an adventure, or perhaps a detective story.

Charles Williams's *War in Heaven* (1930) starts with a dead body found incongruously under the desk of a London publisher named Lionel Rackstraw. Detectives are called in, suspects identified, clues gathered. The scene shifts from London to the Agatha Christie-esque village of Fardles, where another crime is committed: someone knocks the Archdeacon over the head and makes off with the communion chalice. The murder mystery opening gives way to something more mystical—Williams's novels are often called "supernatural thrillers"—when the chalice is revealed to be the Graal, the Holy Grail, come to rest in a place whose original name was not Fardles but Castra Parvulorum, the camp of the children. The name change is accounted for by Grimm's law:

> "Grimms Law," Mornington asked, astonished. "Wasn't he the man who wrote fairy tales for the *parvuli*? But why did he make a law about it? And why did anyone take any notice?" (24).

The law in question deals not with fairy tales but with language shifts, yet Williams reminds us that the two are linked and invites us to speculate on what the laws of the fairy tale might be, especially with regard to magical treasure and acts of violence. Those laws will govern the novel's outcome as much as does the logic of the detective novel. *War in Heaven* frequently calls attention to its own relationship to folklore: along with a dead body, Lionel's office contains the proofs for a book called *Historical Vestiges of Sacred Vessels in Folklore*, by Sir Giles Tumulty, an antiquarian and, as it turns out, a dabbler in occult arts (he is the closest stand-in for Eliot's Madame Sosostris). In Sir Giles's book is the evidence that the Fardles chalice might be more than it seems.

Both crimes in this case are the work of Rackstraw's boss's father, the retired publisher Gregory Persimmons. Persimmons is a would-be mage, who wants the Graal as an object of power. Sir Giles sends him to a shopkeeper referred to as "the Greek," though the ascription is questionable: "he might be Greek, as Sir Giles had said, he might be anything, and the name over the door had been indecipherable" (66). The Greek is associated more with the Middle East than with Greece: he attests, seemingly from firsthand knowledge, to Persimmons's rightful ownership of the Graal by giving it a provenance "from near Ephesus, [having] been brought to Smyrna in the flight before the Turkish advance" (128). Like Eliot's Smyrna merchant, the Greek is decadent, a seller of shady merchandise and a seducer of sorts. His chemist's shop is a black magic store in disguise. Instead of weekends at the Metropole, he offers an ointment that provides both magical and sexual release:

> Gregory smiled, and touched the ointment with his fingers. It seemed almost to suck itself upward round them as he did so. He disengaged his fingers and began the anointing. From the feet upwards in prolonged and rhythmic movements his hands moved backward and forward over his skin, he bowed and rose again, and again. The inclinations gradually ceased as the anointing hands grew higher—around the knees, the hips, the breast. (73)

And shortly thereafter,

> [. . .] the powerful ointment worked so swiftly upon him, stealing through all his flesh with a delicious venom and writhing itself into his blood and heart,

that he had scarcely come to rest before the world was shut out. He was being made one with something beyond his consciousness; he accepted the union with a deep sigh of pleasure. (73–74)

As Gregory works his way toward damnation, the Greek is supplemented by an even more sinister tutelary figure, the Jew. Where the Greek offers sensual release and power, Manassah the Jew offers only destruction. He seeks to destroy the Graal rather than make use of it:

"Destroy it!" Gregory mouthed at them. "*Destroy* it! But there are a hundred things to do with it. It can be used and used again. I have made the child see visions in it; it has power."

"Because it has power," the Jew answered, leaning over a counter and whispering fiercely, "it must be destroyed. Don't you understand that yet? They build and we destroy. That's what levels us; that's what stops them. [. . .] To destroy this is to ruin another of their houses, and another step towards the hour when we shall breathe against the heavens and they shall fall. The only use in anything for us is that it may be destroyed." (144)

This is all too close to Eliot's vision in "Gerontion" (1920), conceived of as a preface to "The Waste Land." In that poem, a bitter old man (modeled after Henry Adams) meditates on the downfall of European civilization, abetted by Jews:

My house is a decayed house
And the jew squats on the window sill, the owner
Spawned in some estaminet of Antwerp,
Blistered in Brussels, patched and peeled in London. (Lines 7–11)

Christian myth is difficult to disentangle from such venom. It shows up in Chaucer's "Prioress's Tale," and it shows up in present-day versions of the same blood libel. If there is corruption and violence and decay, it can't be *our* fault. It must be the work of the Jews or some other outsiders.

The narrative logic of Williams's story, unlike Eliot's poem, does not lead toward dessication and despair. Against the cabal of Jew, Greek, and black magician, another coalition forms, consisting of Lionel Rackstraw's colleague Kenneth Mornington, the Archdeacon, and a poetry-writing duke they enlist in their cause. The three are explicitly compared to the three Grail knights:

"We're carrying the San Graal," Mornington said. "Lancelot and Pelleas and Pellinore—no, that's not right—Bors and Percivale and Galahad. The Archdeacon's Galahad, and you can be Percivale: you're not married, are you? And I'm Bors—but I'm not married either, and Bors was. It doesn't matter; you must be Percivale, because you're a poet. And Bors was an ordinary workaday fellow like me." (120)

As these three bachelor knights oppose the three black magicians, the murder mystery plot returns in the form of an odd sort of caper, complete with a car chase. While the Graal is being stolen, stolen back again, and hidden in plain sight like the McGuffin in a Hitchcock film, the two forces are engaged in a metaphysical struggle between being and nothingness. In lengthy passages of internal monologue, characters try to come to terms with the Graal and its significance. For each, the chalice offers a distilled version of his own relationship to the universe: to Persimmons, it is power; for Manasseh, destruction; to the duke, a restored Catholic church; to the Archdeacon, the consummation of his religious vocation; to Mornington, a vision of myth channeled through literature: "Malory—Tennyson—Chrétien de Troyes—Miss Jessie Weston. *Romance to Reality*, or whatever she called it" (121).

It is Mornington's immersion in the literature of the Grail (including "The Waste Land," implied by the reference to Weston's *From Ritual to Romance*) that overcomes any doubts he might have had about the intrusion of the supernatural into ordinary English reality. Some such rationale is necessary in this second mythic method. Whereas poetry can leave its mythic basis on the figurative level, so that the Grail legend acts as a unifying conceit for all of Eliot's observations and allusions, fantasy has to bring the impossible into the narrative "reality." Magic in a poem can be like background music in a movie: pervasive, unexplained, guiding the viewer's emotional response without being noticed by the characters. Magic in a fantasy is like diegetic music: if there is a string quartet playing on the soundtrack, the camera must at some point pan over to four players whose presence is justified by the occasion. Williams uses Mornington as his camera. As he takes in the diegetic magic, his response calls attention to and simultaneously justifies the break with reality:

> Mornington, listening, felt the story to be fantastic and ridiculous, and would have given himself up to incredulity, had it not been for the notion of the Graal itself. This, which to some would have been the extreme fantasy, was to him the easiest thing to believe. For he approached the idea of the sacred vessel, not as did Sir Giles, through antiquity and savage folklore, nor as did the Archdeacon, through a sense of religious depths in which the mere temporary use of a particular vessel seemed a small thing, but through exalted poetry and the high romantic tradition in literature. This living light had shone for so long in his mind upon the idea of the Graal that it was by now a familiar thing—Tennyson and Hawker and Malory and older writers still had made it familiar, and its familiarity created for it a kind of potentiality. To deny it would be to deny his own past. (100–101)

Williams, through Mornington, is asserting that the Grail legend and its ritual origins can be seen as neither foreign nor antique but rather part of one Englishman's personal and present-day experience. Literature, he suggests, can work as a substitute for oral tradition, though it is necessary to work out how the mythic interacts with the everyday.

Literary texts do not come immersed in belief systems, ways of life, and interpretive schemata, as do myths in oral cultures. That is the other part of fantasy's mythic method, to provide living contexts to replace the ones stripped from myth texts. If the story is to do its work in the present, then not only must the existence of the Graal be explained but we must also see how it relates to the world of shops, motorcars, and newspaper headlines. Williams makes use of a number of fictional techniques to accomplish this end. One is borrowing a plot from a popular formula, the detective story. Another is the adoption of multiple points of view. He freely shifts the narrative focus among his characters, using direct and indirect quotation of their thoughts and letting their perceptions guide the third-person narrator's attention and vocabulary. A third technique is letting the characters themselves puzzle out the symbolic level of events and objects: What does a seemingly random murder mean? What is the value of a religious relic? How are names significant? A fourth is the pairing of black and white magics. Evil rituals are elaborate, coercive, and self-indulgent. By contrast, anything simple, cooperative, and self-denying becomes not only good but magically effective: the Archdeacon's prayers, no different from those he has practiced all his life, become part of the magical armament of virtue because they oppose a magic that would deny all that they stand for. Confronted by black magic, simple virtue becomes a magical force.

Williams draws on another set of legend motifs to reinforce this contrast. As in Eliot's poem, another companion turns up on the road, someone who is both there and not there. A mysterious stranger in gray shows up at Fardles to help the three grail knights. He is Prester John, a warrior-king out of medieval legend, here identified with both John the Baptist and the Graal itself:

> "I am John and I am Galahad and I am Mary; I am the Bearer of the Holy One, the Graal, and the keeper of the Graal. I have kept it always, whether I dwelt in the remote places of the world and kings rode after me or whether I removed to the farther parts of man's mind. All magic and all holiness is through me, and though men stole the Graal from me, ages since I have been with it forever." (204)

Prester John fulfills some of the same functions as Eliot's Tiresias: he combines both genders (Sybil and Fisher King, Galahad and Mary) and represents a point of view beyond that of any of the limited, mortal characters. He is both the object of the quest and the means of achieving it. But to get there, the characters have to come to terms not only with magic and holiness but with evil as well.

Part of the effectiveness of "The Waste Land" is its compelling vision of the modern world as a barren, ruined, empty place: the realm of the impotent

Fisher King. There are glimpses of this wasteland in *War in Heaven*, such as the tawdry urban environment surrounding the Greek's magic shop:

> There were a sufficient number of sufficiently dirty children playing in the road to destroy privacy without achieving publicity: squalor was leering from the windows and not yet contending frankly and vainly with grossness. It was one of those sudden terraces of slime which hang over the pit of hell, and for which beastliness is too dignified a name. But the slime was still only oozing over it, and a thin cloud of musty pretence expanded over the depths below. (65–66)

This description, though, filtered through the perceptions of Gregory Persimmons, represents his snobbery as much as the horrors of modern life. A more compelling vision of a modern inferno comes through Lionel Rackstraw, who lives the apparently model life of a successful publisher, husband, and father. For Lionel, nothing is certain, anything good is likely to be taken away at any time, and the abyss is always there, lurking under the surface reality: "The faces he saw, the words he heard existed in an enormous void, in which he himself—reduced to a face and a voice, without deeper existence—hung for a moment, grotesque and timid" (17).

Lionel's mental state is left unexplored through most of the narrative, but it is significant that Williams returns to it right at the end of the book. In Prester John's last conversation, just before he and the Graal vanish in a vision of the divine, he suggests to Lionel that he has embraced his alienation as a way of feeling alive: "you are afraid of losing yourself in the fantasies of daily life, and you think that these pains will save you" (251). Implied in Prester John's comment is a tripartite hierarchy of realities. Only God and Heaven are truly real, daily life is mere fantasy, and Lionel's paranoid fears are something in between. Therefore it is good to have glimpses of something beyond the ordinary, even if the glimpses are themselves delusive. They are at least a step in the direction of true vision, usually represented in the novel by the perceptions of the Archdeacon. Here is what the Archdeacon sees when he looks into the Graal:

> Faster and faster all things moved through that narrow channel he had before seen and now himself seemed to be entering and beyond it they issued again into similar but different existence—themselves still, yet infused and made one in an undreamed perfection. The sunlight—the very sun itself—was moving on through the upright form before the altar, and darkness and light together were pouring through it and with them all things that were. (253–254)

This is not typical novelistic discourse. It more closely resembles poetry or religious testimony: the visions of Julian of Norwich or William Blake or Eliot at the end of the *Four Quartets*. For some readers it is the real meat of the novel, the justification for the plotting and visits to the minds of unpleasant characters such as Persimmons or problematic ones such as Lionel. For other readers it is mystification, a peculiar habit of Williams, who can write with perfect clarity on some pages and then produce whole paragraphs of nearly indecipherable prose (to the despair of his Inkling friends, who often complained of Williams's obscurity; see Glyer 82–83). One sympathetic reader explained these lapses into incoherence in terms of the limits of language itself: "What he had to say was beyond his resources, and probably beyond the resources of language, to say once for all through any one medium of expression." This reader was T. S. Eliot, in an introduction published with Williams's *All Hallows' Eve* (xi.).

It is no stretch to read *War in Heaven* through Eliot. The two were friends, fellow Christian mystics, and in a sense coworkers:

> My play *Murder in the Cathedral* was produced at the Canterbury Festival in 1935; Williams's *Cranmer* was the play for the following year, and I went down with a party of mutual friends to see the first performance. (Eliot, "Introduction" x)

If Eliot influenced Williams, Williams also influenced Eliot. Williams praised Eliot in his 1930 survey of *Poetry at Present*, and Eliot, working at Faber and Faber, published Williams's novels (Lindop 11). Their works continued to parallel one another after "The Waste Land" and *War in Heaven*. Williams wrote his own mythicized treatment of Tarot in *The Greater Trumps* (including a character named Sybil) and his version of Eliot's "The Hollow Men" in *All Hallow's Eve*. The character of the religious playwright Peter Stanhope in *Descent into Hell* is a blending of Eliot with Williams himself.

Hence Williams's novel can stand for fantasy's mythic method as Eliot's poem represents Modernist poetry's. They tell the same story, or use the same story to tell us how to cope with modernity. That coping strategy has four components. First, the contemporary world must be organized somehow, and myth offers a structure whereas history seems to offer only struggle and accident. Even if, for Eliot, myth itself has shattered, he still suggests that the fragments can be gathered up against ruination. For Williams, myth is more durable, though it tends to lurk half forgotten in places like Fardles. It is residual within the social setting of his fantasy but can be made to emerge into a new vision of the world.

Second, the mythic structure offers a way to isolate and expel undesirable elements of society, which is to say the aspects of the self that can't be acknowledged. These may be projected onto various sorts of outsiders: for Eliot, the merchant, the Jew, and the homosexual; for Williams, the merchant, the Jew, and the power-seeker. Interestingly, the only one of Williams's villains whose story reaches any conclusion is Gregory Persimmons, who turns himself in for murder, resolving the mystery plot. Manasseh and the Greek are last seen prostrate, abashed by the power of the Graal and Prester John, but not explicitly killed nor crying defeat. Persimmons is the true abject, the thing that must be brought down because it is desired. Williams did desire mastery over mystical things: along with his Christian mysticism, he was drawn to notorious occultist Aleister Crowley and groups such as the Hermetic Order of the Golden Dawn (Gauntlett 2008). Persimmons might be a portrait of Crowley or of Williams himself. He is only the first of a string of such figures in Williams's novels: false prophets, black magicians, charismatic leaders who attract and dominate female acolytes. Crowley had several such relationships with young women, and so did Williams. In each of Williams's novels, the mage figure must be defeated and humiliated, but he reappears in the next, as Williams's own inner mage has not gone away.

The third component of the mythic method is its ability to validate moments of glory. Fiction often strives toward such moments. James Joyce called them epiphanies: glimpses of some redemptive truth, often achieved through suffering and hidden in the trivial. Joyce's epiphanies are human and secular; their relationship to myth is usually ironic. For Eliot, they emerge slowly: absent from his early work, hinted at in "The Waste Land," asserted with increasing confidence in "Ash Wednesday" and the *Four Quartets* as he aligned himself with Christian mysticism. Knowing and reading Williams helped push Eliot along this trajectory. Eliot said of Williams, "He knew, and could put into words, states of consciousness which many people have once or twice in a lifetime" (1945 xvii). The reason Williams could put such states into words is that he had a literary model that allowed him to do so: the fairy tale. What we might call Grimm's Other Law states that in a fairy tale, heroes may undergo terrible trials and evil beings might thrive temporarily, but good will triumph in the end. Tolkien points out in his essay "On Fairy-Stories" that this turn to the good is wholly unexpected, beyond hope. He calls it *eucatastrophe*, the good reversal, and connects it with the hope that lies beyond despair in Christian myth. The murder mystery shares this structure (as G. K. Chesterton and Inkling associate Dorothy Sayers knew), so Williams has a double rationale for his happy endings. For Williams, triumph consisted not of wealth or marriage and half a kingdom, as in traditional tales, but in moments of mystical union with God. The mythic pattern, in this case, converges with and underscores his own experience.

But mystical visions cannot truly be shared, only pointed toward. There must be something in the reader's own experience to hang the vision on, or else the moment of glory evaporates into empty rhetoric. Williams was writing for a wider readership than Christian visionaries, whose faith would presumably not need such reinforcement anyway. As Marek Oziewicz says of mythopoeic fantasy generally, Williams's novel "points to the supernatural, but establishes moral premises for the supernatural within the work itself, since in today's world no widely accepted body of belief, including Christianity, can be taken for granted" (85). The novelistic discourse through which Williams affirms the myth demands that it be testable against everyday experience. By invoking the real world through observed scenes and realistically reported streams of consciousness, Williams's novels invite us to judge their outcomes against our own sense of probability and moral rightness. The skeptical reader will not do the work for him; the mystical payoff must be earned.

Though moments of rapture are necessarily private, what can be shared is the mythic pattern that creates a space for such a vision, and, for the fullest degree of sharing, that mythic pattern cannot be a sectarian one. To turn Christian beliefs into fantasy requires the freedom to play with elements of the narrative, something not possible with official doctrines and fixed scriptures. Both Eliot and Williams found the freedom to invent and alter by arriving at Christian images and themes through noncanonical legends: stories associated with Christian belief but not governed by official teachings. This is the fourth component of Williams's mythic method: play. He gains license to play by working not directly with the core beliefs of Christianity but with those beliefs filtered through half-pagan offshoots, such as the Grail legend and the stories of Prester John. Another such legend motif is the figure of Lilith, previously adapted to fantasy by George MacDonald and used by Williams in *Descent into Hell*. These are theologically safer than stories about the Hebrew prophets or Jesus and his miracles, in that there is no investment in justifying them scripturally or putting the right doctrinal spin on them. They are also accessible to a non-Christian readership, which is free to read them metaphorically instead of literally or to look for psychological rather than theological validity.

Williams encodes both sorts of reading into the novel, the psychological and the metaphoric. By employing the novel's capacity to shift among varying points of view, he can affirm Anglican Christianity through one character, while another tries to explain everything in materialistic terms. Inspector Colquhoun, the police detective, is mostly blind to magical events and deaf to their religious resonances, but he doggedly links up the knowable facts to restore justice. He is on the side of good even if he does not understand goodness the same way the Archdeacon does. He also embodies something of a psychoanalytic reading of the story. In a revealing little scene, the inspector muses on the case as he is falling asleep, and his train of thought reflects Freud's ideas on dreams, puns, and displacement:

> At the moment the inspector thought nothing of this; but that night, as he lay half asleep and half awake, the two names which had haunted him arose like a double star in his sky. He felt them like a taunt; he bore them like a martyrdom; he considered them like a defiance. A remote thought, as from the departed day of common sense, insisted still: "Fool, it's his father, his father, his father." A nearer fantasy of dream answered: "He and his father—the name's the same. Substitution—disguise—family life—vendettas—vengeance—ventriloquism . . ." It lost itself in sleep. (126)

Williams invites not only a Freudian reading but also one based in comparative mythology. He invokes, as Eliot does, Frazer's *Golden Bough* and Weston's *From Ritual to Romance*, so that the Grail pursued by the various characters echoes not only the cup from the Last Supper but also other sorts of communion and sacrifice, other roads to vision. The character of Prester John, although associated with biblical figures such as John the Baptist, is also linked with various exotic locales, such as Persia and Ethiopia, and with non-Christian prophecies. Just as Eliot ends "The Waste Land" with a Buddhist sermon and a Hindu blessing, Williams suggests a oneness underlying all mythic traditions. As the trio of villains is trying to figure out who Prester John might be, Gregory comments,

> "I've heard tales—lies, very likely—but tales. Out about Samarcand I heard them and down in Delhi too—and it wasn't the Dalai Lama either that made the richest man in Bengal give all he had to the temples and become a fakir. I don't believe in God yet, but I wonder sometimes whether men haven't got the idea of God from that fellow—if it's the same one." (172)

These are interesting chains of association, not only between the Buddhist sage and the Christian prophet-king but also between the villain's paranoia and the hero's insight. Similar slippages occur in all of Williams's supernatural thrillers. In *All Hallow's Eve*, for instance, a figure much like Prester John turns out to be the Antichrist, but that is not obvious at first, and Simon the Clerk might well have turned out to be a helper rather than an archvillain had he not had both the taint of power and "a hint of the Jew" (52) about him. One can expect to find in any Williams novel both a true and a false hierophant, or spiritual guide, but the two could often change places with little damage to the plot. It all depends on the mythic allusions and the way the story plays with them. Says Eliot:

> There is much which he has invented, or borrowed from the literature of the occult, merely for the sake of telling a good story. In reading *All Hallow's Eve*, we can, if we like, believe that the methods of the magician Simon for controlling mysterious forces could all be used with success by anyone with suitable natural gifts and special training. We can, on the other hand, find the machinery of the story no more credible than that of any popular tale of vampires, werewolves, or demonic possession. ("Introduction" xv)

This freedom is an extension of his free play with mythic motifs, as is the capacity of Williams's stories to "make you partake of a kind of experience that he has had, rather than to make you accept some dogmatic belief" ("Introduction" xiv). It makes the modern world possible, not only for art but for meaning, morality, and vision. Not all modern fantasists found that meaning in Christian doctrine, as did Williams and his fellow Inklings, but all found myths to be powerful tools for investigating morality and transcendence.

Much of what I have claimed about Williams's mythic method and its relationship to literary Modernism could also be said about Tolkien and Lewis, the better known mythopoeic fantasists. Partly because it *has* been said, by Shippey, Oziewicz, Verlyn Flieger, Patchen Mortimer, Kath Filmer, and Patrick Curry, I will not attempt a close reading of *The Lord of the Rings* to try to establish it as a Modernist text, nor to trace its many mythic sources. These and other scholars have not only tracked down inspirations for Middle-earth in Celtic, Latin, Norse, Old English, and Finnish texts, but they have also pointed out significant connections between Tolkien and modern experience. The latter include his transcription of World War I trench warfare into the Dead Marshes and the devastation of Mordor; his representation of evil in terms of totalitarian collectivism; his awareness of the ecological devastation accompanying the industrial revolution; and his depiction of existential doubt or despair in such characters as Frodo and the Steward of Gondor, Denethor. Tolkien himself was aware of the degree to which his imaginative creation reflected present-day realities. In a 1944 letter to his son, stationed overseas during World War II, Tolkien acknowledged:

> I sometimes feel appalled at the thought of the sum total of human misery all over the world at the present moment: the millions parted, fretting, wasting in unprofitable days—quite apart from torture, pain, death, bereavement, injustice. If anguish were visible, almost the whole of this benighted planet would be enveloped in a dense dark vapour, shrouded from the amazed vision of the heavens! And the products of it all will be mainly evil—historically considered. But the historical version is, of course, not the only one. (*Letters* 76)

The other, nonhistorical version to which he refers is a mythic or religious one, and Tolkien was clearly using that perspective to counter his despair over history. Later in the same letter he describes his composition of a scene in *The Lord of the Rings*:

> So far in the new chapters Frodo and Sam have traversed Sarn Gebir, climbed down the cliff, encountered and temporarily tamed Gollum. They have with his guidance crossed the Dead Marshes and the slag-heaps of Mordor, lain in hiding outside the main gates and found them impassible, and set out for a more secret entrance near Minas Morghul [sic] (formerly M. Ithil). It will turn out to be the deadly Kirith Ungol and Gollum will play false. (*Letters* 76)

Frodo and Sam's journey echoes the letter's own trajectory, from despair to unexpected hope (for Gollum's falsity leads directly to the story's eucatastrophe). Though Tolkien always denied he was writing an allegory of the war, he was certainly aware of metaphoric connections between it and his story:

> We are attempting to conquer Sauron with the Ring. And we shall (it seems) succeed. But the penalty is, as you will know, to breed new Saurons, and slowly turn Men and Elves into Orcs. Not that in real life things are as clear cut as in a story, and we started out with a great many Orcs on our side [. . .].
> (*Letters* 78; ellipses in original)

Attuned though Tolkien was to contemporary history, he had little to do with contemporary literature, and so there is a better example to show how his kind of secondary-world fantasy, as opposed to Williams's urban, "real-world" version of the genre, connects with Modernism. A fantasy novel published in 1926 demonstrates how myth's organizational power and potential for play can function within a pagan, rather than a Christian, mythic system. The author of that fantasy, Hope Mirrlees, was as closely connected to major figures within Modernism as Williams was to Eliot, and those biographical links point toward the potentially emergent power of the other mythic method.

Our clearest portrait of Mirrlees was drawn by a not entirely sympathetic acquaintance, Virginia Woolf. An entry in her diaries describes Mirrlees as "over-dressed, over elaborate, scented, extravagant, yet with thick nose, thick ankles; a little unrefined" (cited in Carpentier 172). In a 1919 letter to Margaret Llewelyn Davies, Woolf complains that

> Last weekend [. . .] we had a young lady [HM] who changed her dress every night for dinner—which Leonard and I cooked, the servants being on holiday. Her stockings matched a wreath in her hair; every night they were differently coloured; powder fell about in flakes; and the scent was such we had to sit in the garden. Moreover, she knows Greek and Russian better than I do French; is Jane Harrison's favourite pupil, and has written a very obscure, indecent and brilliant poem, which we are going to print. (Quoted in Boyde 2)

Woolf is clearly irked by the affected stylishness and perhaps jealous of the early literary success of her younger guest. In addition, she and Mirrlees were rivals for the attention of their mutual mentor, the Cambridge don and classical scholar Jane Ellen Harrison. The poem that Leonard Woolf was preparing to publish (immediately after publishing T. S. Eliot's *Poems*) was called *Paris*. It is a montage of the city as it recovers from war, experimental in typography and daring in its choice of detail—hence Woolf's "obscure, indecent and brilliant." Julia Briggs describes the poem as "terribly engaged with the post-war moment, the strike in Paris of 1 May 1919, the demobbed soldiers, President Wilson arriving for the Treaty of Versaille etc etc—also an elegy for the dead, also an assertion of solidarity with the French, and the French avant-garde at that" (quoted in Swanwick 15). Its techniques presage many of Eliot's choices in "The Waste Land," including the inclusion of explanatory (or diversionary) footnotes.

The poem's first lines suggest the brash obscurity of an Ezra Pound:

> I want a holophrase
> NORD-SUD
> ZIG-ZAG
> LION-NOIR
> CACAO-BLOOKER
> Black-figured vases in Etruscan tombs (3)

The obscurity decreases, however, with a footnote that explains "Nord-Sud" as a line of the Paris underground, and "Zig-Zag," "Lion-Noir," and "Cacao-Blooker" as posters, presumably found on the walls of Metro stations. The black-figured vases represent traces of the past beneath the surface of the present, a theme throughout the poem.

Most important, the word *holophrase* is glossed in the work of Jane Harrison, who was not only Mirrlees's teacher but also her collaborator and life companion. A holophrase is simply a single word that carries the meaning of an entire sentence, a phenomenon that Harrison associates with a pre-Modern, unalienated state:

> The Fuegians have a word, or rather holophrase, mamihlapinatapai, which means 'looking-at-each-other,-hoping-that-either-will-offer-to-do-something-which-both-parties-desire-but-are-unwilling-to-do.' This holophrase contains no nouns and no separate verbs, it simply expresses a tense relation—not unknown to some of us, and applicable to any and every one. [. . .] As civilization advances, the holophrase, overcharged, disintegrates, and, bit by bit, object, subject and verb, and the other 'Parts of Speech' are abstracted from the stream of warm conscious human activity in which they were once submerged. (Themis 474).

Mirrlees, therefore, starts her poem with the equivalent of an plea to the Muses: she wants an undivided poetic language to convey her kaleidoscopic vision of Paris past and present. Part of that vision is mythic: it includes not only the Eiffel Tower and cafes and memorials of the recent war but also Etruscan vases and nymphs and newborn fertility gods: "Hatless women in black shawls/Carry long loaves—Triptolemo in swaddling clothes" (17). More important, Paris holds

> Stories. . . .
> The lost romance
> Penned by some Ovid, an unwilling thrall
> In Fairyland,
> No one knows its name. (17)

Mirrlees was to find that lost Ovidian romance—and a holophrase of sorts—in her only major fantasy.

Though Mirrlees was nearly forgotten by the literary world for several decades, her pioneering poem was rediscovered by feminist scholars in the 1970s.
Her third novel, *Lud-in-the-Mist*, was revived independently in 1970, as part of
Ballantine Books' Adult Fantasy Series, which capitalized on the success of the
paperback edition of *The Lord of the Rings* by bringing a number of older fantasies back into print. Since its republication, Mirrlees' work has become a favorite of writers and cognoscenti—one of those books that people acquire
extra copies of to give to worthy recipients. It has not, however, been read as an
important Modernist text, not even in an article on Mirrlees as Modernist poet
(Boyde) or in a book-length study of Jane Harrison's influence on Modernism
(Carpentier).

Nothing about the book proclaims it as Modernist. It is set in an imaginary
country called Dorimare: quaint, charming, and bordered by Fairyland. The
main character is a middle-aged and self-satisfied burgher named Nathaniel
Chanticleer. At the beginning of the book, Nathaniel is primarily concerned
with his duties as mayor of the town of Lud-in-the-Mist and with the quality
of his Moongrass cheeses. Yet there is an underlying unease in both Nathaniel
and the country, and a deeper theme signaled in the epigraph from Harrison's
Prolegomena:

> The Sirens stand, as it would seem, to the ancient and the modern, for the
> impulses in life as yet immoralised, imperious longings, ecstasies, whether
> of love or art, or philosophy, magical voices calling to a man from his "Land
> of Heart's Desire," and to which if he hearken it may be that he will return no
> more—voices, too, which, whether a man sail by or stay to hearken, still sing
> on. (*Lud-in-the-Mist* xiii)

The epigraph not only suggests a mythic dimension to the story but also connects it with Harrison's belief in the present-day relevance of myths. Harrison
was the center of the so-called Cambridge ritualists, a peer of Lang and Frazer
and a major influence on Francis Cornford, Gilbert Murray, and Stanley Edgar
Hyman, among others. Like Eliot, Harrison believed that modern art needed
to return to the mythic. Although it must include, "among other and deeper
forms of life, the haste and hurry of the modern street, the whirr of motor cars
and aeroplanes" (*Ancient Art* 236–237), it must also look back to the rituals that
once grounded men and women in the cycles of nature, allayed their fears of
the dead, and offered glimpses of mystery. Harrison was not certain this effort
could be successful: "Whether any systematized attempt to remind man, by
ritual, of that whole of life of which he is a specialized fragment can be made
fruitful or not, I am uncertain" (*Themis* xix). Nevertheless, it was worth a try,
and Harrison's student found a way to suggest modern alienation and ancient
ritual without depicting either directly. Instead, she constructed a halfway
point, the imaginary land of Dorimare, and gradually revealed connections
forward and backward.

Present-day Dorimare is a practical and prosperous realm on the verge of an industrial revolution. It lacks religion or artistic ambition and is ruled by the middle class, which, two centuries earlier, overthrew the infamous Duke Aubrey, a cruel and capricious ruler but also a poet and priest of sorts:

> For three days a bloody battle raged in the streets of Lud-in-the-Mist, in which fell all the nobles of Dorimare. As for Duke Aubrey, he vanished— some said to Fairyland, where he was living to this day.
>
> During those three days of bloodshed all the priests had vanished also. So Dorimare lost simultaneously its Duke and its cult. (11)

Yet neither Fairyland nor the Duke is completely gone. Both live on in the practices and sayings of country folk:

> He was a living reality to the country people; so much so that, when leakages were found in the vats, or when a horse was discovered in the morning with his coat stained and furrowed with sweat, some rogue of a farm-hand could often escape punishment by swearing that Duke Aubrey had been the culprit. And there was not a farm or village that had not at least one inhabitant who swore he had seen him, on some midsummer's eve, or some night of the winter solstice, galloping past at the head of his fairy hunt, to the sound of innumerable bells. (18–19)

If bourgeois secularism is the dominant culture of Lud, fairy lore is its residual culture. It is connected with the very phenomena Raymond Williams identifies as residual: monarchy, country life, and religion (with an ironic twist, since fairy faith fills the niche occupied in our world by Christianity). And the entire story has to do with the residual becoming emergent, with the reluctant cooperation of the unlikeliest of heroes. Nathaniel, like other members of his class, detests the idea of Fairyland. Fairy fruit is contraband, reference to anything magical or mystical is considered obscene, and "Son of a Fairy" is a deadly insult (14). Yet fairy influences pervade Dorimarean culture. A few years before the book takes place, an anonymous tract called *Traces of Fairy in the Inhabitants Customs, Art, Vegetation and Language of Dorimare* noted the many unnoticed magical references in, for instance, oaths like "by the Sun, Moon and Stars; by the Golden Apples of the West; by the Harvest of Souls" (15). The same tract claimed that a bluish tinge in cattle and red hair on people were marks of fairy descent: both Nathaniel and his son Ranulph are regrettably "ginger" (57). More important, the tract said that "all artistic types, all ritual acts, must be modelled on realities; and Fairyland is the place where what *we* look on as symbols and figures actually exist and occur" (15).

Mirrlees brings in a wealth of knowledge about English fairy lore. No one has identified the source of that knowledge, but Harrison's studies in myth certainly put her, and thence Mirrlees, in contact with folklorists, as well as ethnologists and literary scholars. References to traditional songs, tales, dances, foods, customs, and beliefs help validate the story's magical component: if Dorimare is next door to Fairyland, so too, according to traditional belief, is England. But to Nathaniel and his friends, all of this lore is old-fashioned, countrified, and a little embarrassing: they are too modern to take much stock in it. Gradually throughout the story the rural culture is shown to be older than it appears. Unnoticed among the farms and villages are ruins of castles. Nonsense songs document forgotten rituals. A simple country dance was once "danced in the moonlight when Lud-in-the-Mist was nothing but a beech wood between two rivers" (77). Farmsteads are guarded by ancient stone figures called herms, described thus in a riddle: "What is it that's a tree, and yet not a tree, a man and yet not a man, who is dumb and yet can tell secrets, who has no arms and yet can strike?" (202).

A herm is a column topped by a male head. It is limbless, phallic in shape and often with an erect phallus of its own. The facial expression is usually described as an "archaic smile," reflecting a period in Greek art before naturalistic expression—Mirrlees uses that exact phrase to describe the herm in the story, which is also characterized as "the spirit of the farm" (210). A character named Portunus, whom Nathaniel takes for simpleminded, is often found dancing in front of this herm. But Portunus is not simpleminded, but one of the Silent People—the dead—and both he and the herm point toward Mirrlees' use of myth.

Harrison discusses herms in conjunction with the cults of Hermes and Dionysos, who are aspects of the same deity: "This affiliation is clearly shown by the fact that in art Hermes and Dionysos appear, as they were worshipped in cultus, as herms; the symbol of both gods as gods of fertility is naturally the phallos" (*Prolegomena* 427). Gods are missing from *Lud-in-the-Mist*. Their place is taken by the fairies and by Duke Aubrey, who has become their leader (or always was, as his name suggests: Aubrey equals Oberon). The herm marks an older time when the gods were known and worshipped, but not in the way gods are honored in Greek literature. These are not Olympian figures, distant and beautiful. Instead, the gods of Dorimare, perceivable under the layers of time and cultural shift, are like the cultic gods Harrison sees as the original basis for Greek religion. They are local, dark, and dangerous. The purpose of ritual is not to please them but to ward them off:

> To our surprise, when the actual rites are examined, we shall find that they have little or nothing to do with the particular Olympian to whom they are supposed to be addressed; that they are rites not in the main of burnt-sacrifice, of joy and feasting and agonistic contests, but rites of a gloomy underworld character, connected mainly with purification and the worship of ghosts. The conclusion is almost forced upon us that we have here a theological stratification, that the rites of the Olympians have been superimposed on another order of worship. (*Prolegomena* 10–11)

The gods Harrison describes are not clearly distinguished from spirits of the dead. The same rituals that keep the gods away also fend off angry ghosts. A single word, *ker*, was used for both the dead and godlike beings, as well as a number of other oddly conflated entities: "the term Ker [is] perhaps the most untranslatable of all Greek words. Ghost, bacillus, disease, death-angel, death-fate, fate, bogey, magician have all gone to the making of it" (*Prolegomena* 212). In *Lud-in-the-Mist*, all of these meanings belong to the inhabitants of Fairyland:

> In out-of-the-way country places it was still believed that corpses were but fairy cheats, made to resemble flesh and bone, but without any real substance—otherwise why should they turn so quickly into dust? But the real person, for which the corpse was but a flimsy substitute, had been carried away by the Fairies, to tend their blue kine and reap their fields of gillyflowers. The country people, indeed, did not always clearly distinguish between the Fairies and the dead. They called them both the "Silent People"; and the Milky Way they thought was the path along which the dead were carried to Fairyland. (12–13)
>
> And some of the dead return, especially those who, like Portunus, want revenge upon their murderers. Harrison describes a particular variety of ker that doubles as a Fury: "The Erinys primarily is the Ker of a human being unrighteously slain. Erinys is not death; it is the outraged soul of the dead man crying for vengeance [. . .] (*Prolegomena* 214).

Nathaniel Chanticleer comes into contact with all these mythic forces through the actions of a physician named Endymion Leer. Leer was involved in the death of Portunus; it is he who arranges to have Nathaniel's son eat the addictive and hallucinatory fairy fruit; he courts the foolish and romantic teacher of Lud-in-the-Mist's young ladies and introduces as their dancing instructor the fairy trickster Willy Wisp. He is also the author of the anonymous pamphlet mentioned before, revealing Dorimare's suppressed fairy past. Masquerading as Nathaniel's helper, Leer gradually strips him of his honor and peace of mind. When Nathaniel's daughter dances off with the other enchanted pupils of Miss Crabapple's Academy and Ranulph is sent over the border to Fairyland, Nathaniel must face the fact that his secure life has been an illusion; that Duke Aubrey and the Silent People not only exist but also have the power of life and death over Dorimare. Leer, their agent, plots the overturning of the laws of Lud-in-the-Mist and the downfall of its leader, Mayor Chanticleer.

But there has always been an unpredictable streak in Nathaniel that suggests that, like Tolkien's Bilbo Baggins, he is not to be counted out so easily. Like Dorimare itself, his prosaic surface hides mythic depths. Since childhood, he has been troubled by what he calls the Note, because he first heard it from an antique lute in his family's attic:

> Master Nathaniel seized one of the old instruments, a sort of lute ending in the carving of a cock's head, its strings rotted by damp and antiquity, and, crying out, "Let's see if this old fellow has a croak left in him!" plucked roughly at its strings.
>
> They gave out one note, so plangent, blood-freezing and alluring, that for a few seconds the company stood as if petrified. (5)

The sound of this note changes Nathaniel's life and haunts his dreams:

> It was as if the note were a living substance, and subject to the law of chemical changes—that is to say, as that law works in dreams. For instance, he might dream that his old nurse was baking an apple on the fire in her own cosy room, and as he watched it simmer and sizzle she would look at him with a strange smile, a smile such as he had never been on her face in waking hours, and say, "But, of course, you know it isn't really the apple. *It's the Note*." (5–6)

Nathaniel's reaction to this unsettling experience is to bury himself in the mundane, but he cannot ultimately escape the Note. It returns to his life in the form of his son's illness, his daughter's Pied Piper-like abduction, even the country tune he hears Leer singing to Ranulph on his sickbed. The Note is fairy fruit in another form, and the Fairies are not to be denied, but the Note suggests something more. The cock-headed lute is himself, Chanticleer; he is the Note's herald.

It is this streak of the dreamer and the melancholic, paradoxically, that allows Nathaniel to rouse himself, to solve an ancient murder case (for, like Williams's *War in Heaven*, Mirrlees' book combines fairy tale and detective story), and ultimately to travel to Fairyland in search of his children. He becomes an unlikely Orpheus bringing a loved one back from the dead and reinventing Dorimare's religion, just as Jane Harrison claimed a historical Orpheus reinvented the worship of Dionysos (*Prolegomena* 456). Nathaniel ends up as an agent of Fairyland, replacing Endymion Leer, but in place of Leer's intoxicating physic, he employs the Law to negotiate with the dangerous gods, restraining the Dionysiac side of Duke Aubrey and bringing out the Apollonian.

Many readers of *Lud-in-the-Mist* are puzzled by the climax, in which Nathaniel ventures to Fairyland to rescue first the troupe of schoolgirls-turned-Maenad and then the captive Ranulph. As Nathaniel crosses the border of Fairyland, the crystalline language of the narrative grows opaque, scenes shift and transform as in dreams, and it is difficult to figure out exactly how he effects the rescue. It is clear, however, that the power he invokes against the Silent People is the Law. In an earlier scene, Nathaniel himself refers to the Law as the cure for the Fairies' perfidy: "the homœopathic antidote that our forefathers discovered to illusion" (156). When he sees Willy Wisp auctioning his daughter and the other Crabapple pupils in a Fairy slave market, he cries foul:

> "They cannot be sold until they have crossed over into Fairyland—I say they *cannot be sold."*
>
> All round him he heard awed whispers, "It is Chanticleer—Chanticleer the dreamer, who has never tasted fruit."
>
> Then he found himself giving a learned dissertation on the law of property, as observed in the Elfin Marches. The crowd listened to him in respectful silence. Even Willy Wisp was listening, and the Crabapple Blossoms gazed at him with inexpressible gratitude[. . .].
>
> "Chanticleer and the Law! Chanticleer and the Law!" shouted the crowd. (248–249)

But what has the Law to do with life, death, myth, and magic? Why is it effective against the Fairies' power? How is it related to Nathaniel's role as cult-reforming Orpheus?

Again, the answer can be found in Harrison. She was always interested in the difference between the ranking of gods found in literature and their ritual importance, and she was particularly interested in the cultic goddess Themis, or Justice, who barely registers in Homer. For Harrison, Themis represents the social function of myth, and thus her worship is an advance over the more ancient rites of fear and propitiation:

> The Greek word *Themis* and the English word *Doom* are, philology tells us, one and the same; and it is curious to note that their development moves on exactly parallel lines. *Doom* is the thing set, fixed, settled; it begins in convention, the stress of public opinion; it ends in statutory judgment. Your private doom is your private opinion, but that is weak and ineffective. It is the collective doom, public opinion, that, for man's common convenience, crystallizes into Law. (*Themis* 482)

Furthermore, it is through this Law that the terrible mysteries of life and death are brought into harmony with human needs:

> The mystery, the thing greater than man, is potent, not only or chiefly because it stimulates a baffled understanding, but because it is *felt* as an obligation. The thing greater than man, the 'power not himself that makes for righteousness,' is, in the main, not the mystery of the universe to which as yet he is not awake, but the pressure of that unknown ever incumbent force, herd instinct, the social conscience. The mysterious dominant figure is not Physis, but Themis. (*Themis* 490)

If Endymion Leer is a physician, a follower of Physis or Nature, Nathaniel is the priest of Themis. The sole function of Themis in Homer is to call the gods to assembly and dismiss them afterward (*Themis* 482). By calling on the Law,

Nathaniel dissolves the Fairy assembly and sends his daughter home. When he returns to Lud-in-the-Mist, he enacts a new regime that acknowledges Fairyland and its power. New laws allow the importation of fairy fruit, but in moderation, as homeopathic cure rather than addictive drug. The ecstatic madness of Dionysos is tempered with Apollo's sobriety and creativity; both are seen as necessary parts of the social compact. As Harrison says "the mystery-god and the Olympian express respectively, the one *durée*, life, and the other the action of conscious intelligence which reflects on and analyzes life" (*Themis* ix). Nathaniel's job is to bring these into balance. Calling on human Law on the very borders of Fairyland is a bold and perilous act, but it brings the two aspects of Dorimare and of Nathaniel himself back into a balance that neither has had for some time.

All of this should demonstrate the mythic dimension underlying Mirrlees' fairy tale, but it doesn't show how *Lud-in-the-Mist* relates to the contemporary world. How is this novel a Modernist text? As in *The Lord of the Rings*, the story's images, events, and characters all refer outside the enclosed fantasy world without exactly constituting an allegory. Certain elements stand out as particularly timely. The multivalent symbol of fairy fruit, for instance, manages to convey not only timeless themes of poetic inspiration and Romantic *Sehnsucht* but also youthful rebellion and the cocaine craze of the 1920s. The trial of Endymion Leer suggests any number of tabloid-fodder murder cases. Unrest among the working classes of *Lud-in-the-Mist* brings echoes of Bolshevism and anarchy into the fairy-tale world. The unsettled postwar literary scene is transcribed into the complex relationship between Dorimare's dominant middle class and its residual and emergent subcultures.

But the modern world and Modernist sensibility are most clearly represented in Nathaniel himself and in the winds from Fairyland that he feels sweeping away his beliefs and way of life. Mirrlees constructs a knowing narrator who sometimes merges with Nathaniel's own perceptions and sometimes stays ironically distant from him. From the outside, the narrator paints Nathaniel as "a typical Dorimarite in appearance" (3) and then immediately casts doubt on the reliability of appearances:

> You should regard each meeting with a friend as a sitting he is unwittingly giving you for a portrait—a portrait that, probably, when you or he die, will still be unfinished. And, though this is an absorbing pursuit, nevertheless, the painters are apt to end pessimists. For however handsome and merry may be the face, however rich may be the background, in the first rough sketch of each portrait, yet with every added stroke of the brush, with every tiny readjustment of the "values," with every modification of the chiaroscuro, the eyes looking out at you grow more disquieting. And, finally, it is your *own* face that you are staring at in terror, as in a mirror by candle-light, when all the house is still. (3–4)

This passage, which begins in comfortable companionship and ends in terror, not only portrays Nathaniel's own existential unease but also turns around to implicate readers. We paint the portrait; we are the subject; it is ourselves that we fear. And at the same time, this meditation on art is itself a portrait: the experience it relates defines Nathaniel's character. He is already in Fairyland and has been so all his life, no matter how desperately he clings to conviviality and convention. As he falls by degrees under the spell of Duke Aubrey, he becomes more and more himself: the outsider, the alienated artist, the man of modern sensibility. By the time he comes to Fairyland, he is ready to see its deceits as deeper truths.

The setting of *Lud-in-the-Mist* resembles a Dutch genre painting, with jolly burghers sitting in front of their substantial houses, but it is as deceptive as the mental miniatures we paint of our friends. What Nathaniel always fears—that life is uncertain and chaotic, that the reassuring epitaphs in the graveyard are lies, that even death is not a release from change—turns out to be precisely true. Mirrlees uses Nathaniel's thoughts, sometimes quoted exactly, sometimes borrowed by the narrator in passages of free indirect discourse, to bring the modern world into Lud-in-the-Mist. He resembles Williams's Lionel Rackstraw or one of Virginia Woolf's characters in crisis—perhaps Septimus Smith quietly going mad in *Mrs Dalloway*. The Waste Land is there in Nathaniel's thoughts:

> With which familiar object—quill, pipe, pack of cards—would he be occupied, on which regularly recurrent action—the pulling on or off of his nightcap, the weekly auditing of his accounts—would he be engaged when IT, the hidden menace, sprang out at him? And he would gaze in terror at his furniture, his walls, his pictures—what strange scene might they one day witness, what awful experience might he one day have in their presence? (6)

This stream of Nathaniel's consciousness takes the narration over entirely when he crosses the border. As he rides into the Elfin Marches on the edge of Fairyland, the narrative discourse becomes a sort of Modernist poem. Its imagery is disturbing: silent crowds, a solitary child trapped on a merry-go-round, human souls advertised as if they were a carnival attraction, a house full of "creatures made of red lacquer" (250). The Fairyland chapter invokes both medieval dream vision and Eliot's image of the "Unreal City" where "I had not thought death had undone so many" (itself an echo of Dante). Yet when these frightening surrealistic scenes lead Nathaniel at length to Duke Aubrey, their source, the meeting is a moment of tenderness and vision:

> At these words the uplands became bathed in a gentle light and proved to be fair and fertile—the perpetual seat of Spring; for there were vivid green patches of young corn, and pillars of pink and white smoke, which were fruit trees in blossom, and pillars of blue blossom, which was the smoke of distant

hamlets, and a vast meadow of cornflowers and daisies, which was the great inland sea of Faerie. And everything—ships, spires, houses—was small and bright and delicate, yet real. It was not unlike Dorimare, or, rather, the trans-figured Dorimare he had once seen from the Fields of Grammary. (254)

We are back with the peaceful burghers in a landscape that is now revealed to be both real and magical, sunny and shadowed, transparent and swathed in mystery.

The four components of Williams's mythic method likewise operate in Mir-rlees' novel. *Lud-in-the-Mist* uses myth to organize and interpret a disguised version of the contemporary world. Instead of the half-Christian, half-pagan myths of the Grail and the Priest-King, she employs a combination of English fairy tradition and archaic ritual as interpreted by Jane Harrison. Christianity is ostensibly absent but suggested by the residual and reemergent social roles played by fairy beliefs and folk rituals.

Part of myth's organizing power is its ability to isolate and expel the dan-gerous and disturbing. Mirrlees makes use of this power in a way quite dif-ferent from Williams's. One character is indeed unmasked, humiliated, and ultimately killed: Endymion Leer. Leer is the foreigner, the poisoner, the hyp-ocrite. Yet he is also revealed to be the true priest and agent of Duke Aubrey. He is Nathaniel's unacknowledged double and predecessor: the only other thoroughly Modern and indeed scholarly point of view in the novel. His down-fall is as much due to his master's fickleness as to the power of the society to reform itself, and in the process of bringing him down, Nathaniel also brings back the previously exiled Silent People and their forbidden fruit. Abjection, for Mirrlees, is part of an ongoing cycle, along with rediscovery and restora-tion. The difference between this and Williams's version of abjection is linked to Mirrlees' choice of myth: neither classical myth nor fairy lore is moralized in the way Christianity is, with its insistence on sorting everything into black and white, good and evil. Leer is evil but he also does good; fairy fruit is both poison and cure; Duke Aubrey is both cruel and tender.

And existential angst is also epiphany. On the first pages of the novel, as the narrator lovingly details Dorimare's charms, she drops a hint about the inter-connectedness of terror and transcendence in the description of the Chanti-cleer gardens:

To the imaginative, it is always something of an adventure to walk down a pleached alley. You enter boldly enough, but very soon you find yourself wishing you had stayed outside—it is not air that you are breathing, but si-lence, the almost palpable silence of trees. And is the only exit that small round hole in the distance? Why, you will never be able to squeeze through *that*! You must turn back . . . too late! The spacious portal by which you en-tered has in its turn shrunk to a small round hole. (3)

So the most familiar of scenes can transform without warning into Fairyland. This is exactly what Nathaniel most fears—and most badly needs. He combines Williams's opposing figures, the mage and the priest. In the mythic system underlying this novel, the Grail can be approached by either route: dark magic or light, occult ritual or spiritual discipline. The result will be the same. Nathaniel finds this a rather bitter lesson. The mythic method makes the modern world possible for art, but it does not make it comfortable.

The fourth component of Modernist fantasy is play. Authorized by Harrison's theories, Mirrlees playfully tosses together classical Greek myth and English folk tradition, seeing both as the mild and aestheticized remnants of ancient rituals of fear and propitiation. By setting up the cult of Duke Aubrey as Dorimare's suppressed religious past, roughly equivalent to English Catholicism, she puts Christianity into the same category of rationalized primitive ritual, thereby freeing us to tinker with Christian myth. Mirrlees also sports with levels of reality, making history a mask for myth and letting magic leak into the daylight world. She invites us to extend the game into our own reality. As we share Nathaniel's experiences, we too begin to question appearances and to doubt common sense. We sense hidden forces at work, or at play, in the world. Fantasy is a game, and a game is a form of ritual. As we play the game, we venture, more or less safely, into the ancient world of gods and sacrifices, but we retain the prerogative of changing the rules: for instance, introducing a power such as the Law to alter the game's outcome. The old becomes the new, and Modernist despair turns around to reveal its other face: mythic vision.

Williams and Mirrlees offer two versions of fantasy's mythic method, one of which gradually transforms the known world into a battleground for competing visions of the divine, whereas the other constructs an imaginary realm as a ludic space in which observed reality and symbol interact on the same plane. Fantasies from the first half of the twentieth century use one technique or the other, or sometimes a combination of the two. A representative of the former mode was G. K. Chesterton, whose *The Man Who Was Thursday* (1908) influenced Williams and was a primary source of C. S. Lewis's *That Hideous Strength* (1945). In the latter mode, Lord Dunsany's *The King of Elfland's Daughter* (1924) resembles *Lud-in-the-Mist* in juxtaposing a real-ish world against a disruptive fairyland. Similarly, James Branch Cabell's imaginary kingdom of Poictesme sometimes suggests real areas of France and sometimes becomes a sort of fairy realm, doubling, in *Jurgen* (1919), as a gateway to both heaven and hell. E. R. Eddison constructs a self-contained fantasy world in *The Worm Ouroboros* (1922) but mixes modes by starting off with an earthly observer named Edward Lessingham. In later novels, such as *A Fish Dinner in Memison* (1941), Lessingham's twentieth-century England is contrasted with a more passionate and adventurous world in which Zeus and Aphrodite take human form; eventually Lessingham is reborn into that world. C. S. Lewis's Narnia stories, starting with *The Lion, the Witch, and the Wardrobe* (1950), move characters between the real world and a secondary fantasy world. The latter serves as the backdrop for transcribed versions of Christian stories of Creation, the Fall, and the Apocalypse.

What all these fantastic tales have in common is the presence of a viewpoint character (sometimes the narrator) who brings to the world of myth and magic a contemporary sensibility and skepticism. These characters ask, on behalf of the reader, what the myth has to offer here and now. For Jane Harrison, myth was something to *do*, rather than something to believe. Hence a myth enacted was a living myth, still potent against darkness and despair. This concept struck a chord with many twentieth-century thinkers and artists, from D. H. Lawrence to Virginia Woolf. Hope Mirrlees put the idea into a form that was pleasingly old-fashioned, yet conceptually innovative and attuned to a modern consciousness. For Mirrlees, Williams, Tolkien, and others of their generation, fantasy became a way of living out, rather than simply retelling myths. By exploring perilous enchanted landscapes and negotiating fairy-tale laws, characters forged new relationships with archaic mysteries. Fantasy makes it new by making it old, and this version of the mythic method was to prove useful to an ever-growing number of readers and writers through the rest of the twentieth century and into the twenty-first.

{ 3 }

Silver Lies and Spinning Wheels: Christian Myth in MacDonald and Lewis

One of the most surprising facts about Christian fantasy is that it exists at all. The decision to write what Tolkien called "fairy-stories" based in Christian myth is a risky one, and the dangers lie on all sides. One obvious hazard is being accused of trivializing religion—turning profound matters of faith into entertainment. Another is getting it wrong—any version of, say, Jacob and the angel other than the exact text of Genesis will include interpolations and inter-pretations that inevitably collide with some readers' understanding of the story and its significance. Those who read the Bible literally will object to any attempt to shift components from the category of history to that of parable. Those who read it metaphorically will object to an overly faithful transcription—the re-sulting fantasy will seem to them more like a sermon than a fully realized mythic romance. Those who disbelieve entirely will wonder why anyone would bother. Yet despite the risks, two fantasists whose works are landmarks in the history of the genre repeatedly incorporated Christian motifs and symbols in their work. The stories of George MacDonald and C. S. Lewis, along with Lewis's attempts to come to terms with the earlier writer, show how fantasy can work as a sort of theological thought experiment. It provides a framework for exploring and testing narratives of faith, sometimes with surprising results.

Lewis and MacDonald followed very different trajectories in their per-sonal religious histories. MacDonald grew up in a strict Calvinist tradition—Congregationalist rather than the official Church of Scotland. He studied for the ministry and served a pulpit for a time before losing his job because of increasingly unorthodox views, especially on damnation. A love for poetry and for literary fairy tales like those of Novalis led him toward Romanticism; at the same time he grew interested in science. He took university degrees in chemistry and natural philosophy, rather than literature or theology (Reis 23). Afterward he kept abreast of developments in medicine, especially the works of William Gregory, professor of chemistry at the University of Edinburgh, whose interest in mesmerism led him to anticipate Freud in formulating a concept of the unconscious (Broome 89). MacDonald associated with free-thinkers during a stay in Manchester, including the Swedenborgian Henry Sutton (Johnson 39), and occasionally preached to Unitarian congregations. He corresponded with Ralph Waldo Emerson in America and read Thoreau, whose "Walking" provided an epigraph to MacDonald's *Lilith* (1895). Though never ceasing to consider himself a Christian, he formulated a personal faith with elements of all of these things: a Romantic view of myth and fairy tale, an embrace of science, traces of Swedenborgian and Emersonian transcenden-talism, and his own brand of Universalism—the belief that all beings can and perhaps will be saved. Many of these ideas show up in his last book, *Lilith*, which is both his most explicitly biblical and his most heretical treatment of Christian myth.

Lewis, by contrast, started his adult life as an atheist and then worked his way toward orthodoxy, becoming one of the most famous Christian apologists in the world. His early childhood faith was an unexamined Protestantism, which was severely tested by the death of his mother and which he gave up entirely at school. In his autobiography, *Surprised by Joy*, he describes a set of discoveries that amounted to an unofficial course in comparative religion and led him away from belief: first, the enthusiasm of the school matron for var-ious forms of spiritualism and the occult and, second, guided by his tutor Wil-liam Kirkpatrick, readings in mythology and classical poetry:

> Here, especially in Virgil, one was presented with a mass of religious ideas; and all teachers and editors took it for granted from the outset that these religious ideas were sheer illusion. No one ever attempted to show in what sense Christianity fulfilled Paganism or Paganism prefigured Christianity. [. . .] But the impression I got was that religion in general, though utterly false, was a natural growth, a kind of endemic nonsense into which hu-manity tended to blunder. (*Surprised* 63)

Where MacDonald might have viewed all these spiritual paths as leading toward some sort of larger insight, Lewis saw only confusion. If there was no single truth about religion, there was no truth at all. As he wrote to his friend Arthur Greeves, "There is absolutely no proof for any of them, and from a phil-osophical standpoint Christianity is not even the best. All religions, that is, all mythologies to give them their proper name are merely man's own invention— Christ as much as Loki" (*Letters* 231).

Lewis's search for spiritual truth was more than mere intellectual curiosity. He describes his religious impulses in terms of two powerful affective re-sponses: desire and lust. Though these terms are often interchangeable, Lewis, a very precise and self-aware writer, takes considerable pains to show that they are nothing alike, at least in his usage. Lust seeks fulfillment, whereas desire, for Lewis, is that which cannot be fulfilled. Neither is overtly sexual. Lewis writes rather coyly of sexual matters: when he confesses that he went through, at school, "a violent, and wholly successful assault of sexual temptation" (*Surprised* 68), there is no indication that he was in direct contact with any young women, and he disavows any interest in the homosexual activity that was widespread among his peers (89), so he is most likely speaking of sexual fantasies and masturbation. The connection between physical lust and its spiritual analogue is addressed most directly when Lewis talks of mistaking the desire raised by reading William Morris's romances or Greek myths for sexual arousal:

> It was quite easy to think that one desired those forests for the sake of their female inhabitants, the garden of Hesperus for the sake of his daughters, Hylas' river for the river nymphs. I repeatedly followed that path—to the end. And at the end found pleasure; which immediately resulted in the discovery that pleasure (whether that pleasure or any other) was not what you had been looking for. (169–170)

So, rhetorically, he equates lust with the pleasure of "auto-eroticism" (168), which is ultimately unsatisfying. Desire, by contrast, is associated with pain (to a degree that hints at masochism) but ultimately leads to, or is revealed to be, joy. He frequently uses the metaphor of piercing: the "stab of Joy" (78). The importance of desire is that it takes one out of oneself: "All the value lay in that of which Joy was the desiring. And that object, quite clearly, was no state of my own mind or body at all" (220). Rather it is "that unity which we can never reach except by ceasing to be the separate phenomenal beings called 'we'" (221–222).

Lewis is aware that a Freudian would read all this in sexual terms. The contrast between desire and lust, for instance, could be equated with the contrary pulls of libido and death wish. Lewis does not deny the sexual connection but reverses the direction of the metaphor: "Joy is not a substitute for sex; sex is very often a substitute for Joy" (170). His self-awareness in this regard suggests that it makes less sense to try to psychoanalyze Lewis than to trace his conscious and deliberate use of the paired concepts of desire and lust to assert something about the proper and improper uses of myth.

As Lewis describes his spiritual growth, he enumerates a number of encounters that generated lust, defined as an attraction that is "erotic in rather a morbid way" (35). The first he mentions is his reading of historical fiction, specifically fiction set in ancient Rome (35). The second is science fiction: he explains his youthful interest in other planets as something "psychological, not spiritual; behind such a fierce tang there lurks, I suspect, a psychoanalytical explanation" (35–36). Third comes the occult, the desire for the supernatural that "like the lust of the body [. . .] has the fatal power of making everything else seem uninteresting while it lasts" (60). Next is the attraction of what Lewis calls the World: "the desire for glitter, swagger, distinction, the desire to be in the know" (68). When Lewis reached university, an acquaintanceship with a man who was going mad and who shared several of Lewis's supernatural interests reinforced the association of occultism with dangerous lust. Among the branches of the occult Lewis lists psychoanalysis: "He had flirted with Theosophy, Yoga, Spiritualism, Psychoanalysis, what not? Probably these things had in fact no connection with his insanity, for which (I believe) there were physical causes. But it did not seem so to me at the time" (203).

What these diverse ideas and experiences have in common is that Lewis was tempted by them. Furthermore, he disliked being tempted by them. As he underwent his conversion first to theism and then specifically to Christianity, he examined himself repeatedly and found "what appalled me; a zoo of lusts, a bedlam of ambitions, a nursery of fears, a harem of fondled hatreds" (226). The remedy for lust was desire. To some degree, the turn from lust to desire was a return to childhood, for his earliest experience of what he was to term Joy came in his prelapsarian, presexual boyhood. It first took the form of a response to a distant vista:

> the low line of the Castlereagh Hills which we saw from the nursery windows. They were not very far off but they were, to children, quite unobtainable. They taught me longing—*Sehnsucht*: made me for good or ill, and before I was six years old, a votary of the Blue Flower. (7)

Thus Lewis sets up an equation between German Romanticism (represented by both the catchword *Sehnsucht* and the reference to Novalis's dream blossom) and spirituality that prepared the way for his next experience of desire, which came through Romantic literature and its admixture of revived Northern myth.

Presaged by a keen response to Beatrix Potter's evocation of autumn in *Squirrel Nutkin* (16), Romantic desire really overwhelmed Lewis when he came across a passage from Longfellow's translation of the Swedish poet Esaias Tegnér:

> I heard a voice that cried,
> Balder the beautiful
> Is dead, is dead— (17)

Without knowing the full myth to which Tegnér is referring, Lewis responded powerfully to the Nordic setting, the mystery, the powerful sense of loss, and, I suspect, the way the god's death is encountered: as an overheard report from an anonymous voice. The voice—of god or oracle—was like an adult speaking in hushed tones of something children are not supposed to know and are therefore all the more eager to find out. Says Lewis,

> I knew nothing about Balder, but instantly I was uplifted into huge regions
> of northern sky, I desired with almost sickening intensity something never

to be described (except that it is cold, spacious, severe, pale, and remote) and then [. . .] found myself at the very same moment already falling out of that desire and wishing I were back in it. (17)

This experience became Lewis's touchstone. Everything spiritual was, as it were, rubbed against the memory to see if the streak indicated gold or dross, the true desire or the baser lust. If science fiction and the occult were illicit pleasures, fantasy and myth reproduced the moment of sublime remoteness that meant Joy. Lewis sought out such experiences, first in Arthur Rackham's illustrations and Wagner's musical settings of the stories of Siegfried and the twilight of the gods (72) and then in other mythic traditions. He discovered Finnish and Celtic and eventually Greco-Roman myth, though "Northernness still came first" (114). An interest in the sagas led him to William Morris and thence into medieval literature. Lewis flirted with the Celtic twilight, but Yeats's interest in magic put him on the wrong side of the scale: instead of "the imaginative longing for Joy, or rather the longing which was Joy," Yeats represented (at least in retrospect) "the ravenous, quasi-prurient desire for the Occult, the Preternatural as such" (175).

After Lewis was reconverted to a belief in God, he resisted committing himself to Christianity. The story of Christ's incarnation and sacrifice still seemed to him only one of many dying-god myths, and of those, not the one he most desired. Humphrey Carpenter reconstructs a conversation between Lewis and J. R. R. Tolkien, recorded, after a fashion, in Tolkien's poem "Mythopoiea." In Carpenter's version, Lewis complains that:

> When he encountered the idea of sacrifice in the mythology of a pagan religion he admired it and was moved by it; indeed the idea of the dying and reviving deity had always touched his imagination since he had read the story of the Norse god Balder. But from the Gospels [. . .] he was requiring something more, a clear meaning beyond the myth. (*Tolkien* 147)

He describes all myths as "lies, even though lies breathed through silver" (147). Tolkien disagrees. To him, the myth-making imagination is a source of insight into creation itself; if the Christian story resembles other myths, it was not because all are lies but because a great truth is gradually revealing itself. Lewis accepts the argument and throws himself wholeheartedly into Christianity as the proper source and object of his previously inchoate desires—and the cure for his lusts.

It is likely that this division between lust and desire was retroactive: something the later Lewis thought his younger self ought to have felt. The distinctions are not obvious: why would science fiction fall on one side of the line and fantasy on the other, except that for Lewis the one led toward conversion and the other did not? Why should philological studies of myth generate insight while anthropological readings of the mythic underpinnings of romance are only a useless exercise ("The Anthropological Approach" 301)? Why is Wagner's Romantic excess any more valid than Maeterlinck's symbolism? Lewis (despite his distaste for sports) is always lining up teams. He chooses for the home team not only Morris but also Plato, Aeschylus, Vergil, Spenser, and Milton. Playing for the occultist opposition are Yeats, Maeterlinck, Haggard, and Wells, as well as comparative mythologists such as Frazer. But the captain and hero of team Desire is George MacDonald.

Lewis's MacDonald is an artless writer of great spiritual insight along conventional Christian lines. He shows up in *Surprised by Joy* as the catalyst for Lewis's conversion. Picking up a copy of MacDonald's *Phantastes* in a railway bookstall, he finds himself embarking on a threefold journey: his own train trip, MacDonald's wandering tale, and a crossing from unbelief to faith, "as if I were carried sleeping across the frontier, or as if I had died in the old country and could never remember how I came alive in the new" (179). The enchantment goes on after both trip and book are finished: "now I saw the bright shadow coming out of the book into the real world and resting there, transforming all common things and yet itself unchanged" (181). Lewis credits MacDonald with a quality he calls "holiness" and pays him the ultimate tribute: "That night my imagination was, in a certain sense, baptized" (181).

But MacDonald is only the Baptist crying out in a Romantic wilderness (and who does that make Lewis?). Lewis is willing to give his precursor credit for mythic, even salvific, power, but not literary craft. In an introduction to his book of selections from MacDonald, Lewis comments that

> If we define Literature as an art whose medium is words, then certainly MacDonald has no place in its first rank—perhaps not even in its second. There are indeed passages [. . .] where the wisdom and (I would dare to call it) the holiness that are in him triumph over and even burn away the baser elements in his style: the expression becomes precise, weighty, economic, acquires a cutting edge. But he does not maintain this level for long. The texture of his writing as a whole is undistinguished, at times fumbling. (Preface xxvi)

I agree with William Gray in finding MacDonald "a much better writer than Lewis would have us believe" (118). By making MacDonald into a sort of untutored rustic sage, however, Lewis turns his predecessor into a wellspring from whom he can draw freely. "I have never concealed the fact that I regarded him as my master" says Lewis; "indeed I fancy I have never written a book in which I did not quote from him" ("Preface" 20). MacDonald's imagination fuels the fantasy worlds of Narnia and Perelandra, and Jeffrey Bilbro suggests that Lewis's first overtly Christian fantasy, the allegorical satire *The Pilgrim's Regress*, is directly modeled on *Phantastes* (2). MacDonald is quoted throughout Lewis's essays, and he even becomes a character in *The Great Divorce* (1946), playing Vergil to Lewis's Dante on a trip through heaven and hell. Such an overwhelming influence needs to be tamed, and Lewis tames MacDonald by misreading him. Lewis brought many readers to MacDonald but carefully channeled their response. We are, he suggests, to read MacDonald for evocative imagery, mysteriously charged symbols, and religious aspirations but not for good writing or reliable dogma.

In *The Great Divorce*, Lewis even has MacDonald repudiate his own statements on salvation. In this allegorical novella, the narrator finds himself in a great, gray, joyless city: a vision of the modern world as hell. The only way out is a bus excursion to a place resembling the Castlereagh Hills of Lewis's childhood, a beautiful green place where everything is so substantial that the ghostly passengers cannot even bend the blades of grass. The other passengers represent all manner of minor (but, for Lewis, damnable) sins: there is the "Tousle-headed poet" (7), the religious liberal (34), the urban planner (13), the former Communist (8), and even the "two young people [. . .] trousered, slender, giggly, and falsetto" (3)—unsubtle code for homosexuality. As the bus arrives, each of these fallen souls is met by some loved one and encouraged to renounce the city and come away to heaven. The narrator's guide is MacDonald. The two engage in an extended theological dialogue in which the narrator— obviously Lewis himself—questions MacDonald about some of his own writings: "In your own books, Sir," says Lewis, "you were a Universalist. You talked as if all men would be saved" (124). And MacDonald promptly recants, confessing that "every attempt to see the shape of eternity except through the lens of Time destroys your knowledge of Freedom. Witness the doctrine of Predestination which shows (truly enough) that eternal reality is not waiting for a future in which to be real; but at the price of removing Freedom which is the deeper truth of the two. And wouldn't Universalism do the same?" (125). With that difficulty resolved, Lewis can follow MacDonald's lead and set out for the higher hills.

The trouble is that, as Catherine Durie observes, "the MacDonald who makes such forceful points is a ventriloquists's dummy" (175), uttering only what Lewis wishes he had said. The real MacDonald, rather than giving up this flirtation with universal redemption, wrote it into each of his major fantasies. From the early *Phantastes* through *Lilith*, MacDonald continued to explore different routes toward heaven, many of them unorthodox. Using a variety of forms, including comic fairy tale and sentimental novel, he traced the spiritual development of each of his aspiring characters. Some of these are naively good, like the Princess Irene of *The Princess and the Goblin*, whereas others are willful and selfish, like the spoiled Princess Rosamund of "The Wise Woman." Though they occasionally go astray, all are led ultimately toward self-knowledge—and hence the chance of salvation—by some mentor figure, nearly always a woman. These mentors indicate which strand of myth Mac-Donald found most useful for exploring moral and spiritual issues. His values are derived from Christianity, but his model is not Old or New Testament narrative but the fairy tale tradition that he, like feminist commentators such as

Marina Warner and Angela Carter, associates with female storytellers and feminine power. Though the passive heroines of the Grimms' published versions might lead us to think, with Roderick McGillis, that "the female [in fairy tales] is passive and in need of protection and rescue; the male is active and skilled in the manly arts of war" (86), that is not necessarily true of the stories MacDonald would have heard in his youth. One of the best-known Scottish tales, for instance, is the story of the female giant-killer "Mollie Whuppie." What McGillis sees as a departure from tradition might actually be a reflection of MacDonald's own heritage: "MacDonald allows his female characters agency, and he invests his male characters with characteristics we might think of as 'feminine'" (McGillis 86). All of MacDonald's fantasies are "old wives' tales" in that they look to older women for wisdom.

MacDonald's settings, like those of folk Märchen, are both concrete and portentous. Any object might suddenly undergo surprising transformations and reveal symbolic depths. Worms take wing, a lamp shines as bright as the moon, burning coals are also roses, spinning wheels spin invisible threads of faith, yet each of these things remains its ordinary, familiar, substantial self. MacDonald's stories feel like allegories, but it is impossible to pin them down to a single significance or a direct biblical or other mythic reference. Colin Manlove says of MacDonald's tales: "it is perhaps impossible to extract a connected meaning or 'allegory' from them: they are full of hints, but once one tries to capture these, the story either escapes or fades, like the radiant 'bird-butterfly' that, when caught by Vane in *Lilith*, loses its light and becomes 'a dead book with boards outspread'" (83). Though Manlove's wording implies that this is a fault, I think it is one of MacDonald's great strengths.

The Princess and the Goblin is MacDonald's most coherent work of fantasy, yet it too defies reading in allegorical terms. It tells of a young princess, raised by servants in a mountainside castle, who finds her way one rainy day up a previously unknown stairway to a tower room where she meets an old woman spinning in a bare garret. Unlike the spinning witch in the "Sleeping Beauty" tale-type, this woman is benevolent. She introduces herself as Irene's great-great-grandmother. Later in the story, she offers Irene the product of her labor, an invisible thread that will guide her through danger: "But remember, it may seem to you a very roundabout way indeed, and you must not doubt the thread. Of one thing you may be sure, that while you hold it, I hold it too" (105). The thread helps Irene rescue the young miner Curdie when he has been imprisoned by the goblins. Together she and Curdie foil the goblins' plans to kidnap her and marry her to their prince.

Many of the story's elements are clearly symbolic: not only the narrator but the characters themselves comment on the way things seem to change according to what one thinks they mean. If the perceiver is not ready to accept the symbol, the object itself might not be available. For instance, of her moon lamp, the great-great-grandmother says, it does not happen above five times in a hundred years that any one does see it. The greater part of those who do take it for a meteor, wink their eyes, and forget it again. Besides, [. . .] if that light were to go out you would fancy yourself lying in a bare garret, on a heap of old straw, and would not see one of the pleasant things round about you all the time. (80)

But all the symbols are plurisignificant: there is no one answer to the mystery. The story has been read as a representation of the church in the world, of the Romantic imagination, and of psychoanalytic models of the psyche. All of these readings work; none fully accounts for the book's power. Robert Wolff's Freudian interpretation is a good example of how overly systematic analyses go astray. He asserts that the goblins represent

the greedy, cunning side of our own human nature tunneling away in the secret subterranean chambers of the subconscious and always threatening to take possession of the castle of our minds, unless we, like Curdie, remain on our guard against them, with the aid of our higher selves, which dwell like grandmother in the lofty towers of our personalities (166).

Wolff is both trivially right and significantly wrong. Of course the goblins are the baser side of humanity; it doesn't take a psychoanalyst to point out what is evident in every legend about goblins. MacDonald's spatial metaphor, which places moral guidance in the castle tower and blind bestiality in the cellars, is a deliberate construction rather than a veiled message from the unconscious. Either Wolff's Freudianism or his own sexist assumptions cause him to eliminate Princess Irene from his summary and to place the masculine Curdie in the role of protagonist, and his allegorical model forces him into a misreading of the goblins' motives. As Manlove points out, they do not want to take possession of the castle, nor does the castle belong to Curdie but to Irene and her father (85).

More important, each of these readings necessarily leaves out symbols that don't fit. A Freudian reading doesn't explain why Irene's great-great-grandmother in the tower is both young and old, why she keeps pigeons as her poultry and lives on their eggs, or why she has a lamp that can shine through walls and a bathtub full of the night sky. A Christian reading accounts for the thread of faith, the burning roses (the Virgin Mary's rose cross-pollinated with the burning bush of Exodus), and the pigeons (as signs of grace, doves of the Holy Spirit) but doesn't explain why the goblins fear Curdie's songs and rhymes or why the divine is glimpsed exclusively through images of femininity: the womblike bath, the healing roses, the umbilical thread, the spinning-wheels worked by both the grandmother (as Irene calls her for short) and Curdie's mother.

But we are not allowed to read these merely as erotic or maternal images, either. Like Lewis, MacDonald invites us to look at the Freudian symbol as reversible, rather than always pointing toward the sexual. Female sexuality is expressed through, but also stands for, spiritual insight, which comes, literally, from the distaff side of the family. The spinning mother's distaff and wheel signify creativity and the Romantic imagination. MacDonald's spinning wheels, like those of Romantic composers, make music. Irene hears her grandmother's wheel before she sees it:

> as she stood, she began to hear a curious humming sound. Could it be the rain? No. It was much more gentle, and even monotonous than the sound of the rain, which now she scarcely heard. The low sweet humming sound went on, sometimes stopping for a little while and then beginning again. It was more like the hum of a very happy bee that had found a rich well of honey in some globular flower, than anything else I can think of at this moment. Where could it come from? [. . .] She was rather afraid, but her curiosity was stronger than her fear, and she opened the door very gently and peeped in. What do you think she saw? A very old lady who sat spinning. (9)

MacDonald's narrator sustains a set of metaphoric equivalencies among spun thread, melody, natural processes (the sounds of rain and bees, the spider silk from which the thread is spun), femininity, faith, and poetic vision. In regard to the last of these, the grandmother's wheel is paired with her moon lamp: both the thread from the wheel and the light from the lamp act as guides when characters are in danger. The grandmother says that "I don't work every night—only moonlit nights, and then no longer than the moon shines upon my wheel" (77), and she tells Irene that the lovely things in her room would disappear if the lamp went out, leaving her in "a bare garret, sitting on a heap of straw" (80). When the grandmother sings to Irene, her song is as elusive as the hum of the wheel: "And from somewhere came the voice of the lady, singing a strange sweet song, of which she could distinguish every word; but of the sense she had only a feeling—no understanding. Nor could she remember a single line after it was gone. It vanished, like the poetry in a dream, as fast as it came" (162).

Everything said about the grandmother is also true, on a more modest scale and in an earthier realm, of Curdie's mother. Just as her grandmother's invisible thread guides Irene, a humble ball of string guides Curdie through the goblins' tunnels—a trick he learned from the stories his mother has told him (83). In the sequel, *The Princess and Curdie*, Curdie finally meets the grandmother firsthand and hears her spinning wheel, but its song is not new to him:

> He knew it at once, because his mother's spinning-wheel had been his governess long ago, and still taught him things. It was the spinning-wheel that first taught him to make verses, and to sing, and to think whether all was right inside him; or at least it had helped him in all these things. Hence it was no wonder he should know a spinning-wheel when he heard it sing—even although as the bird of paradise to other birds was the song of that wheel to the song of his mother's. (*Curdie* 30)

Different in degree but not in kind, the two spinning songs teach Curdie to look beyond his father's mining trade and the material concerns of daily life. Unlike Irene, Curdie is able to hold onto the song's words, perhaps because he has been schooled as a rhyme maker by his mother's wheel.

> "What is it saying?" asked the voice.
> "It is singing," answered Curdie.
> "What is it singing?"
> Curdie tried to make out, but thought he could not; for no sooner
>   had he got a hold of something than it vanished again. (76)

But though he says he couldn't understand, the grandmother tells him: "Oh, yes, you did, and you have been telling it to me! Shall I tell you again what I told my wheel, and my wheel told you, and you have just told me without knowing it?" (76) She sings it again to the accompaniment of the wheel, and the song turns out to be about creation and rebirth:

> The stars are spinning their threads,
> And the clouds are the dust that flies,
> And the suns are weaving them up
> For the time when the sleepers shall rise. (77)

If this is represents a Christian message, it arrives via a very unorthodox mythic route. Though the risen sleepers are part of Christian belief, they also suggest other sleepers of legend, such as King Arthur or Frederick Barbarossa and his knights. The stars, clouds, and suns represent divinity working through natural process instead of miraculous fiat. The context associates creation and resurrection with women's crafts, rather than men's commands.

Goddesses and guides resembling Irene's great-great-grandmother show up in many European myths (the Fates, Arachne, the Norns) and folktales (the Grimms' Mother Holle, the fairies of Perrault's "Sleeping Beauty"). Though it is unlikely that MacDonald knew anything about American Indian mythology, this complex of symbols closely resembles Navajo beliefs about Spider Woman, the ancestor and creator goddess who spins the universe from her own body. Many mythic traditions associate spiders with storytelling. Some, like the Anansi stories of Africa, make the spider figure masculine, but more often the webmaker is a female figure, benevolent if the culture invoking her approves of female power but sinister where women are devalued. Irene's grandmother is kin to other female authority figures in fantasy—we can see echoes of her in H. Rider Haggard's *She* and in both the wise and protective Galadriel and the devouring spider Shelob of Tolkien's *The Lord of the Rings*. For Lewis (as for Walt Disney), adult female power was evil: the White Witch of Narnia or the brutal lesbian Fairy Hardcastle of *That Hideous Strength*. But MacDonald's versions of the goddess are nearly always both good and wise.

Even in *Phantastes* and *Lilith*, in which the good aspect of the goddess is paired with an evil twin, the good is ultimately more potent.

There is nothing in Christian scripture and very little in doctrine to support MacDonald's vision of the female savior or mentor. Tolkien, strongly Catholic, could look to the Virgin Mary, the Queen of Heaven, as a precedent for Galadriel and Middle-earth's mother goddess Varda, but MacDonald, coming from a Protestant background, had no such backing. Yet MacDonald trusted the truthfulness of fairy tales—both traditional Märchen and his own invented stories—and the symbols they cast up, including women rulers and adventurers. Where those stories and their inner logic diverged from biblical authority, he followed the former. The difference between his concept of mythic fantasy and Lewis's can be found in the titles of their respective essays on the form: Lewis's "Sometimes Fairy Tales May Say Best What's to Be Said" versus MacDonald's "The Fantastic Imagination." For Lewis, there was always something "to be said"—some lesson to be conveyed. Hence, all of his imaginative creations are ultimately pulled into the gravitational field of Christian myth. Aslan reenacts Christ's sacrifice in *The Lion, the Witch, and the Wardrobe*, and we get the apocalypse in *The Last Battle*, the Garden of Eden in *Perelandra*, and the confusion of tongues at the Tower of Babel in *That Hideous Strength*.

MacDonald, instead, asks us to follow the imaginative tale wherever it may lead:

> "Suppose my child ask me what the fairy tale means, what am I to say?"
>
> If you do not know what it means, what is easier than to say so? If you do see a meaning in it, there it is for you to give him. A genuine work of art must mean many things; the truer its art, the more things it will mean. ("Fantastic" 25)

"A fairytale," he insists, "is not an allegory"; hence it is a mistake for the artist to seek to impose a message that is not already there in the structure of the story:

> If my drawing, on the other hand, is so far from being a work of art that it needs THIS IS A HORSE written under it, what can it matter that neither you nor your child should know what it means? (25)

Those who explain fairy tales allegorically treat them as objects of utility rather than beauty: cabbages instead of roses. "To ask me to explain," he says, " is to say, 'Roses! Boil them, or we won't have them!'"(28).

For MacDonald, narrative art was a single operation, unanalyzable. By contrast, Lewis described his own fictional practice as involving three steps and two identities: creative artist and moral man. First, the artist as dreamer generates pictures, the "bubbling stuff" of pure imagination ("Sometimes" 46). Next, the artist as organizer looks for an appropriate form to contain the pictures "as the housewife longs to see the new jam pouring into the clean jam jar" (46).

Finally, "the author as man, citizen, or Christian" (45) seeks some moral justification for the tale. At that stage, the images are linked to religious teaching:

> I thought I saw how stories of this kind could steal past a certain inhibition which had paralyzed much of my own religion in childhood. Why did one find it so hard to feel as one was told one ought to feel about God or about the sufferings of Christ? [. . .] But supposing that by casting all these things into an imaginary world, stripping them of their stained-glass and Sunday school associations, one could make them for the first time appear in their real potency? (47)

Thus, according to Lewis, his Narnia stories started with pictures of "a faun carrying an umbrella, a queen on a sledge, a magnificent lion" (46), and only afterward did the lion become an analogue of Christ and the queen a stand-in for Satan. Likewise, in his space trilogy, the images of Martian canyons and the floating islands of Venus emerged first, and only afterward did they suggest to him an allegorical scheme for replaying the stories of Creation and Fall.

Out of the Silent Planet (1938), the first book in the trilogy, was written as Lewis's part of an agreement with Tolkien that each should write a modern romance, Lewis dealing with travel through space and Tolkien with time. Tolkien started a romance called "The Lost Road," in which a modern Englishman visits successively earlier and increasingly legendary eras, from Alfred the Great's time to the fall of Atlantis. He abandoned the project after a handful of chapters, though the idea of a modern sensibility encountering history and myth fed into the layers of legendary and mythic time in *The Lord of the Rings*. Lewis stuck to the plan, at least at first. His hero Ransom travels to Mars with two companions in a private spaceship reminiscent of the one in H. G. Wells's *The First Men in the Moon* (1901). There he meets the three intelligent races of Martians and learns that all the planets except Earth are guided by angelic spirits. Our own fallen angel, or *oyarsa*, is Satan, and the universe turns out to resemble medieval cosmology more than the particles and processes of scientific materialism. Weston, the scientist who built the spaceship of the first volume, shows up on Venus in the second, *Perelandra* (1943), as a demonically possessed tool bent on bringing Satan's message to Venus. Ransom is transported there by angelic means to prevent a second Fall. By the third book, Lewis pretty much disavows any science fictional influences by invoking biblical myth (the Tower of Babel), Arthurian legend (Ransom has become the wounded Fisher King and modern-day Pendragon, aided by a revived Merlin), and alchemy (as the *oyéresu* of the other planets descend to Earth and take on their astrological roles). The scientific organization NICE, or National Institute for Co-ordinated Experiments, is revealed as a front for a Satanic conspiracy and its leader Horace Jules—a caricature of H. G. Wells though bearing the name of his French rival Jules Verne—is shown to be the dupe of the dark magicians who wish to destroy all life.

An unnamed co-conspirator on the science fiction side might be David Lindsay, best known for his extraordinary Gnostic fantasy *A Voyage to Arcturus*, which was published in 1920, roughly midway between MacDonald's *Lilith* and Lewis's *Out of the Silent Planet*. Lindsay is a conduit between MacDonald and Lewis, though his own beliefs and the philosophical speculation embodied in that novel are far from either the former's Universalism or the latter's orthodoxy. The form of *A Voyage to Arcturus* is an astral voyage, half science fiction adventure and half visionary fairy tale, which harkens back to MacDonald's hybrid of Darwinian evolution and biblical adventure in *Lilith* and which anticipates even more precisely Lewis's method in *Out of the Silent Planet*. We need not speculate about these influences: in his study of Lindsay, Gary K. Wolfe points out that Lindsay claimed MacDonald as "his greatest influence" (11) and quotes a 1944 letter from Lewis acknowledging that "The real father of my planet books is David Lindsay's *V oyage to Arcturus*" and that "it was Lindsay who first gave me the idea that the 'scientifiction' appeal could be combined with the 'supernatural' appeal" (7). Yet for Lewis, Lindsay, even more than MacDonald, would have represented the right materials used for the wrong ends. *A Voyage to Arcturus* takes imagery from Genesis and language from Norse myth ("Surtur," "Muspel") and uses them to send the reader on a journey of exotic eroticism, pain, and disillusionment. Lewis's space trilogy, especially the middle volume *Perelandra*, is an attempt to redirect the power of Lindsay's space allegory toward an orthodox affirmation of faith.

Lewis's discrediting of the fathers of science fiction in both his memoir and his space trilogy bears out his admission that the novels became a way to exorcise his hunger for exotic worlds and extraordinary voyages, a hunger that he later came to characterize (perhaps recalling Lindsay's sexually charged landscapes) as lust. It did not start out that way—the turn comes somewhere in the middle of *Perelandra*, when the charm of discovery gives way to theological debate. The gap between *Perelandra*'s vivid opening and its turgid middle—a seminar on obedience with nods to Milton—suggests that Lewis is being honest about his method. The images do seem to have arisen first, with the commentary of *Paradise Lost* being imposed on them afterward.

Lewis's method of composition thus contrasts strongly with MacDonald's practice, in which even a tale as obviously allegorical as "The Golden Key" resists reduction to any one schema. Bonnie Gaarden offers two readings of that tale, as both Bunyanesque pilgrimage and Romantic Bildungsroman: "A devout theist but one who emphasized God's immanence over God's transcendence, MacDonald created literary images that can be read with or without reference to the Christian God" (36). Instead of naming his allegorical pilgrims Christian or Eve, MacDonald calls them Mossy and Tangle—probably, according to Stephen Prickett, a reference to Goethe's *Wilhelm Meister* (Gaarden 51 n.1). Both names suggest spiritual confusion but also natural abundance and beauty; one would not mind going astray in a tangle of moss.

In MacDonald's last fantasy, *Lilith*, he invoked biblical myth explicitly for the first time, but he did so in a way that reaffirms his particular Romantic and scientific take on Christianity. It is useful to pair that work with an earlier, semiautobiographical novel called *Robert Falconer* (1868). One of MacDonald's realistic stories of the Scottish countryside, *Robert Falconer* was a particular favorite of Mark Twain and his wife Livy (Lindskoog 1). It might not seem to have much to do with a mystical tale of dimensional crossings, magical transformations, and Adam's demonic first wife, but there are surprising connections between the two books. Both focus on young men—the title character of *Robert Falconer* and Mr. Vane of *Lilith*—who undertake similar quests for spiritual insight and redemption. In both cases, it is not the protagonist's own soul that must be redeemed but that of an ancestral figure, Robert's father and Mr. Vane's prospective mother-in-law, Lilith. Both protagonists work through versions of Christian myth to arrive at decidedly unconventional understandings of the divine will. In both novels, MacDonald invites us to read such myths conditionally, critically, even skeptically, and he counterbalances scripture with two other sources of inspiration: first, the processes and motifs associated with folklore, and, second, natural phenomena, which he reads both scientifically and emblematically.

Robert Falconer wishes to be a musician and is on his way to becoming a traditional performer, learning tunes and techniques from his neighbors. His stern grandmother disapproves of his learning the fiddle, the devil's instrument. She even burns the fine old violin he has inherited from his black-sheep father. When Robert finally confronts her and claims the right to learn music, he is also implicitly rejecting her Calvinist faith in favor of a Romantic commitment to the folk imagination and a Transcendentalist belief in nature as a source of revelation. And it is in the battle between these forms of belief that MacDonald reveals his aims and methods of fantasy writing, even though there is little that is overtly fantastic in *Robert Falconer* outside of the main character's dreams and visions. One important clue is that, despite his very sincere search for faith, Robert rebels against Milton's version of the Fall, because, "in reading the Paradise Lost, he could not help sympathizing with Satan, and feeling [. . .] that the Almighty was pompous, scarcely reasonable, and somewhat revengeful" (93). One can feel MacDonald getting ready to rewrite Milton, as he eventually does in *Lilith*.

MacDonald uses vernacular traditions to counter Milton and the Bible. He approaches the story of the Fall through Lilith, a figure from medieval Jewish legend. He adds major players to the drama: a daughter of Eve named Mara and a daughter of Lilith named Lona, and both characters resembles figures out of folktale: Lona the cast-out heroine and Mara the witch in the woods. The whole story is framed as a Märchen, with the biblical and invented characters playing parts described in Vladimir Propp's morphology of the folktale: Adam as Dispatcher, Mara as Donor/Tester, Lilith as Villain, and Lona as Princess. Vane thinks Lona is the kind of princess who must be rescued by a male hero—the role in which he casts himself—but she is actually the more independent female hero of stories such as "Tattercoat."

MacDonald gives to his alter ego Robert Falconer his own familiarity with and love for oral tradition. Like Curdie, Robert learns to dream from the tunes and tales he hears as a child; the fiddle is his equivalent of the magical spinning wheel. When he learns to read, his imagination is first fully engaged not by religious writings but by secular folk literature, including Arabian Nights tales: "He read on, heart and soul and mind absorbed in the marvels of the eastern skald; the stories told in the streets of Cairo, amidst gorgeous costumes, and camels, and white veiled women" (137). Other folk narratives, from closer to home than Cairo, also strike a chord, such as the highland ballad sung by Robert's friend and tutor Ericson, in which

> a young man fell in love with a beautiful witch, who let him go on loving her till he cared for nothing but her, and then began to kill him by laughing at him. For no witch can fall in love herself, however much she may like to be loved. (233)

The narrator says that "while Ericson told the story the room still glimmered about Robert" (234). MacDonald is suggesting that such a magical story casts a "glimmer"—or glamour—on its listeners. This storyteller's glimmer is an illustration of the transformative power of the imagination, especially the collective imagination. Like the light from the moon lamp of *The Princess and the Goblin*, it is a source of deeper truth, rather than illusion.

The second great source of spiritual nourishment for MacDonald, as attested in his portrayal of Robert, is nature—the scenic route to the divine. Like folk tradition, natural beauty becomes a point of departure from, and a source of resistence to, orthodoxy. Out in the hills, Robert loses himself in *Sehnsucht*:

> He lay gazing up into the depth of the sky, rendered deeper and bluer by the masses of white cloud that hung almost motionless below it, until he felt a kind of bodily fear lest he should fall off the face of the round earth into the abyss. A gentle wind, laden with pine odours from the sun-heated trees behind him, flapped its light wing in his face: the humanity of the world smote his heart; the great sky towered up over him, and its divinity entered his soul; a strange longing after something 'he knew not nor could name' awoke within him [. . .]. (122–23)

The sky, in particular, always triggers not only desire but also fancy. Looking at a cloud, Robert startles a friend by imagining himself up there digging earthworms of lighting—or, in Scots: "wadna ye like to be up in that clood wi' a spaud, turnin' ower the divots and catchin' the flashes lyin' aneath them like lang reid fiery worms?" (65–66). Part of what is interesting in this image is the yoking of heaven and earth—airy cloud castles and humble earthworms. It is a link that reappears as a fully concretized fantasy in *Lilith*, when Mr. Vane is startled to see his spiritual guide Adam, in raven form, digging up a worm and casting it into the air, where it suddenly "spread[s] great wings, gorgeous in red and black, and soar[s] aloft" (20).

Rather than simply being astounded at the transformation, or accepting it as a material parable of the soul and the body, Mr. Vane critiques it on scientific grounds:

> "Tut! Tut!" I exclaimed; "you mistake, Mr. Raven: worms are not the larvae of butterflies!" (20)

Though this comment says more about Mr. Vane's vanity at this point in his story than about the relative values of religion and science, MacDonald characteristically balances his transcendental visions with scientific observation. *Lilith* is, in some ways, as autobiographical a work as *Robert Falconer*, and Mr. Vane resembles his author in being a student of science: "It was chiefly the wonder they woke that drew me," Vane says; "I was constantly seeing, and on the outlook to see, strange analogies, not only between the facts of different sciences of the same order, or between physical and metaphysical facts, but between physical hypotheses and suggestions glimmering [!] out of the metaphysical dreams into which I was in the habit of falling" (5).

Part of the charm of *Lilith* is the way its strange and symbolic images are rooted in natural phenomena, such as the metamorphosis of caterpillar (or worm) into butterfly. Many creatures in *Lilith* are in the process of evolving from lower to higher states of being (including the protagonist), although a few are devolving. Mr. Raven's description of life on the "steppes of Uranus" is a portrait of evolution on fast-forward:

> It is a great sight, until you get used to it, when the earth gives a heave, and out comes a beast. You might think it is a hairy elephant or a deinotherium—but none of the animals are the same as we have ever had here. I was almost frighted myself the first time I saw the dry-bog-serpent come wallowing out—such a head and mane! and such eyes! (19)

In the light of such descriptions, it is surprising to find a commentator on a creationist website asserting that "Darwin and his teachings might as well never have existed as far as MacDonald is concerned" (Myers 2). Richard Reis comes closer to the truth when he says that "MacDonald understood the uneasy fascination with Darwinism which so disturbed his readers, and he found it another convenient means of symbolizing his ideas about the spiritual education" (132). In other words, rather than rejecting Darwin's ideas on biblical grounds, MacDonald found them a rich source of metaphor. This view is supported in *Robert Falconer* when the protagonist asks, regarding seemingly unredeemable prostitutes: "Shall it take less time to make a woman than to make a world? Is not the woman the greater? She may have her ages of chaos,

her centuries of crawling slime, yet rise a woman at last" (354). Evolution becomes an alternative, and perhaps feminist, myth of redemption and growth.

Alongside Darwinian theory, the new science of psychology makes its way
into MacDonald's writings. In *Robert Falconer*, MacDonald speculates quite
explicitly on the operations of the unconscious. He refers to "the bit and bridle
of the association of ideas, as it is called in the skeleton language of mental philosophy" (402). As an instance of the workings of the unconscious mind, he
cites a case in which a convict is reformed by looking at a carpet "of the same
pattern as that in the church to which he had gone as a boy [. . .]. It was not the
matting that so far converted him [. . .] but [. . .] memories of childhood, the
mysteries of the kingdom of innocence which that could recall" (402–403).
MacDonald here anticipates not only psychoanalysis but also more recent
neurological studies of how memories are formed and accessed.

Schooled in both "mental philosophy" and German Romantic symbolism,
MacDonald was so very aware of the dynamics of dream that Freudian and
Jungian readings of his fantasy tend to fall flat, either by belaboring the obvious ("Lilith is an anima figure") or by warping the text to fit expected patterns (e. g., Robert Wolff's Freudian decodings). MacDonald's fantasy offers its
own theory of the unconscious, one that is less doctrinaire than orthodox psychoanalysis. His willingness to look at religious issues from a scientific perspective results, in *Lilith*, in a narrative that departs in significant ways from its
scriptural sources.

On the one hand, we have a story of fall and redemption, with Adam and
Satan as major actors. On the other, the title character comes not from biblical
authority but from religious legend. Lilith is not a biblical character. There is
only a single reference to a *lilith*, meaning some sort of night demon, in Isaiah.
Nothing in Genesis hints at a first wife for Adam, or proposes a feminine version of Lucifer the fallen angel, which Lilith becomes in MacDonald's retelling.
He alters Judeo-Christian tradition to produce not just one but three major
feminine powers: proud Lilith, nurturing Eve, and Eve's stern daughter Mara.
By introducing Lilith into the story, he is able to remove the onus of the Fall
from Adam and Eve, who thus become the perfect parents and caretakers of
the dead, as those, like the sleepers of Curdie's song, await eventual resurrection. Resurrection is depicted as a natural process in a scene in which Vane
observes the dead returning to life. MacDonald's precise descriptions of the
way two skeletons gradually reacquire flesh and act out an old quarrel render
the scene more science fictional than theological.

Another departure from canonical Christian myth has to do with who gets
to be redeemed. There is no casting of multitudes into outer darkness in Mac-
Donald, no agony of burning. Everybody gets in. MacDonald's Universalism
goes beyond saving just the nice characters, or the weak but salvageable ones
like Mr. Vane. At the end of his novel, Lilith herself gives up her ego and her
stolen immortality to sleep with the other mortals, and Adam prophesies that

even the Archenemy will one day be redeemed: "When the Shadow comes here, it will be to lie down and sleep also.—His hour will come, and he knows it will" (217–218). If we are not sure MacDonald means it, a check with Vane's double Robert Falconer shows Robert asking his friend Shargar, "Gin a de'il war to repent, wad God forgie him [If the Devil were to repent, would God forgive him]?" (79), to which Shargar sensibly replies, "There's no sayin' what fowk wad du till once they're tried" (79). MacDonald was not merely doubtful of the justice of eternal damnation; he seems to have found the idea of being saved at others' expense downright distasteful: "I did not care for God to love me if He did not love everybody," as he says in another novel *(Weighed and Wanting* 1882; quoted in Reis 33).

There is no hell in MacDonald, except a psychological one. In *Lilith*, he offers us a set of powerful symbols for understanding a divided and tortured self. Lilith's hell is the mirrored, egg-shaped chamber in which she contemplates herself, which is also the hoarded life she carries like an egg in her hand (resembling the egg in which the magician Koshchei, in the Russian tale of "The Firebird," has hidden his life). Ultimately, she is unable to open her hand to release herself; the hand must be cut off and buried to bring flowing water back to the land. Her redemption involves pain and renunciation but not punishment. The chamber of the sleeping dead is a sort of purgatory, but it is not a place of torture, rather of peace and dreaming and the cycles of nature: "I lay at peace, full of the quietest expectation, breathing the damp odours of Earth's bountiful bosom, aware of the souls of primroses, daisies and snowdrops, patiently waiting in it for the Spring" (230). This vision of immersion in nature mirrors the book's opening epigraph, which comes not from the Bible or some religious authority but from Thoreau's essay "Walking"—the Scottish mystic and the American scientist/philosopher share a view of the natural world as an Eden that was never lost but only forgotten by self-absorbed humans.

It is no wonder that Lewis felt the need to rewrite MacDonald into a more appropriate spiritual guide. Though Lewis credits MacDonald with having baptized his imagination, Lewis's imagination works in a very different way. MacDonald's fantasies resist any orthodox reading. The same characters will look, from one angle, like biblical references; from another, like psychoanalytic categories or natural symbols; from a third, they will assert themselves as realistically unpredictable individuals. Trying to fit them into a strict allegorical scheme would be, as MacDonald says, boiling roses. To keep his roses unboiled, MacDonald plays fast and loose with sources, altering mythic characters and changing the outcomes of both Fall and Apocalypse. Adam becomes not only an ancestral mentor but a shape-shifting raven, a Trickster of sorts. Lilith is a combination of seductive vampire and murderously jealous mother (reminiscent of the queen in "Snow White")—yet with the help of Mr. Vane and her daughter she finds her way toward self-renunciation. Even the Shadow, MacDonald's version of Satan, will be redeemed in time.

By contrast, Lewis's Narnia books sometimes look like a Classics Illustrated comic-book version of the Bible. One can almost see him checking things off a list: OK, there's the Crucifixion done (*The Lion, the Witch, and the Wardrobe*); now we need to get through the Creation (*The Magician's Nephew*) and the Apocalypse (*The Last Battle*). Laura Miller describes her reaction as a child when she discovered that her beloved Narnia books had a secret doctrinal message: "I'd been tricked, cheated, betrayed" (99). The betrayal is not merely the discovery of a dose of medicine hidden in the confection or that Lewis was in league with the forces of conformity that Miller was already beginning to reject in her encounters with official religion. It was that the overtly Christian parts contradicted what she understood from the rest of the books. For the young Miller, "Narnia was liberation and delight. Christianity was boredom, subjugation, and reproach. [. . .] The Christianity that I knew—the only Christianity I was aware of—was the opposite of Narnia in both aesthetics and spirit" (96). Her more mature reconsideration is that her initial aesthetic response might have been truer to the text than the allegorical reading that substitutes an abstract God for the furry immediacy of Aslan:

> So when Lewis's child readers don't see Christianity in the Chronicles, they are in fact perceiving a truth about Narnia that adults usually miss. The Christianity in Narnia has been substantially, rather than just superficially, transformed—to the point of being much less Christian, perhaps than Lewis intended. (91)

Miller goes on to offer readings of Narnia that emphasize the stories' undermining of their own doctrinal messages. George MacDonald's work, though, rarely requires such resisting readings (to borrow a term from Judith Fetterly's feminist critique of American literature). Lewis tries to keep his symbols under conscious control, but he does not always succeed. Sometimes those symbols go romping off on their own, like the parade of Bacchantes at the end of *Prince Caspian* who threaten to turn the Sunday-school session into a pagan orgy. They do not quite do so, because Lewis diverts our attention back to Aslan and the right kind of desire. Bacchus and his maenads come dangerously close to lust, and lust is the route to damnation. MacDonald too invokes dangerously seductive symbols, such as Lilith herself in her guise as succubus or vampire. Rather than looking away quickly, the text dwells on her, pondering what forces might create such a being and how her evil power might be transformed into something good.

Whereas MacDonald redeems even evil itself, Lewis is always eager to exclude those he thinks should not get into Heaven. *The Great Divorce* reads as if he wrote it during a particularly irksome faculty meeting and took special glee in consigning his philosophical opponents to hell. MacDonald's approach to Christian myth is, in many ways, closer to such critical and creative reworkings as Charles Williams's treatment of the Grail legend than to Lewis's

Perelandra or *The Last Battle*. MacDonald invites us to rethink myths and our relationship to them, rather than simply to accept them as given. Readers from Jewish or Christian backgrounds are used to having fantasy writers refurbish myths from other cultures for our enjoyment and edification. We are less accustomed to fantasy that asks us to investigate and reinhabit the myths that formed us, but that is what George MacDonald's asks us to do.

It is also what Lewis does in his atypical late work *Till We Have Faces*. This 1956 novel reverses many of the patterns readers of Lewis's earlier fiction would have come to expect. It retells the Greco-Roman myth of Psyche, included as an embedded narrative in Apuleius's *The Golden Ass*, rather than any biblical topos; it presents a number of viewpoints on religion without dismissing any of them outright; it is narrated by an adult woman who is a strong and complex character (albeit one whose primary relationships are with men); and it offers the possibility of a feminine, as well as a masculine, face for God. Most surprisingly, it acknowledges and even validates doubt. Orual, the central character, learns to doubt her own perceptions, her good faith in interacting with others, and the precepts she has been taught by a trusted mentor—and all of these doubts bring her closer to the divine, rather than driving her away.

Till We Have Faces takes place in the small barbarian kingdom of Glome in the backwaters of Greek civilization. Its king, like Henry VIII, is obsessed with producing a male heir but ends up instead with three daughters: Orual, Redival, and Istra, or Psyche. Orual is taught by a Greek slave called the Fox, brought in to tutor the son who never arrives. Plain, strong, and intelligent, she learns to handle a sword, negotiate a treaty, and argue philosophy with the Fox. She earns a measure of respect from her father but never his affection. The great loves of her life are the Fox, her loyal guard Bardia, and the preternaturally beautiful Istra. Her great enemy is the goddess Ungit, represented by a hulking, featureless figure—ancient statue or natural formation—in a dark and smoky temple. Ungit is a primitive mother goddess who demands blood sacrifices and sends a plague for which the only cure, according to the high priest, is the sacrifice of Istra to the Shadowbeast on the mountain—which is, unknown to the citizens of Glome, really Ungit's divine son, Cupid to her Venus.

In this novel, Lewis pioneered the now popular fantasy mode of retelling fairy tales from unexpected points of view: "Sleeping Beauty" narrated by the evil fairy (Sheri S. Tepper's *Beauty*), "Cinderella" from the perspective of the transformed coachman (David H. Wilson's *The Coachman Rat*, 1989), and so on. In Lewis's reworking of Apuleius's text, Orual is Psyche's jealous older sibling, the sister who, in a related tale, tricks Beauty into betraying her Beast. Only this sister is motivated primarily by a desire to protect Psyche. She is devastated when she thinks Istra has been devoured, even more disturbed by what she thinks is madness when Istra tells of her divine lover and his invisible palace. Of course, none of this motivation is unmixed. Part 1 of the novel is Orual's story as she tells it to the gods, with herself as innocent victim; part 2 depicts her painful journey toward the awareness that she has been not only a protector but also a user of other people. She has more in common with the devouring Ungit than she has ever admitted to herself, though at her best she also resembles the newly deified Psyche.

Till We Have Faces is quite extraordinary for its depiction of Orual as a powerful, complex, spiritual woman. It is unusual both for its time, the mid-1950s, and for its author, who had earlier ejected one of his heroines (Susan Pevensie in *The Last Battle*) from Narnia for showing signs of adult sexuality and advised another (Jane Studdock in *That Hideous Strength*) to forget her dreams of academic success and to submit in proper medieval fashion to the authority of her clearly inferior husband. Orual's doubts and her rebellion against Ungit and the God of the Mountain are treated sympathetically and eventually lead toward her spiritual awakening. The catalyst for this turnabout in Lewis's views of womanhood was probably Joy Davidman, the book's dedicatee and the first woman he seems ever to have viewed as an equal. Davidman was a challenge to Lewis in many ways: not only female but also American, Jewish (though a convert to Christianity), divorced, politically radical, and a poet. The story of their meeting and marriage and her untimely death is now part of the Lewis mystique, thanks to William Nicholson's television play *Shadowlands* (1985) and Lewis's own discussion of his loss in *A Grief Observed* (published pseudonymously in 1961). *A Grief Observed* is a much less confident treatment of faith than *Surprised by Joy*, though still affirming Lewis's Christianity. Its writer, unlike the earlier ebullient and sometimes bullying Lewis, is slow to judge, to divide the world into friendly and enemy camps. Even before Davidman's death, Lewis had stopped drawing an absolute distinction between desire and lust and their mythic implications, to judge by the figure of Ungit in *Till We Have Faces*.

Ungit embodies everything Lewis has earlier banished as lust. Her worship is primitive, her acolytes temple prostitutes. She is always associated with blood and animal nature: the messy facts of birth, sexuality, and death. Orual hates her, as she hates her own femininity. In a revealing passage late in the novel, Orual looks at the stone figure and sees her childhood nurse Batta, a stupid, greedy, fleshy woman:

> she was very uneven, lumpy and furrowed, so that, as when we gaze into a fire, you could always see some face or other. She was now more rugged than ever because of all the blood they had poured over her in the night. In the little clots and chains of it I made out a face; a fancy at one moment, but then, once you had seen it, not to be evaded. A face such as you might see in a loaf, swollen, brooding, infinitely female. It was a little like Batta, as I remembered her in certain of her moods. (270)

This oppressively female deity, like Batta, is worst when the mood is a loving one: Orual is desperate to evade "her huge, hot, strong yet flabby-soft embraces, the smothering, engulfing tenacity of her" (270).

I think we have to take Lewis at his word here and examine the sexual symbolism—the female body as object of disgust and abjection—not as the end of
the semiotic path but as the beginning. The scene is too obvious for any Freudian uncloaking: sex is the surface meaning, and the dreaming truth lies somewhere else, or somewhere beneath. The novel is not a diatribe against women
or their bodies, though Orual is uncomfortable thinking of herself as a woman
or a physical being. Nor is it a lesson in Christian orthodoxy, though it can be
read in Christian terms. The book's title tells us where to look for the central
issue. "How can they [the gods] meet us face to face," Orual asks, "till we have
faces?" (294). This metaphor, like Freudian symbolism, is reversible. We cannot
meet the gods face to face until they too have faces. Lewis, through Orual,
teaches us that we rely on the divine to provide us with identities: the very
selves that defy God are reflections of God's greater self. But at the same time
we learn from Ungit that the faces of the gods are our own faces projected onto
the universe.

Tom Shippey suggests that the novel can be read as a survey of myth criticism. Each major character understands Ungit in a way that parallels some
school of interpretation. The Fox represents the Stoic take on myth, the old
priest of Ungit is a pagan fundamentalist, his successor Arnom is a solar my-
thologist, the priest of the new Istra cult reflects Jane Harrison's ritual theory,
and so on ("Imagined" 313–316). Only Psyche comes close to voicing a Christian perspective on myth, and even then the novel does not unequivocally
endorse her views over all the others. In Orual's final vision, it is the skeptical
Fox who counsels her on the nature of the gods. At this point, Lewis has revised his old idea of myth as "lies breathed through silver" into something like
"lies transmuted into truth"—a position closer to those of Tolkien and Owen
Barfield than to Lewis's in his earlier fantasies. A chain of equivalencies and
substitutions links the pagan gods with the Christian and the worshiper with
the worshiped. Psyche is Orual, who is Ungit, who is both Batta and the Shadowbeast, who is Cupid, who anticipates Christ.

The Christian idea of union with Christ the Bridegroom is, in this case,
unabashedly carnal. "He comes to me only in the holy darkness," says Psyche
(123). Orual—a virgin herself— fills in the details with her memories of the
House of Ungit: "You ought to have lived in there—in the dark—all blood and
incense and muttering and the reek of burnt fat. To like it—living among
things you can't see—dark and holy and horrible" (125). There is still a contrast
between lust and desire—between the primitive Ungit and her more refined
son—but the narrative implies that they are two aspects of the same deity,
stages of development rather than opposing forces. Orual cannot come to an
understanding of the higher god without confronting the lower. In a poignant
moment late in the novel, she spends the night in Ungit's temple, where there
is now a new, Greek-style statue of the goddess: "wonderfully beautiful and
lifelike, even when we brought her white and naked into her house; and when

we had painted her and put her robes on, she was a marvel to all the lands about and pilgrims came to see her" (234). Yet this new sanitized Ungit does not have the power of the old. A grieving peasant woman sacrifices a pigeon not to the new statue but to the old stone figure. Orual asks why:

> "Do you always pray to that Ungit," said I (nodding toward the shapeless stone), "and not to that?" Here I nodded towards our new image, standing tall and straight in her robes and (whatever the Fox might say of it) the loveliest thing our land has ever seen.

"Oh, always this, Queen," said she. "That other, the Greek Ungit, she wouldn't understand my speech. She's only for nobles and learned men. There's no comfort in her." (272)

The ancient bloody goddess brings healing as well as plagues. Her language is women's language, her presence close and comforting, as well as smelly and stifling. Psyche's traditional task of bringing a box of beauty from Persephone to Venus becomes, in Lewis's retelling, the transformation of terrible Ungit into a higher form of godhood. "And will the gods one day grow thus beautiful, Grandfather?" Orual asks the ghost of the Fox. He replies,

> "They say . . . but even I, who am dead, do not yet understand more than a few broken words of their language. Only this I know. This age of ours will one day be the distant past. And the Divine Nature can change the past. Nothing is yet in its true form." (305)

This is Lewis the Christian coming to terms with the problem of the virtuous pagan, a problem he had dealt with less satisfactorily in the Narnia series via the single honorable worshiper of the Calormene god Tash, whose service Aslan simply takes for his own. "Whenever you said Tash you meant Aslan," Aslan/Lewis says in effect. In this novel, though, there is no sense of religious error corrected but rather of differing levels of understanding. As MacDonald says of fairy tales, "Everyone [...]who feels the story, will read its meaning after his own nature and development: one man will read one meaning in it, another will read another" ("Fantastic" 25). The same is true, Orual discovers, of myths, and of the gods themselves.

There are two corollaries to MacDonald's claim about tales and their significance. The first is that a myth need not mean what the authorities say it means, or even what the author says it means. The story of the Fall, for instance, can be repurposed into an exploration of evolution, physical and spiritual, instead of a lesson in obedience. The second corollary is that any tale might turn out to contain a seed of truth unanticipated by its original tellers—even a Christian truth, if that is what the listener is able to understand from it. These are the lessons MacDonald learned from the fiddles and spinning wheels of his youth. They correspond to claims by feminist scholars such as Hélène Cixous about women's language: unlike the father tongue of law and church and logic, women's language, they say, is indirect, polyvocal, allusive, tied to the body and its senses. This sort of women's language is Ungit's language. That is why there is comfort in her. Lewis too learned the lesson of the spinning wheel and the language of the mothers, though he learned it late. *Till We Have Faces* says that if myths are lies breathed through silver, the silver is more important than the lies, and the body's breath more important than either. A biblical myth can be a fairy tale, and a pagan myth can become a Christian parable. Lewis's last work of mythic fantasy tells us that lust is ultimately not different from desire, that the longing that draws us upward toward the divine also anchors us in blood and stone and darkness.

For both writers, fantasy functioned as an entry into the highest realms of the spirit. Concocting entertainments for children did not seem to them a lesser enterprise than composing sermons for adults; indeed, the right kind of grown-up was the one who retained a child's delight in imaginative play. More surprisingly, these two men were willing to pour their beliefs into fairy tale, a form that assumes unbelief: to let "once upon a time" replace "credo" as an introduction to statements of faith. If such framing invited comparison between biblical narrative and Norse myth, or invited readers to see Christian tropes in psychoanalytic terms, or elevated the fairy godmother to divine status, the risk was worth it (as Lewis might see it) or was no risk at all (as MacDonald suggests). In that artistic decision lies the key to fantasy's emergence as a major literary form and as a locus of controversy. Lewis and MacDonald opened a path for religious fantasists such as Madeleine L'Engle and Nancy Willard, but they also paved the way for fantasies questioning biblical authority and Christian belief, such as James Morrow's *Towing Jehovah* and Philip Pullman's Northern Lights trilogy. There is room within the fantasy genre itself for a range of responses to religious myth. Outside the pages of books, things have not always been so civil, as will be seen in later chapters.

Romance and Formula, Myth and Memorate

You don't belong here. You're destined for something greater. You aren't
who everyone thinks you are. True love waits for you. Ancient and
powerful forces are at work in the world, and you can touch them.
All you need is the talisman, the doorway, the secret word.

This is the call of romance, and it is a call that elite literature forgot for much of
the twentieth century. One of the attractions of fantasy as a genre is its promise
to reconnect the pleasures of literary narrative—insight into character, poetic
precision, ironic observation—with those of romance, which had otherwise
been given over to forms perceived as subliterary. Because pulp magazines,
dime novels, comics, children's books, and the movies never stopped spinning
tales of mystery and marvel, they have been labeled nonliterature, paralit-
erature, even subliterature, yet their practitioners often have a sophisticated
awareness of connections to earlier forms of romance and to myth. Versions of
romance emerged within each of these venues and met with literary traditions
of allegory and mythic vision to help form the modern genre of fantasy.

The word *romance* has so many shadings and applications that it usually
requires a modifier: medieval romance, Gothic romance, scientific romance,
Harlequin romance. What these have in common is a conception of storytelling fundamentally different from a realist model. Realism says literature
exists to tell truths about the everyday world; romance says that literature
should supplement the world of experience. All the forms of romance take us
out of the ordinary, the probable, the realm of common sense. Romance tends
toward, longs for, mystery and myth. This is not to say that romance is less true
than realism, only that its truths are likely to come in disguise and to concern
the extraordinary and the improbable.

Because nothing is more improbable than a happy ending or more extraordinary than heroism, romance frequently reproduces the traditional narrative

patterns of fairy tale and heroic legend. The great innovation of the Inklings and their generation was to assert that contemporary fiction could not only reproduce those patterns but rehabilitate and reinhabit older mythic texts. Their turn toward medieval and classical sources was a deliberate attempt to reinvent romance for an era of scientific skepticism and technology run amok. Yet they did not reject the many techniques developed by novelists in the eighteenth and nineteenth centuries for representing consciousness, including various sorts of internal monologue and what Dorrit Cohn calls "psycho-narration," in which the narrator summarizes a character's thought process while demonstrating "superior ability to present it and assess it" (29). By combining traditional motifs and story patterns with the novel's rhetoric of interiority, Tolkien, Eddison, and other early twentieth-century fantasists did what Chrétien de Troyes and Marie de France had done in the twelfth century: fuse popular and literary traditions into a single narrative form. The resulting fantasies turned out to meet a need that no one had quite anticipated, certainly not the critics who confidently predicted a quick fall into obscurity for everything wizardly or "hobbitish."

Even though *The Lord of the Rings* was published in the mid-1950s and its underlying mythos gestated for four decades before that, it found its niche in the 1960s. A controversy over rival paperback editions helped kick off the craze, but word of mouth carried it on. The reasons that Tolkien's work resonated so strongly with readers in that decade have less to do with counter-cultures and the baby boom (as often assumed) than with a powerful renewal of interest in myth. That was the moment when psychoanalysis met structuralism and philosophy converged with anthropology. Claude Lévi-Strauss, Joseph Campbell, Northrop Frye, and Mircea Eliade were all active during the decade, as, in a sense, was Carl Jung, with the aid of posthumous collaborators such as Carl Kerényi and Marie-Luise von Franz. Myth criticism was an important component of literary studies, although such criticism usually did not go much further than pointing out the use of particular myths in modern texts. Charles Moorman commented in 1960, "Myth is currently used as a sort of universal literary solvent; the unspoken assumption would seem to be 'Let us reduce this poem, this novel, this play to its basic mythical, structural, ritual ingredients and there will then be an end to all critical problems'" (7).

The assumption was that all myths are psychically available to modern writers and readers. Jungian psychology said that they were common property; Freudian analysis said that we couldn't avoid them if we tried. Outside the academy, popularizers and pseudo-shamans offered do-it-yourself trips into indigenous cultures and their mysteries. The Esalen Institute and the Findhorn Foundation, both founded in 1962, helped to popularize the eclectic spiritual movement known as the New Age, incorporating many neo-pagan elements. Emerging ecological and feminist movements, seeking to detach themselves from Judeo-Christian history and hierarchies, found validation in Hinduism or South American animism or Wicca.

In this intellectual climate, readers gobbled up Tolkien's brand of mytho-poeic fantasy, and publishers sought other works to satisfy their hunger for more of the same. The readers wanted to revisit Middle-earth, or, better yet, travel to the mythic lands from which Tolkien derived his world. In this regard, the genre's debt to Ballantine Books, Tolkien's authorized American publisher, can hardly be overstated. Fantasy became a commercial category when publishers Ian and Betty Ballantine and editor Lin Carter began reprinting earlier works that more or less fit the profile of *The Lord of the Rings*: literary texts set in imaginary worlds incorporating motifs and themes mostly from Arthurian legend and from Celtic and Germanic mythology. Ballantine reprinted E. R. Eddison, Evangeline Walton, William Morris, Hope Mirrlees, James Branch Cabell, and many other neglected writers. As the supply of forgotten fantasy classics dwindled, Ballantine's Adult Fantasy series began to include new works such as Peter Beagle's *The Last Unicorn* (1969) and Joy Chant's *Red Moon and Black Mountain* (1971). The market for fantasy was born, although the academic world was not ready to accept nonrealistic genres as potentially equal to the kinds of fiction for which its critical and pedagogical tools were adapted.

Most particularly, critics did not know how to deal with formula, except to deplore it. Oral traditional stories are always formulaic: repeated retellings will push any narrative into a shape that fit the needs and expectations of listeners. Yet traditional storytellers work with formulas in creative ways, developing some scenes and eliding others, for instance, as audience attention and context demand. A good storyteller can make even a fairy tale—one of the most rigidly structured of oral forms—into something surprising by choosing the lesser known among alternative formulaic elements and taking indirect paths to the inevitable outcome. Popular romances share oral narrative's tendency toward formula, with the guiding power of the marketplace taking on the role of the attentive and demanding audience. From a marketing standpoint, it would be ideal if books within a genre were truly interchangeable and predictable, so that they could be sold like cans of soup. However, like oral narrators, writers of popular fiction are not interchangeable. They—at least the good ones—know how to create variation within predictability and how to turn traditional structures to new purposes. Yet despite the pioneering efforts of Western literature scholar John Cawelti, most academic criticism in the 1960s had no way to differentiate between effective and sloppy uses of formula or to explain how the formulaic aspects of a romance might interact with nonformulaic components.

Publishers were equally uncertain, at least for a time. The Ballantine Adult Fantasy series was a mixed success, because it relied on discovering stories that were, by definition, eccentric—any kind of fiction other than realism was out of the center. Additionally, some of the older texts reprinted in the series were dense and difficult. Fans of *Lud-in-the-Mist* were not necessarily going to warm to Ariosto's *Orlando Furioso*. Another Ballantine editor, Judy-Lynn del Rey, is said to have figured out that predictable mediocrity was easier to sell than unique genius and thus created a commercial fantasy line, starting with Terry Brooks's Tolkien imitation *The Sword of Shannara*. Conceived of as a popular formula, fantasy could be David Eddings or Piers Anthony rather than E. R. Eddison or Hope Mirrlees, just as stories of courtship could be Barbara Cartland instead of Anthony Trollope. Commercial fantasy might not produce a breakout success, but like other forms of formulaic storytelling it could reliably pull in the steady readership that oddball classics could not. Yet even the most abstruse and eccentric fantasies are formulaic insofar as they draw on traditional narrative forms and aspire toward romance.

When we say that a particular story is a work of romance, we really mean that the story seeks to produce the *effect* of romance: a heightened sense of possibility and a longing for something that can never be wholly encompassed within the work itself. The romance effect is related to estrangement—Brecht's *Verfremdungseffekt*—and to nostalgia, though it is nostalgia for what has never been experienced (like C. S. Lewis's desire for the unvisited vistas near his childhood home). Like sexual arousal or religious vision (both of which can contribute to it), the romance effect is highly individualized, unpredictable, and mysterious. Commercial writers and publishers therefore seek ways to make it more universal and reliable, and they usually do so by trying to reproduce previous successes; hence the heavy reliance on formula within both popular fiction and Hollywood film. It is safer to follow a time-tested recipe than to invent a new dish. Nonetheless, like oral storytellers, creators of popular media can be creative within, and sometimes even because of, formulaic constraints. All forms of romance function within the tension between predictability and surprise, between formula and creative play. At the predictable end, romance soothes and flatters, whereas at the innovative end, it is more likely to challenge readers to confront their own failings and remind them of obligations. Such distinctions were lost on critics who looked only for F. R. Leavis's "great tradition" of serious, moral, and realistic fiction. Leavis's perspective dominated literature classrooms in the 1960s (as those of us who were in classrooms at the time can attest). Playfulness was suspect, and formula was beyond the pale. The effects valued by the literary establishment were irony and ambiguity (all seven types) rather than romance.

By 1960, Modernism, which specialized in ambiguity and irony, was no longer emergent but dominant within literary culture. The fiction writers who were anthologized and taught included such realist Moderns as Woolf and Forster in Britain and Hemingway and Faulkner in America, as well as nineteenth-century realists such as Eliot, James, Dickens, and Twain, who could be read as anticipating a Modern sensibility. People conveniently forgot that Woolf also wrote fantasy (*Orlando*), James ghost stories, and Forster science fiction. *Bleak House* and *Huckleberry Finn* overshadowed their own creators' *A Christmas Carol* and

A Connecticut Yankee in King Arthur's Court. Fantasy struggled to establish its version of the mythic method as an accepted literary form, although institutional barriers could sometimes be bypassed by sticking with older materials, such as classical or medieval texts (fantasy has always been more palatable to the mainstream when it is old or foreign). Hence, as mentioned previously, writers interested in myth and romance frequently found models and markets in the less prestigious—and therefore less restrictive—genres such as children's literature, adventure stories, women's fiction, and science fiction. The fantasy movement of the 1960s was as much an attempt to recuperate those forms as a rediscovery of neglected literary treasures.

Defenders of romance have always struggled to explain why acts of compensatory imagination should not be dismissed as "wish fulfillment" or "escape." It does not seem to dawn on many critics that the only wish that can truly be fulfilled by a story is the wish for a story. As for escapism, C. S. Lewis pointed out that escaping into fiction is neither harmful nor permanent and occurs with all genres (*Experiment* 68), and Tolkien observed that those who condemn escapism seem to confuse "the Escape of the Prisoner with the Flight of the Deserter" ("On Fairy-stories" 79). The sticking point for certain types of readers, besides a mistrust of inventive play, is that romance makes desire and the satisfaction of desire into a structural principle. In such stories, character, setting, and circumstance serve the plot, as they do in fairy tales, rather than generating it, as critical convention says they do in realistic fiction.

Genres outside the canon of realism generally tap into three kinds of desire: the desire for erotic satisfaction with a perfect mate, the desire to perform great deeds in exotic places, and the desire to exchange one's identity for a more interesting and important version of the self. Each of these is associated with particular story structures or genres and a specific audience. The first, the Romance of Erotic Fulfillment, is so prominent within popular storytelling that it often takes over the term *romance* entirely. It is usually thought of in connection with women readers and with a generic pattern aimed at those readers: the formula sometimes referred to as Gothic romance because of its indebtedness to the haunted love stories of Ann Radcliffe, Charlotte and Emily Brontë, and Daphne du Maurier. Janice Radway and Tania Modleski were the first scholars to take this genre seriously, analyzing its formulas in terms not only of the satisfaction of desires but also of the unacknowledged anxieties that come with finding one's erotic other. A variation on this form of romance is the romantic comedy, in which the desire for a soul mate is both fulfilled and interrogated through humor and satire. Both of these genres have roots in oral tradition. Gothic romance reproduces the titillating terror and erotic tension of a story such as "Bluebeard," whereas romantic comedy combines the dueling wits and mistaken identities of fabliaux with the deferred consummation of Milesian fables.

The second form of desire, for unconstrained action in an exotic locale, marks the Romance of Adventure, typically aimed at a readership of men. It can take several generic forms, such as the western, science fiction, the spy story, and the lost-world story typified by Edgar Rice Burroughs and H. Rider Haggard. In his groundbreaking studies *The Six-Gun Mystique* and *Adventure, Mystery, and Romance*, John Cawelti identified several formulaic elements of the Romance of Adventure: symbolic spaces such as the western's open landscape, character types such as the femme fatale and the hard-boiled hero, and ritualized actions such as the shoot-out at high noon. The lines between genres of adventure romance are often blurred. Many of the science fiction writers of the 1920s and 1930s also wrote for the detective, adventure, and western pulp magazines. Writing for those same pulps, Dashiell Hammett invented the hard-boiled detective story by fusing classic mystery fiction with the violence of the western, and Raymond Chandler followed by making explicit reference to earlier forms of romance, bringing out the knight-errant qualities of the streetwise private eye. However, the Romance of Adventure more commonly sends its heroes farther afield than the mean streets of Los Angeles. It is no accident that much adventure romance emphasizes modes of transport, from Jules Verne's undersea Nautilus to Wells's time machine. Getting there is all the fun, and the "there" the reader gets to, vicariously, is the realm of myth. Science fiction writer Stanley Weinbaum summed up the Romance of Adventure and its mythic origins in the title of his 1934 story "A Martian Odyssey." Every hero of adventure romance is another Odysseus or Jason; every spaceship an Argo.

The third type of romance is the Romance of Hidden Identity. The desire to uncover a secret and superior identity for oneself is common among children, who not infrequently convince themselves that the desire is fact. Freud called such beliefs "family romances." One form of family romance is imagining that one is adopted and that one's real parents are kinder, wealthier, and more aristocratic than the people one lives with. Though "children's literature" names an audience, rather than a genre, many generic patterns do function within children's literature, and most involve some version of the family romance, such as rags-to-riches orphan stories from *Oliver Twist* to Harry Potter. These too have their traditional sources and analogues. Fairy tales are often based on the family romance (Tatar *Hard Facts* 75)—think of Cinderella. In myth, the typical hero's biography, as Lord Raglan pointed out in "The Hero of Tradition," involves unknown parentage and obscure upbringing up to the point where the hero is revealed to be semidivine: the ultimate hidden identity. The fosterlings and stepchildren of heroic legend include Moses, Theseus, Arthur, and Oedipus, just for starters.

The three forms of romance are not identical to the genres in which they are frequently embodied. Genres hybridize freely, and an individual work can start out, for instance, as a Romance of Adventure and move into Romance of

Erotic Fulfillment. Nor is their appeal restricted to the particular groups of readers with which they are most closely associated. Men write and read stories of eternal love, women desire adventure, and both are susceptible to the attractions of the family romance long after they disown any childhood dreams of being lost heirs.

Mythic Fantasy before and after the Boom: Continuity and Change

As pointed out previously, the extracanonical genres often turned to myth for models and motifs even before the fantasy/romance revival of the 1960s. The Tolkien boom encouraged more elaborate world building and grander plotting within each of the romance genres, and it brought many new writers into the field, but these were shifts of emphasis, not wholly new practices. For instance, early superhero comic books referred explicitly to classical or other myths, as in Wonder Woman's Amazon Island and Captain Marvel's acronymic incantation "Shazam," which calls eclectically on powers derived from Solomon, Hercules, Atlas, Zeus, Achilles, and Mercury to account for its hero's Romance of Hidden Identity. After Tolkien, comics writers, especially those at Marvel Comics, raided myth more systematically, turning the Norse god Thor into a superhero in 1962 and bringing whole pantheons into the universe of Doctor Strange (*Strange Tales*, starting in 1963).

A similar melange of myths lurks in the background of the late-nineteenth- and early-twentieth-century masculine Romances of Adventure by H. Rider Haggard, Talbot Mundy, Edgar Rice Burroughs, Abraham Merritt, and Robert E. Howard. These are all based on the assumption that travel to the farther reaches of empire is also travel in time. The idea that "the relation of the colonizing societies to the colonized ones is that of the developed, modern present to its own undeveloped, primitive past" is, as John Rieder points out, an ideological fantasy—that is, something that influences the behavior of even those who disbelieve it (30). Haggard regularly tapped into that ideological fantasy in his colonial adventure stories. His romances, especially the novels cowritten with Andrew Lang, also exploit the longing for myth, which is perceived as belonging to that lost but recuperable past. By traveling to the farthest reaches of the world, the colonial hero finds an atavistic part of himself, so that the journey is also "a return to a lost legacy, a place where the travelers find a fragment of their own history lodged in the midst of a native population that has usually forgotten the connection" (Rieder 40).

Mundy copied the travelog part of Haggard's formula—the journey across desert and mountain in search of adventure—but added an element related to his own interest in theosophy. Mundy's heroes find not only exotic scenery and mysterious women but also mystical truth. Merritt sometimes left out the travel and simply whisked modern American men magically into lost realms of gods and warriors, as in *The Ship of Ishtar* (1924). Howard started out by writing Haggard-style adventure journeys but then, in his Conan stories, displaced his hero entirely into an imaginary prehistory, the Hyborian Age. Conan is already a barbarian warrior, rather than a Modern man reverting to barbarism. Burroughs wrote about a similar atavistic hero in his Tarzan stories (which also incorporate the Romance of Hidden Identity) but also displaced colonial empire to outer space in his planetary romances. In *A Princess of Mars* (serialized as *Under the Moons of Mars* in 1912), Burroughs's John Carter leaves the Earth through astral projection; once on Mars, however, the magical premise gives way to exotic science (a nonexistent "eighth ray" powers flying machines and helps the Martians maintain their thin atmosphere). A longing for myth lies at the heart of the Mars books, as acknowledged in the second volume in the series, *The Gods of Mars* (1912), but the titular gods turn out to be scientifically advanced frauds, and myth is perpetually deferred.

Science fiction often retells specific myths with a scientific rationale, so that gods become aliens and magic is explained as advanced technology. A small subgenre nicknamed by Brian Aldiss the "Shaggy God story" (Langford) is devoted to retelling parts of Genesis in science fictional terms so that, for instance, a crash-landed spaceman meets an alien Eve. A different sort of Shaggy God story involves reenacting myths other than biblical ones. The hero of A E. van Vogt's *The Book of Ptath* (1943) discovers himself to be a reincarnation of an Egyptian divinity. Henry Kuttner's protagonist in *The Mask of Circe* (1948) is both himself and Jason, the Greek Argonaut. Both of these stories thus strongly invoke the Romance of Hidden Identity in its most Freudian form. Casey Fredericks points out the connection of such stories to both myth and psychoanalytical theory:

> This kind of story [. . .] depicts the heroic development of a modern protagonist within the conventional monomythic initiatory pattern, but with the result that the modern man rediscovers and recovers an older identity in himself which is that of some superhuman being. The "hero" or "god" is not acquiring his unique personality and asserting it in the world for the first time, but regaining and reasserting his own older, preformed superhuman identity. For all the initiatory character of the trials, quests, or adventures, these narratives exhibit a fundamental psychiatric quality and presuppose popular psychoanalytical themes like identity crisis, multiple personality, recovery from amnesia, or therapeutic abreaction. (125–126)

Van Vogt's story was published in 1943 in John W. Campbell's pulp magazine *Unknown*, an offshoot of the science fiction magazine *Astounding*. During its brief run, *Unknown* played a major role in directing American fantasy toward the hybrid genre of science fantasy, usually with a comic tone. For instance, Campbell published a series of stories by Fletcher Pratt and L. Sprague de Camp featuring a psychologist-turned-magician named Harold Shea. In the first story, "The Roaring Trumpet" (1940), a new form of symbolic logic sends Shea across a dimensional divide into a world that turns out to be that of the Norse gods just before Ragnarok. Later stories in the series send Shea to various other literary and mythological worlds, using deliberate anachronisms to critique the myths while drawing on their color and narrative power. The point of the Harold Shea stories is that myth is a mode of thought like science, another way of organizing the universe.

Pratt and de Camp also framed stories as straight fantasy rather than rationalized or science fantasy. Their collaborative novel *Land of Unreason* (published in a shorter version in *Unknown* in 1941) lands a modern-day American in a world compounded of *Through the Looking Glass* and *A Midsummer Night's Dream*. Pratt's *The Well of the Unicorn* (1948) takes place in a medieval world that "resembles Viking Scandinavia in its geography and sociology though the names are often ancient Greek in sound and construction" (Fredericks 111). *The Tritonian Ring* (1953) by de Camp inserts Poseidon and the Gorgons into an adventure story modeled after Howard's swords-and-sorcery fantasies. In the same swashbuckling mode, Fritz Leiber's story "Two Sought Adventure," published in *Unknown* in 1939, introduced two characters to whom Leiber returned repeatedly over the next fifty years: the barbarian swordsman Fafhrd and his thief companion the Grey Mouser. Leiber essentially invented the subgenre of swords-and-sorcery by combining Burroughs's and Howard's underdressed warrior heroes, Lord Dunsany's forgotten and malevolent gods, and Pratt and de Camp's irreverent attitude.

Others explored the same bodies of myth in less humorous fashion. Poul Anderson's *The Broken Sword* (1954) is a complex and sober fantasy set in a medieval England that, like Tolkien's Middle-earth, blends Celtic and Scandinavian influences. Anderson is one of a number of writers who bridged the pre- and post-Tolkien eras, continuing to write myth-related fantasies and science fantasies through the 1960s and beyond. Another such transitional figure is Andre Norton, who began writing historical romances in the 1930s, moved to science fiction in the 1950s, and, with 1963's *Witch World*, started a series that after the second volume (in which witchcraft repels alien technology) switched from science fantasy to straight fantasy. Marion Zimmer Bradley's similar Darkover series, starting with *The Planet Savers* in 1958, keeps its science fictional framework throughout but invokes many fantasy tropes, from enchanted swords to fire spells.

In the post-Tolkienian 1960s, Bradley unveiled a history and mythology for her invented world. She also began to develop what had been simple adventure stories into more complex studies in myth and sexuality, a trend that reached its culmination in a non-SF work, *The Mists of Avalon* (1979). In that feminist revision of Arthurian legend, Bradley drew on her experience as a writer of science fiction, adventure stories, and lesbian romances to supply the female experiences and viewpoints missing from medieval texts. Like Mary Stewart, another popular writer of both romance fiction and Arthurian retellings, Bradley used the formulas of women's romance fiction in a not-quite-formulaic way to develop subplots and to give her characters interior lives. Whereas characters in most medieval romances and virtually all myths simply act, their novelized namesakes *think*: imagining their actions beforehand, pondering each experience as it takes place, and second-guessing their choices afterward. Bradley's Morgaine is a modern romance heroine transported into the Middle Ages, just as her science fictional heroes are twentieth-century American women and men transported to the alien forests and crags of Darkover. Using these characters as narrators or focalizers, Bradley offers her readers vicarious travel to the magical past, in the Avalon novels, or an archaic future, in the Darkover stories.

Unlike most writers of women's romance fiction, Bradley was usually more interested in the Romance of Adventure or the Romance of Hidden Identity than that of Erotic Fulfillment, explaining that her own reading as a child tended more toward boys' books than girls', which were too focused on finding the right man ("Responsibilities" 33). When she did write love stories, they concerned unconventional or forbidden relationships, such as the bond between her Darkovan hero Regis Hastur and his bodyguard Danilo Syrtis. Bradley's love stories are invariably accompanied by political standoffs or environmental crises, so that scenes can shift between erotic tension and swashbuckling action. Completing the romance hat trick, any lead character within the Darkover universe is likely to have latent telepathic powers and an unguessed alien or aristocratic ancestry.

Erotic fulfillment is more central to the Norse-inspired *Brisingamen* (1984), by Bradley's sometime collaborator Diana Paxon. In it a colorless heroine blossoms with the aid of Freyja's necklace and finds true love with a motorcycle-riding incarnation of Odin after sleeping with nearly every male character. Rather than using Bradley's mode of science fantasy, Paxon's novel, half women's romance and half fantasy, anticipates a major publishing category of the late twentieth century, the paranormal romance. An even earlier example of paranormal romance is Sanders Anne Laubenthal's *Excalibur* (1973), a Ballantine fantasy original. The opening of Laubenthal's novel is indistinguishable from that of any romantic thriller by Mary Stewart or Barbara Michaels. In such romances, a female character, green- or gray-eyed and with a touch of extrasensory perception, arrives at a grand but haunted mansion, where she is courted by one charming but unreliable suitor and one surly but intriguing man who is linked to the house and its secrets and who turns out to be her soul mate. The cover of the book inevitably shows the young woman running down a hill, cloak outspread, with the house and the dark hero looming behind her. The cover of Laubenthal's novel sends mixed signals. It has a young cloaked woman, a shadowy male figure, and a dark castle, but it also has a dragon and a glowing sword—not a bad iconic representation of the novel's generic ambivalence. The characters and primary setting are pure Gothic romance, whereas the quest for Arthur's sword and glimpses of another world (where the dragon lives) indicate fantasy. Throughout the novel the reader's attention alternates between the heroine's love interests and the power of Excalibur to destroy or preserve the world.

Within children's fantasy, the same patterns of romance that appeal to adults also engage children, with the partial exception of the Romance of Erotic Fulfillment. I say partial exception because the desired other can be hinted at—for instance, in the form of a perfect friendship or an idealized "crush" like Ozma of Oz. Ozma, in the later books by L. Frank Baum, such as *The Emerald City of Oz* (1910), is exquisitely beautiful and powerful but at the same time the perfect girlish chum. A nonparental adult can also be a displaced erotic object: for instance, the Grandmother in George MacDonald's tales or, in a more sinister incarnation, the White Witch in Lewis's Narnia. In each case, the glow that in adult romance would be imparted by adult sexual desire is replaced or represented by magical power. A more surprising example is the nursery goddess who first appeared in P. L. Travers's *Mary Poppins* (1934). As imagined by Travers, rather than Disney, Mary Poppins is secretive, vain, capricious, stern, and, within her sphere, nearly omnipotent, much like the gods of oral tradition, and that is no accident. Her creator was closely associated with the Irish Renaissance and was interested, like her friends W. B. Yeats and George Russell, in mysticism and mythic revivals. Hence Mary Poppins can go from pushing a pram in the park to hobnobbing with demigods; indeed, she is "Cousin Mary" to a number of powerful beings, from snakes to stars. She takes her charges on miniature versions of the Romance of Adventure, always with a safe retreat to the nursery at the end and, if one were lucky, a tuck-in, accompanied by the scent of "her crackling white apron and the faint flavour of toast that always hung about her so deliciously" (102).

The fantasy boom of the 1960s spilled over into children's literature, resulting in the reissuing of all these earlier works, as well as fostering the shift toward fantasy of established juvenile science fiction writers such as Norton and Eleanor Cameron. A newer crop of children's fantasists included Susan Cooper, Lloyd Alexander, Jane Louise Curry, and Alan Garner, all of whom reworked traditional mythic stories, especially the Welsh myths and legends collected in the four branches of the Mabinogion and the Anglo-Breton traditions of King Arthur and Merlin, already transcribed into children's fiction by T. H. White in *The Sword in the Stone* (1938). Garner mixed Celtic and Scandinavian myth in his first children's fantasies *The Weirdstone of Brisingamen* (1960) and *The Moon of Gomrath* (1963) and went directly to the Mabinogion for source material in *The Owl Service* (1967). Alexander's Prydain Chronicles begin with *The Book of Three* (1964), also based on an incident in the Mabinogion. The story of Taran, Alexander's Assistant Pig-Keeper hero, ended up generating four sequels of increasing depth and complexity. Cooper created a modern-day Merlin in *Over Sea, Under Stone* (1965) and brought the character back in *The Dark Is Rising* (1973). Curry introduced the medieval Welsh to the New World Mound Builders in *Beneath the Hill* (1967), the first of seven books of time travel and treasure seeking.

Curry's books primarily invoke the Romance of Adventure, as do Garner's, Alexander's, and Cooper's early volumes. The Romance of Hidden Identity becomes more important in Cooper's second and fourth books, in Alexander's later stories about Taran, and in Garner's *The Owl Service*. In each of these, a principal character is marked by unusual birth circumstances: an orphan, a bastard, a foundling, or, like *The Dark Is Rising*'s Will Stanton, a sort of changeling. The seventh son of a seventh son, Will discovers on his eleventh birthday that he is not human but one of the Old Ones, like Merlin. Another character in the series turns out to be the lost son of Arthur and Guinevere, carried by Merlin into the modern world. Alexander toys with and then rejects the Romance of Hidden Identity in *Taran Wanderer* (1967), when his hero decides that he will be identified by his actions, not by some absent and possibly royal or magical father.

C. W. Sullivan identifies three ways in which modern fantasy incorporates Celtic and other myths. First, a writer can simply expand a traditional story by "add[ing] detail and texture, filling in the background, developing major and minor characters more fully, borrowing from other compatible sources, and creating new material that complements the original" (14). To this description I would add the novelistic depiction of characters' interior lives. Second, the writer can reconstruct the story's cultural context, adding motifs from related stories along with beliefs and practices from the same society (Sullivan 35); an examples of this method is Nancy Bond's time-travel fantasy *A String in the Harp* (1976). The third choice, according to Sullivan, is to compose a new, modern-day plot "supported or rounded out by a great deal of material drawn largely from the mythology, folklore, and culture of the Celtic peoples" (54). This option is typical of romances that focus on more or less ordinary characters who wander into a mythic milieu. Particularly interesting are the ones in which the two components of the story, mythic formula and character-driven fiction, come into conflict. Instead of assuming that a modern character can easily and safely tap into the collective unconscious, some writers make us aware of the dangers and difficulties that come with mythic vision. In their later volumes, Alexander, Cooper, and Garner work their characters over pretty roughly: those characters have to grow and adapt and confront their own weaknesses. The most powerful scenes in their stories are moments when ordinary life suddenly drops away and something grander and more dreadful is glimpsed. I will come back to those threshold moments later on, for such liminality is the key to fantasy's ability to reanimate myth and make formula into something personal and profound.

Sullivan draws his examples from both children's and adult fantasy, and rightfully so, for one of the unanticipated results of the fantasy rediscovery of the 1960s was to create a crossover audience that read freely within both categories. The same writers, such as Andre Norton, wrote for both markets, and the same texts could be packaged as children's books in hardcover and adult fantasy in paperback. *The Hobbit* was enjoyed by preteens and professors, and so were complex newer fantasies such as Ursula K. Le Guin's *A Wizard of Earthsea* (1968), Patricia McKillip's *The Forgotten Beasts of Eld* (1974), and most of Diana Wynne Jones's fiction. When Jones began to write specifically for an adult audience, the only adjustment she had to make was to explain her elaborate plots more carefully, because, as she said, "Children are used to making an effort to understand. They are asked for this effort every hour of every school day and, though they may not make the effort willingly, they at least expect it" ("Two Kinds"). Adults are, if not lazier, at least out of practice in solving puzzles.

Jones's body of work is a useful corrective to many critical notions about formulas. She was alert to the prevalence of formula in popular fantasy and scornful of unthinking uses of formulaic elements. Both are hilariously sent up in her critical volume disguised as a tour book, *The Tough Guide to Fantasy-Land* (1996), and in an accompanying novel *The Dark Lord of Derkholm* (1998). The pattern Jones identifies is mostly derived from Tolkien, or, more precisely, Tolkien's imitators (she also makes note of the green- or gray-eyed heroines of paranormal romance). Essential ingredients include a quest, a mixed band of travelers, a lost heir, a wizard guide, and a prophecy concerning the overthrow of an evil overlord. In *The Tough Guide*, fantasy clichés become trademarks or Official Management Terms marked with the appropriate symbol—for instance, the Reek of Evil[OMT] that hangs around marshes and ruins. Every one of the clichés skewered in *The Tough Guide* becomes an element in the plot of *The Dark Lord*, and yet that novel is fresh, funny, and original because Jones builds in a measure of resistence in both characters and plot. The characters know they are caught in a rigid and dehumanizing schema, and they actively work to deconstruct it while fulfilling its terms to the letter. They also have dreams and desires not fully accounted for in the formula. The title character, for instance, only plays Dark Lord for the groups of tourists who come through a dimensional portal from our world; left to himself, he is a loving father and husband and a sort of wizardly genetic engineer working to create new varieties of magical beings to enrich his world. The novel is both a clever metafiction and a surprisingly satisfying execution of the formula. It expands the possibilities of the genre by testing the formulaic limits.

Monomania and Mary-Sue

The formula outlined in *The Tough Guide to Fantasy-Land* is ubiquitous in commercial fantasy fiction and gaming. It is also the monomyth described by

Joseph Campbell and self-consciously employed in Campbell-influenced texts such as George Lucas's script for *Star Wars*. Combining the structuralist analyses of Lord Raglan and Vladimir Propp with the psychoanalytical systems of both Freud and Jung, the monomyth reduces all mythic texts (including fairy tales) to a single plot. According to Campbell in *The Hero with a Thousand Faces*, every hero has a similar mysterious birth and childhood, is called to adventure, is sent across a threshold into a magical dreamlike realm, undergoes trials, confronts a monstrous opponent, and returns to the daylight world with some sort of boon for mankind.

The problem with Campbell's monomyth as an analytical tool is that it always works because it simplifies every story to the point where nothing but the monomyth is left. It ignores the many mythic stories that do not have questing heroes, and it leaves out the culturally defined values and symbols that make each tradition unique. In *The Hero with a Thousand Faces*, Campbell makes much of the Navajo story about the Twin War Gods who go on a quest for their father the Sun. They fit his pattern. He says nothing about Coyote, who doesn't. Other Navajo figures get turned into accessories to the hero's tale. Spider Woman, for instance, the great weaver who created everything, is dismissed as "a grandmotherly little dame who lives underground" and whose function is primarily to help the Twin Heroes (69).

In Karen Joy Fowler's novel *Sarah Canary* (1991), a character in nineteenth-century Washington Territory, hearing a tale from his Chinese companion, hits on something like Campbell's structuralist reductionism:

> "I heard a story like that once," B. J. said. "Only instead of a poet it was a princess, and instead of eight Immortals it was seven swans, and instead of having to jump off a cliff she had to be silent for twelve years, and instead of immortality it was love she wanted. Except for that, it was the same story."
> (*Sarah Canary* 76)

B. J. is right in a way, but he is also delusional (literally delusional; he is an escaped madman). There is no universal grammar of story that makes all myths into one super-entity, one monomyth. You might as well say that Mayan jaguar carvings and Easter Island colossi and Greek marbles are identical expressions of religious impulse. They are all made of stone; let's call it the *monolith*. If one strips away everything distinctive, then of course all stories become the same. If every myth is the monomyth, then everybody can have the home version of a myth quest, with no personal danger and no obligation to follow the rules of the society whose myths one has bought. And that is what much formula fantasy becomes: a quick and safe trip into myth, with no risk and no transformation.

That which is disguised in professional writing is usually more obvious in amateur work. Fans have created a term for a particularly inept form of fiction in which a new character, an idealized version of the author, is inserted into an existing science fictional world. Such a story is called a "Mary-Sue," as in

"Ensign Mary-Sue gulped nervously as she stepped onto the deck of the Starship Enterprise and saw her hero James T. Kirk sitting in the captain's chair." In some ways all fantastic romance is myth fan fiction, and all its heroes are Mary-Sues, as they get to do what writers and readers do not: enter into mythic worlds and interact with gods and heroes. Looking across the spectrum of romance from the derivative to the subversive, we can see how protagonists become increasingly complex and self-critical while still mediating between the self and the mythic realm. The Mary-Sue version of the monomyth simply plumps the reader down in the middle of a romance; the best modern fantasy investigates what happens to both character and world as a result.

Alan Garner's first four fantasies follow an instructive trajectory from Mary-Sue romance to a richer and more disturbing kind of mythic fantasy. In *The Weirdstone of Brisingamen*, two children, Colin and Susan, stumble across a magical plot cobbled together from various mythic sources including—most convincingly—local Cheshire legends. There is no particular reason for their involvement except that Susan has an heirloom bracelet that everybody wants to get hold of. The bracelet is named for Freyja's necklace in Norse myth, but one of the chief villains who is pursing it is an Irish war goddess, the Morrigan. At this point in his career, Garner mixed mythologies indiscriminately; the cast also includes Nordic dwarves, Celtic elves, a Tolkienian evil force named Nastrond, and a Merlinesque wizard who guards a cave of sleeping warriors like those of the Germanic Frederick Barbarossa. A series of chases ends with the status quo restored and the children largely unaffected by what they have been through. In the second volume, *The Moon of Gomrath*, though, they begin to be altered by their encounters with myth. Susan is possessed by a creature out of Scottish legend, the Brollachan, and can be restored only by another bracelet, this one a gift from a Welsh nature goddess. In putting on the bracelet Susan also takes on a new identity as one of a band of divine huntresses, and she does not want to go back to mortal life. Colin is also changed by undertaking the quest to bring her back. Both end up as more interesting characters than the Susan and Colin of the first book, though not necessarily happier characters. They also find themselves at odds with the wizard Cadellin, who was their guide in the first novel; their actions bring back the nature-based Old Magic that is beyond the control of his rational High Magic.

Such tensions are among the chief differences between a Mary-Sue romance and a fully realized fantasy. In the latter, characters are not fully congruent with the roles they must play, they are changed by their experiences with magic, and they cease to take the rules and values of the myth entirely on faith. It becomes more difficult to speak simply of the use of myth *in* such fantasies; instead, they become stories *about* myth. After Garner's first two books, which throw in traditional motifs whenever the plot requires them, his fantasy begins to question the relationship between myth and psychology, and the friction between character and preordained role becomes greater. For instance, Garner's third novel, *Elidor* (1965), takes four children from a Manchester slum to the magical world of the title, where they find themselves fulfilling a prophecy to restore the ruined realm. The first third or so of the book resembles many formula fantasies, with a wizard guide, ordinary protagonists thrust into the role of heroes, a force of darkness, and a plot that mostly involves going around and collecting magical treasures about which neither the heroes nor the readers care very much. Such items have been aptly termed "plot coupons" by Nick Lowe. The idea is that magical objects need not be given any symbolic weight or historical significance. Instead, a lazy author can "write into the scenario one or more Plot Coupons which happen to be 'supernaturally' linked to the outcome of the larger action; and then all your character[s] have to do is save up the tokens till it's time to cash them in" (Lowe).

In *Elidor*, though, once the coupons have been exchanged for savior points, the story is less than half done, and everything we have been assuming is called into question. The four indistinguishable child heroes begin to differentiate themselves, with one, Roland, emerging as both the truest believer in Elidor and the most damaged by their adventure. Their guide Malebron becomes even more ambiguous than Cadellin in *The Moon of Gomrath*—what kind of "good" wizard knowingly exposes children to dangers they do not understand to serve his own ends? The treasures, brought across to contemporary England, turn into pieces of trash but continue to serve as magnets for the shadow beings who follow them across the portal from Elidor. Though Garner wraps up the plot in a way that saves both the children and Elidor, it is at a high cost, including Roland's peace of mind and possibly his sanity.

Garner's next novel, *The Owl Service*, takes up similar issues—myth's obligations, dangers, and impact on sanity—in relation to a specific mythic text: the Welsh story of Blodeuwedd, a woman made of flowers by the wizard Gwydion. I say it is about Blodeuwedd, although Campbell's monomyth would have us focus on the male hero, Lleu Llaw Gyffes, Gwydion's protegé. The conflict between male power and female autonomy runs throughout the Welsh tale, and Garner picks up on it in his reworking.

Lleu's mother is an enchantress, Arianhrod, niece of the King of Gwynedd. As the story begins, she has neither child nor consort, nor desires either. At the king's behest, her brother Gwydion devises a test of her virginity that results in two retroactive pregnancies, as it were. As she steps over an enchanted rod (no Freudian symbolism here), she gives birth to a fully formed baby and an embryo that Gwydion catches and stows away in a sort of magical womb until it is ready to be born. Furious at the trick, Arianhrod vows that the younger child will never have a name or weapons until she gives them to him, nor will he ever marry mortal woman or goddess. Gwydion finds ways to trick her again into naming and arming Lleu. To solve the third riddle, he makes a woman out of flowers and gives her to Lleu, who falls in love with her. But no one considers whether Blodeuwedd loves Lleu, or wants to be a woman at all.

She betrays her husband with another man, Gronw Pebyr, and finds out how Gronw can kill the nearly invulnerable Lleu. Gwydion steps in once more, revives Lleu, and punishes Blodeuwedd by transforming her into an owl.

Garner's novel sticks mostly to the second half of the tale, after Blodeuwedd is given a woman's form. The tragic triangle of Lleu, Blodeuwedd, and Gronw is reproduced among three present-day teenagers: Gwyn, Alison, and Roger. Gwyn is bright and ambitious, but he is the illegitimate son of a housekeeper, Nancy, who resents his existence. He is also Welsh, and the Welsh are a dispossessed underclass in their own land. The fact that his mother is a servant to outsiders is another reason he has a major chip on his shoulder. Alison is English and wealthy; her mother owns the estate where Nancy works. Roger too is English. His father Clive has recently married Alison's mother after Roger's own mother ran off with another man. Alison and Gwyn are friends, though the class difference is a continual source of friction. Gwyn is attracted to Alison; it isn't clear how much she reciprocates. Roger patronizes Gwyn, partly as a way of hiding his own insecurities. Everyone in the household, including Clive, tiptoes around, trying to avoid upsetting Alison's mother, a terrifying presence who never makes a direct appearance in the novel.

So we have Gwyn as Lleu, Alison as Blodeuwedd, Roger as Gronw, and Nancy as Arianrhod. In this version of the Romance of Hidden Identity, the identity that emerges for Gwyn is that of a tragic and sacrificial hero: not exactly the mythic role one would wish to play. Nor is Gwyn particularly happy to have the part of Gwydion, wizard-king and father figure, be filled by the local handyman, Huw. Huw's nickname Halfbacon indicates both his scattered wits and his connection to a story in the Mabinogion about Gwydion's magical pig thievery. Huw makes little sense because he lives only partly in the present time: the myth is always taking place all around him. As the other characters get swept up in mythic forces, Huw's madness becomes insight: no longer a handyman, he is a king in disguise. He knows from his father and grandfather that the original story took place right where they are living, and he knows from their experience and his own that it recurs in every generation—he now plays the part of Gwydion, but he was once Lleu, and Nancy was his Blodeuwedd. Huw is the first to see that all the characters have reassembled, that the myth is wound up like a watch and ready to be set in motion.

It is Alison who sets it off by finding an old set of plates in the attic: the Owl Service of the title. Alison discovers that the floral design on the plates can be traced, cut out, and rearranged to look like owl faces. She does so, compulsively, but the paper owls keep disappearing, and the plates become blank afterward. The valley's power has manifested physically, and the whole story of desire, betrayal, and transformation is launched once again.

One complaint made by some critics when the book first came out was that the three characters were too young, too shallow, to reenact a classic story of love and betrayal. Those critics had evidently not read *Romeo and Juliet* recently,

but they were right in a way. Young Gwyn and Alison and Roger can only im-
perfectly inhabit the roles of Lleu and Blodeuwedd and Gronw. That is precisely
the point: the distance, the dissonance between the powerful, dangerous world
of myth and the hopes and frustrations of ordinary young people.

The two levels of the story are mirrored by two different narrative modes.
The characters' daily lives are rendered in tense but deliberately flat dialogue,
like a Beckett play. Between *Elidor* and *The Owl Service*, Garner worked as an
interview transcriber for the BBC, and he used what he learned about the way
people actually talk in the latter novel. Here, for instance, is an exchange between the two boys that manages to convey family tension, class conflict, Welsh
defensiveness and English condescension, and general adolescent prickliness
while actually saying almost nothing:

> "After all, she is your mother."
> "After all," said Gwyn. "She is."
> "What did you want your money for?"
> "Ten lousy fags."
> "Oh."
> "Ten stinking fags."
> "Look," said Roger. "If that's all it is, I can lend you—"
> "No thanks."
> "You needn't give it me back. I get plenty."
> "Congratulations." (40)

Here Garner's language reminds us that real life is formulaic, too. Conversa-
tional gambits and behavioral scripts are as rule-bound as any fantasy role-
playing game, but the rules are so internalized that the degree of formularization goes unremarked. Realist fiction—just imagine an entire novel of such
conversations—colludes in hiding the tyranny of the ordinary.

In contrast, the mythic level of the novel is represented by the old-fashioned,
academic prose of a book of Welsh legend that Gwyn has been reading for
school. Garner quotes a conversation between Lleu and Gronw:

> "Lord," said he, "since it was through a woman's wiles I did to thee that which
> I did, I beg thee in God's name, a stone I see on the river bank, let me set that
> between me and the blow." "Faith," said Lleu, I will not refuse thee that.'
> "Why," said he, "God repay thee." And then Gronw took the stone and set it
> between him and the blow. And then Lleu took aim at him with the spear,
> and it pierced through the stone and through him, too, so that his back was
> broken,— (47)

Thus on one level people can't say what they feel, but only what their habitual
scripts allow them to say, while on the other level everything is formal, distant,
literary. That is part of the problem for the modern-day characters: even when
their lives are being taken over by the myth, it remains impenetrable to them.

They can't break through the barriers of time and formality to the mythic level on which their emotional turmoil would have at least a tragic meaning. But as the story unfolds, myth increasingly penetrates ordinary reality, and these intrusions are signaled by a new kind of language that is both violent and beautiful. Garner is adept at conveying the moment of transition when a powerful emotion or a work of art or sheer physical sensation takes characters out of themselves and into the numinous:

> Gwyn [. . .] was dazzled by the glare of the sun when he tried to find what Huw was looking at. Then he saw. It was the whole sky.
>
> There were no clouds, and the sky was drained white towards the sun. The air throbbed, flashed like blue lightning, sometimes dark, sometimes pale, and the pulse of the throbbing grew, and now the shades following one another so quickly that Gwyn could see no more than a trembling which became a play of light on the sheen of a wing, but when he looked about him he felt that the trees and the rocks had never held such depth, and the line of the mountain made his heart shake.
>
> "There's daft," said Gwyn.
>
> He went up to Huw Halfbacon. Huw had not moved, and now Gwyn could hear what he was saying. It was almost a chant.
>
> "Come, apple-sweet murmurer; come, harp of my gladness, come, summer, come." (31–32)

In these few sentences, Gwyn has entered into the world that half-mad Huw inhabits most of the time: the world of myth.

Memorates and Mythic Avatars

Garner uses his considerable command of image and rhythm to show characters being called out of ordinary experience into underlying strangeness. The most magical and most terrifying passages in the story are these moments of ecstasy, of standing outside oneself. They are also recognizable as the kinds of experiences people describe when they talk about encounters with the unknown. These are not moments of full immersion in the myth—signaled within the novel by archaic diction and convoluted sentence structure—nor are they merely incidents from everyday life, which would be rendered in the flattened dialogic mode. Instead, they represent a third level of discourse within the novel that functions analogously to Von Sydow's *memorate*.

Memorates reframe traditional supernatural motifs by adding concrete images as corroborative detail. These may involve any of the ordinary senses. Disembodied voices, glowing lights, horrible or entrancing smells, the nightmare sensation of something sitting on one's chest—all can be part of a memorate. Elaine Lawless cites a number of memorates used as testimony in fundamentalist churches;

in them, physical sensation reinforces the spiritual experience: "when I walked into that room it was just full of light, a radiant light in that room," says one testifier (14), and another says,

> I'll never forget the night I got the Holy Ghost I saw a light off to the left of me and I felt just a beautiful light and a beautiful feeling and then I started speaking once I saw this light. And it just rolled out like, just like, you know, and then I felt good, way better than even when I was baptized. (14)

In addition, memorates often involve *extra*sensory perceptions: prophetic or clairvoyant visions and feelings of dread or reassurance, similarly recounted in terms of physical presence and the senses, physical and metaphysical:

> I saw nothing unusual with my outward eye, but I nevertheless knew that there was someone else in the room with me. A few feet in front of me and a little to the left stood a numinous figure, and between us was an interchange, a flood, flowing both ways, of love. There were no words, no sound. (Hufford 35)

Memorates like these link supernatural or sacred legends to the teller's memories and ground them in bodily existence and emotion. They also interpret extraordinary experiences in terms of the beliefs and narrative structures traditional to the teller's own culture. An experience that might be called a visit from the Nightmare or the Hag by someone with European cultural roots could be explained instead as a ghost, a skinwalker, a demon, or even an alien from a UFO by someone with a different set of what David Hufford calls "core beliefs" (29). Memorates tie legend motifs to the teller's convictions and utilize the audience's "belief language" (Oring 9). Elliott Oring points out that a "legend about ghosts, for example, is more likely to seem true if ghosts are an accepted conceptual category and behave like ghosts are expected to behave" (9).

Writers such as Garner use the structure of the memorate to mediate between the poetic and psychological discourse of realistic fiction and the symbolic discourse of myth. The more skilled they are at naturalistic discourse, the less likely it is that their stories will fall into "Mary-Sue" triviality; the better their mythic discourse, the more powerfully the stories will challenge social norms and commonsense assumptions. Romance supplements reality partly by defamiliarizing it. Like a conversion memorate, it records the moment when everything changes, including the storyteller and listener. When fantasy transforms folk narrative into written literature, traditional motifs and plot structures gain novelistic resources such as elaborate physical and social settings, interior monologues, focalizing characters, and various manipulations of time. Such tools for representing a character's sensory existence, social identity, and belief system can be utilized to bridge the gap between mimetically conceived characters and traditional stories of magic and the supernatural. Fantasy, in essence, occupies the gap, just as memorate does within oral culture.

The Owl Service is somewhat unusual in the degree of attention it pays to the different levels of experience—the ordinary, the numinous, and the space between—but it is not the only work of fantasy to exploit these narrative possibilities. Other writers who play overtly with thresholds and contrasting realities include Neil Gaiman, Sean Stewart, Ellen Kushner, John Crowley, Ursula K. Le Guin (especially in *The Beginning Place*, 1980), Robert Holdstock, Delia Sherman, Guy Gavriel Kay, Greer Gilman, and Kelly Link. Within children's literature, L. M. Boston's *The Children of Green Knowe* (1954), Diana Wynne Jones's *Fire and Hemlock* (1985), David Almond's *Skellig* (1998), and Roderick Townley's *The Great Good Thing* (2001) stand beside *The Owl Service* as sophisticated and subtle explorations of the inner experience of myth. The more the writer calls attention to the disjunction between firsthand experience and traditional myth, the closer a work comes to postmodern metafiction, a category that is taken up at greater length in chapter 8. Because of the double-layered structure, however, all stories about thresholds and overlapping realities can be said to function both as fantasy and as metafantasy: that is, as critical exploration of how the fantastic works and what it means to us. All the writers just listed address questions of belief, perception, and sacred tradition, especially as those are reformulated in the context of cultural change and a scientific worldview.

A memorate is itself a threshold, a portal into another world. By imitating the structure of memorate, fantasy takes the reader from the real world to a mythic one. In a story such as *The Owl Service*, the realistic opening acts like a personal experience story, to surround and validate a self-contained fairy tale or legend and, at the same time, to justify the characters' movement from one narrative mode to another. In crossing the threshold, characters move from Northrop Frye's low mimetic to romantic or mythic modes. They become heroes and interact with gods. When they return to their ordinary lives, they narrate their adventures, which means that the fantasy not only mimics but also embeds memorate. Interestingly, the characters are often disbelieved, which means that their memorates fail to do what folklorists say they should: validate the supernatural narrative. At the end of the 1939 film version of *The Wizard of Oz*, for instance, everyone laughs at Dorothy's story. When the hobbits return to the shire in *The Return of the King*, nobody quite understands what Frodo has accomplished or sacrificed, though they quite admire the more dashing Pippin and Merry. Yet the stories have to be told, and not necessarily for the benefit of the listeners. The comparison with memorates suggests something important about the uses of fantasy, about the cultural work it can do.

As I pointed out in chapter 1, most of us in the modern world lack direct connections with most bodies of myth. We do not worship Odin; we cannot consult the priests of Isis; we know no rituals by which to enter into the Dreamtime. We know of these things only through written texts, which are to living myths as fossil footprints are to dinosaurs. Yet people respond even to traces of myth and look for ways to integrate such myths into their own worldviews. Many readers are looking for, and writers are trying to construct, mythic ways of seeing that are compatible with narratives of rationality such as evolutionary theory, cognitive science, history, comparative anthropology. Often this effort involves creating a new relationship with traditional materials: something that allows commitment without literal belief; some new way to pay the toll that myth demands of its followers, short of sacrificing the beasts of the field, one's firstborn, or one's intellectual capacity. By using romance's fictional memorates to connect with sacred stories, writers can engage in a form of cultural criticism. They remind us that the great narratives that shape the world are, after all, texts: the things that, as Jacques Derrida informs us, have no outsides. (That is the other, lesser known translation of his famous "*Il n'y a pas de hors-texte*," usually translated as "There is nothing outside the text.") It is very hard to take hold of something with no outside, so it is no wonder that myths seems to be slipping out of our grasp. If myth were a location, it would be a country that shares no border with the real world.

But myths do have insides, and writers can show us how to place ourselves inside of stories, how to get to myth, as it were. The only way to do so is by becoming stories ourselves, as we do when we transform memory and experience into memorate. As I said before, most of us do not have direct access to living myth traditions. I cannot cross over into the spirit world of my Shoshone-Bannock neighbors. But I can drive out to the Portneuf Bottoms some night and park the car. I might see eyes shining beyond the headlights. Perhaps I will hear a sobbing sound, like a baby crying among the reeds and cattails. If I come back home and describe my experiences, something strange happens. I am still in the real, modern world, but I am also in the world of story. My narrated self does not have to get to myth: it is already there, waiting. The story version of me—like a computer avatar—can walk across thresholds, travel at the speed of thought, talk with spirits. It lives in the gap between ordinary experience and the Dreamtime. Fantasy writers spin cultural memorates to remind us that we are, and have always been, part substance and part story.

That is a different sort of romance from the simpler tales of great adventure, true love, and secret inheritance. It does not always turn out well. At the end of *The Owl Service*, Gwyn cannot break out of the role of Lleu Llaw Gyffes to end the cycle of betrayal and revenge. A stand-in for the writer, who has written about his own use of fantasy as a kind of psycho-autobiography, the character in the story is no fan-fiction Mary-Sue. Like Lleu, Gwyn is made proud and selfish by his needs. When Alison is so possessed by the angry Blodeuwedd that she lies in a coma in the midst of a maelstrom of rocks and feathers, Gwyn cannot give her release. It is the less intelligent, less appealing Roger who throws off his own psychic baggage and finds the solution: Blodeuwedd does not want to be owls or someone's erotic reward; she wants to be flowers. The myth has to be unwound all the way back to Gwydion's first meddling with the forces of generation. It is not a comforting ending. We would rather see Gwyn triumph over adversity and prejudice, win the heart of the princess, defeat his enemy, take up his hereditary kingdom; but this is a myth, not a fairy tale. The myth ends with violence and emotional wreckage: nobody ends up with anybody. The best the characters can do is to adapt to a new reality, which necessitates telling and retelling the story of their collision with forces of nature and the psyche.

This too is romance. The romance effect comes with a kick, like the recoil of a powerful weapon. Not every form of modern romance acknowledges the pitfalls and psychic costs—that is one difference between simply reproducing a formula and reinventing it. The best modern fantasy turns romance formula into a dialogue with myth. Each siren call has an echo in a minor key:

> You don't belong here.
> Maybe you don't belong anywhere.
> You're destined for something greater.
> You're doomed to something greater.
> You aren't who everyone thinks you are.
> You aren't who you think you are.
> True love waits for you.
> But you may end up pouring out your life for a beloved who does not love you in return.
> Ancient and powerful forces are at work in the world, and you can touch them.
> Ancient and powerful forces are at work in the world, and they will surely touch you.
> All you need is the talisman, the doorway, the secret word.
> Talismans can be trash, death and madness are also doors, the most secret word of all is silence.

Expanding the Territory: Colonial Fantasy

> He is called the Prince Who Was A Thousand, and he dwells beyond
> the middle worlds. His kingdom lies beyond the realm of life and death,
> in a place where it is always twilight. He is difficult to locate, however,
> for he often departs his own region and trespasses into the Middle
> Worlds and elsewhere. (*Creatures of Light and Darkness* 37)

The Prince Who Was A Thousand makes his appearance in Roger Zelazny's *Creatures of Light and Darkness* (1969), which transcribes Egyptian mythology into an immeasurably far future. By the time this novel appeared, Zelazny was already conducting something of a one-man tour of world mythologies, having drawn on Greek legend in *This Immortal* (1966), Norse myth in *The Dream Master* (1966), and the Hindu pantheon (with a guest appearance by the Buddha) in the award-winning *Lord of Light* (1967). In subsequent novels Zelazny focused mostly on invented mythologies (though still incorporating motifs from existing myths), such as the dysfunctional family of world builders in the Chronicles of Amber, but he was to return to the exploration of traditional cultures in *Eye of Cat* (1982), which draws on Navajo beliefs. *Creatures of Light and Darkness*'s thousandfold Prince is Thoth, the divine scribe. Yet he is not only Thoth, the Egyptian god of wisdom and writing, but also, as his title suggests, all heroes, all gods. His kingdom is the twilight realm of the unconscious. It is he who mediates between humanity and the forces of the universe:

> In the days when I reigned
> as Lord of Life and Death,
> says the Prince Who Was A Thousand,
> in those days, at Man's request,
> did I lay the Middle Worlds within a sea of power,
> tidal, turning thing
> thing to work with peaceful sea change

the birth,
growth,
death
designs upon them;
then all this gave
to Angels ministrant,
their Stations bordering Midworlds,
their hands to stir the tides. (*Creatures* 98–99)

Not particularly Egyptian, this oceanic cosmos is reminiscent of a number of mythological conceptions, and its mediating deity with his angelic ministers combines features from Buddhist, Christian, and Hindu belief, as well as motifs from the *Book of the Dead.* The source and authorization for Zelazny's Prince is undoubtedly Joseph Campbell's *The Hero with a Thousand Faces* (1949). As mentioned in the previous chapter, Campbell's theory of the monomyth rests on shaky folkloric and ethnographic grounds, but his captivating style and adventurous spirituality captured the imaginations of readers seeking new ways of connecting with the cosmos. Campbell told us we were all heroes: "The mighty hero of extraordinary powers—able to lift Mount Govardhan on a finger, and to fill himself with the terrible glory of the universe—is each one of us; not the physical self visible in the mirror, but the king within" (315). In Campbell's retelling, we all walk with Theseus and Krishna and Jesus: their journeys outline our spiritual biographies. Campbell and other comparative mythographers invite us to think of all traditions as equivalent—though not exactly equal, as indicated by Campbell's description of "unilluminated [and] stark-naked Australian savages" (141). Campbell says, comparing a ritual from Western Australia with practices from what he calls "higher cultures," that "the great themes, the ageless archetypes, and their operation upon the soul remain the same" (142). It does not matter, in this view, whether one starts from the Aboriginal Biyami or the Hindu Rama or the Egyptian Thoth: the endpoint of maturation and enlightenment is the same. Zelazny's novel actually focuses not on Thoth but on Set, the god of chaos, depicted as Thoth's son and (time-traveling) father. Set has returned from near annihilation and a thousand-year servitude to the death god Anubis. Recovering his memory and identity, he seeks to punish Anubis and Osiris, the lords of death and life, for their betrayals and to complete a quest to defeat the Nameless, a formless being (possibly a forgotten Yahweh) that "cries out within the light, within the night" (*Creatures* 49). Neither this overall plot nor the various subplots regarding Isis, Horus, and the few mortals who make an appearance can be found in Egyptian sacred texts; rather, Zelazny has taken divine attributes and used them as mechanisms for characterization. If this is what the old stories say Isis is like, he asks, what kind of human character would possess her blend of divine maternity, wifely loyalty, arbitrary anger, and sexual rapacity? For the novel implies that all these gods were once men and women. Their lives have been extended and their powers infinitely expanded through devices so potent that they do not read as machines at all but rather, as Arthur C. Clarke suggested about any sufficiently advanced technology, as magic (*Profiles* 39).

This fusion of magic and advanced engineering marks the story, like many of Zelanzy's works, as science fantasy rather than either science fiction or fantasy proper.[1] The hybrid form allows Zelazny to sustain a thread of commentary on human potential and scientific hubris even while telling a tale that is half fairy tale and half Jacobean revenge tragedy (the subject of his master's thesis at Columbia). Science fiction provides the rationale; Egyptian and other myths provide the characters and atmosphere; and Campbell's monomyth provides the justification for assimilating yet another culture's sacred traditions. If all the world's mythic beings are merely, as Campbell said in another title, masks of god, then anyone can try on whichever mask suits the occasion. Why limit oneself to Celtic or Germanic myths? There is a whole world of sacred transformations and divine avatars to be explored. Campbell invites the reader to "depart his own region," like the Prince Who Was A Thousand, and "trespass into the Middle Worlds" or Middle-earth, or anywhere myth might take him or her.

Zelazny was not the only post-Tolkienian writer to seek out new sources for mythic romance. There were a number of reasons for writers to look further afield. One of the most important was the desire to avoid simple imitation: it is difficult to write a Celtic or Arthurian or Eddic mythic fantasy without repeating what others have already done, especially if one's sources are other fantasies rather than the primary texts that Eddison, Morris, and Tolkien had consulted. As fantasy became a marketable commodity, sameness was salable, but originality still counted as a way to distinguish oneself from the swords-and-sorcery pack.

A second reason was the desire for new sensations. Like jaded tourists tired of trips to Paris or diners seeking new and exotic tastes, readers wanted to savor more varieties of myth. If Western-style fire-breathing dragons began to seem too predictable, there were those wise and watery Eastern dragons. If wizards all began to sound like Gandalf and Merlin, they could be replaced by tribal shamans. Local nature spirits such as the Greek *kallikanzaroi* could do duty as elf-substitutes. So long as the central character functioned as a stand-in for the reader, the rest of the dramatis personae could be recast and the sets replaced with more exotic backdrops.

A third motivation was an interest in exploring one's cultural roots, especially for the many U.S. and Canadian writers whose ancestors did not come from the the British Isles. One of the first to look to the myths of his own ancestors rather than rewriting Malory or Tolkien was the Finnish-American science-fantasy writer Emil Petaja. Though Finnish legend was one of the ingredients used by Tolkien to concoct his epic (following the common practice of grouping linguistically and culturally distinct Finland with its Scandiana-vian neighbors), he disguised its characters and altered its events to fit into a Celto-Germanic narrative arc. The character of doomed Túrin Turambar, in *The Silmarillion* (1977), is based on the legend of doomed Kullervo from the *Kalevala* (Tolkien, *Letters* 214), but the setting is moved to Middle-earth, based on the Nordic/Germanic Midgard, and the cultural background is the wars of Men and Elves against the Dark Lord Morgoth rather than the world of Finn-ish gods and heroes. Petaja, however, explicitly invoked the *Kalevala* and its Finnish settings—both physical and cultural—in a series of short novels bring-ing four legendary heroes into a space opera future. In each of these stories, an ordinary man discovers himself (in classic romance fashion) to be one of the old heroes reborn. Each confronts aliens that are the old monsters in new guise: the troll-like Hiisi, Vipunen the giant, Louhi the Hag. The novels are full of references to Finnish lore, as the heroes struggle to connect their tasks with the traditional narratives. Here is Carl Lempi, handsome and empathic but a misfit in his time and place, figuring out that he is an incarnation of Lemminkainen:

> Carl's mind churned with *Kalevala* legends. Lemminkainen, son of Lempo. Lemminkainen the beautiful, the golden apple of Ilmatar, creatrix of the universe. Swordsman and brash warrior. Vainomoinen, the wizard, who had dared to cross the black lake, defying even the rulers of the dead. Ilmarinen, the wondersmith, who had fashioned the arch of the sky over the universe. The magic Sampo— (*Saga* 35)

Petaja introduced each of the novels with a note acknowledging his sources. In the first, *Saga of Lost Earths* (1966), he also declared his own birthright con-nection to Finnish traditions—"I have heard these song-stories since child-hood, know great passages by heart"—and expressed his intention of making them better known—"One of the great epics of world literature, *Kalevala* is much neglected these days" (1).

Other writers of fantasy and science fantasy have similarly drawn on myths representing their own ancestry or family history. Lisa Goldstein used Eastern European Jewish magical legends to address the Holocaust in the award-winning *The Red Magician* (1982). Stephen Brust has employed the lore of his Hungarian ancestors in a number of fantasies, including *The Gypsy* (1992), cowritten with Megan Lindholm. Laurence Yep, who made his name as a writer of historical novels about Chinese immigrants, wrote a fantasy tetralogy, the Dragon series (1982–94), based on Chinese lore and including both Asian-style dragons and the character of Monkey from the sixteenth-century novel *Journey to the West*. Like Petaja, Yep grew up hearing the legends and tales of his ancestral homeland: "I first heard about dragons and other magical crea-tures from my maternal grandmother. From her, I learned that Chinese drag-ons were benevolent creatures who brought the rains and helped make crops grow" ("Dragons" 386). For Yep, however, this knowledge was part of the dissonance that kept him from feeling fully part of either world, American or Chinese: "Though I couldn't have put it into words back then, dragons made me aware that my Chinese culture might not be in sync with my American culture—that instead, they might clash" ("Dragons" 387). Fantasy allowed him to explore this disjunction:

> Because of my background, I've always been fascinated by the figure of the Outsider, and I've pursued that figure in both my writing and my studies. For me, the key question has always been how do we know who we are? How much do outside forces shape us? Do we even have the ability to shape ourselves? That dragon legend contained all these issues. (391)

Fantasy thus becomes a borderland, a meeting place where cultures struggle and change. In a fantastic narrative, the contradictory identities constructed by Chinese myth and American reality can meet and exchange pieces of themselves, like cells undergoing syzygy.

A fourth reason to turn away from Celtic and Nordic sources in fantasy was to forge a new relationship to the roots of Western civilization, both Hellenic and Hebraic. The latter, in the form of biblical narrative, has exerted its influence primarily through the institution of the Christian church, but it has also played a part in shaping Western storytelling traditions, a process I discussed in chapter 3 and return to in chapter 6. The Hellenic tradition, the body of myth born in Greece and adopted by Rome, was disparaged by the church but never ceased to influence literary art. Unlike the Northern myths rediscovered by Jacob Grimm and favored by Lewis and Tolkien, those of the South continued to be circulated throughout Europe even between the rise of Christianity and the Renaissance rediscovery of classical forms and motifs. The Matters of Rome and Greece, including Ovidian myth, the Trojan War, and the exploits of Alexander the Great, were as much a part of medieval romance as were King Arthur and the Matter of Britain, and indeed not much distinction was made among these various assemblages of heroic deeds. The fourteenth-century romance "Sir Orfeo," for instance, turned Orpheus into a proper medieval knight and surrounded him with Celtic-style fairies. Later, after the rediscovery of Greek texts supplemented the Latinized traditions that had carried on since the fall of Rome, the world of the Olympians became ubiquitous. Nymphs and satyrs cavorted across palace ceilings, Jove seduced maidens on the operatic stage, and straightforward descriptions of sun and sea gave way in poetry and oratory to references to Phoebus's car and Tethys's watery retreat. As mentioned in chapter 1, myth became part of the standard curriculum not only for the gentlemen who were expected to know their Latin poets but also for the working classes and for women, many of whom gained access through Bulfinch's *Mythology*.

Fantasy offered a way to strip myths of aesthetic associations and the taint of the schoolroom. Instead of pretty painted gods and florid poetic similes, the myths could supply danger and psychological truth. One fantasist of the post-Tolkien era who saw those possibilities was Richard Purtill, a philosopher with classical training. Before venturing into fiction, Purtill had written a book on Tolkien and Lewis called *Lord of the Elves and Eldils* (1974), and his fantasies borrowed something from each of those predecessors. He acknowledges learning from Tolkien the power of naming and the usefulness of an un-adorned style (*Lord* 41–42); from Lewis the affinity between myth and the fantastic (33). Lewis's *Till We Have Faces* (1956) in particular showed how to reframe Greek myth, juxtaposing the Athenian view of the gods with the more primal deities of cultic worship. This technique allowed Lewis to explore Christian ideas of morality and godhood indirectly, without the doctrinal constraints that came into play in his space trilogy and Narnia stories. Retelling the myth of Cupid and Psyche, he combined archaeological fact with psychological insight to create a convincing setting, his most complex character (Psyche's sister Orual), and a satisfactory adventure story that doubles as an allegory of spiritual growth.

Purtill's first fantasy novel is less ambitious than Lewis's, but it likewise takes place just outside the sphere of Athens and retells a familiar myth from an unexpected point of view. *The Golden Gryphon Feather* (1979) is the story of Theseus and the Minotaur, but Theseus does not make an appearance until the next-to-last chapter of the book, and the Minotaur is not a monster but an insolent prince who can produce the illusion of a bull's head on his shoulders. The other characters from the myth make their appearances as well: Minos the King, Ariadne his daughter, the craftsman Daedalus who designed the Labyrinth, and Dionysos, the god who rescues Ariadne after an ungrateful Theseus abandons her. The focus of the narrative, however, is on one of the fourteen Athenian youths—nameless in the original texts—sent as tribute to Minos. Purtill revises the story to make them not mere sacrifices to the Minotaur but designated substitutes for the Cretan bull-leapers, known to moderns through their depiction in the rediscovered frescoes and statuary of Knossos.

As foreigners, these Athenians are not expected to be able to complete the ritual dance without being gored, so in effect they are intended as sacrifices, but it turns out that one of them, the narrator Britomartis, has unexpected gifts in managing both bulls and humans. With Ariadne's help she turns her team into a creditable troupe of dancers and averts catastrophe; along the way she also discovers the truth of her parentage. Her mother is a minor goddess and her craftsman father the son of Pandion, King of Athens, which makes Theseus her cousin. The core of the story is her coming into power as a demigod and then a full deity as her mother steps aside to rejoin her mortal husband. Britomartis is aided by some of the Olympians and hindered by others, and she learns that both Earth and the Bright Land where the gods dwell are threatened by Those Below, older gods or Titans who have been exiled to a lower world. Thus Purtill diverts the myth into moralized romance—the story of a hero who is more than she appears and her enlistment in a fight between divine and demonic powers. Like Lewis, Purtill reads Christian notions of good and evil as separate and opposing forces back into the universe of Greek myth, where such divisions were originally less distinct.

Purtill comments on his intentions in another fictional work, a young adult novel called *Enchantment at Delphi* (1986). This novel does explicitly what *The Golden Gryphon Feather* does covertly: it inserts a modern viewpoint character into Greek myth. In place of Britomartis the Athenian visitor to Crete, *Enchantment* offers Alice Grant, an American teenager studying in Delphi: both are stand-ins for the reader. Like Britomartis, Alice finds herself drawn into the world of the gods, especially Apollo, the presiding deity at the Delphic oracle. Also like the earlier heroine, Alice discovers unexpected powers in herself, though she stops short of divinity. Both characters take part in the battles among the gods, which Purtill divides into alliances of dark and light. Lest we miss the moral dimension, Purtill has his heroine, in one of her time-traveling adventures, aid in the Greek resistance to Nazi occupation.

Purtill also signals to his young readers how they are to read his mythic fiction: that is, to read it just as they have learned to interpret the fantasies of C. S. Lewis. Alice is not completely disoriented by her first glimpses of the Olympians because, as she explains, "Unlike Eustace Scrubb in *The Voyage of the Dawn Treader*, I *had* read the right books—the ones in which someone from our world is snatched away by science or magic to another world or another time: to Narnia, to Oz; to the prehistoric past or the distant future" (*Enchantment* 10; emphasis in original). Immediately we know not only what sort of story we are in for but also what generic context to read it in: as fantasy but also as science fiction or, more precisely, science fantasy, in which time itself—projection into the misty past or the unimaginably far future—functions as a sort of enabler for magical operations not allowed in more strictly extrapolative near-future fiction. A few pages later, Alice finds herself discussing fantasy and its relationship to myth, talking about Lewis's *The Silver Chair* to her Greek friend Nikos:

> "This book isn't about Greek myths really," I told him, "but the man who wrote it knew a lot about mythology, and he used bits from lots of myths. Maybe the silver chair does come from the Theseus story because it is in an underworld and it does imprison the person in it" (39).

Just so—Purtill's book isn't about Greek myths really but about the way they might function in the modern world. Purtill writes himself into the novel—with a gender switch—as Athena Pierce, a philosophy professor who has written two novels suspiciously similar to Purtill's own:

"I used the premise that the Greek gods were real and that they were basically of human stock, but with what some people call psionic powers—telepathy, precognition, and so on. I tied this up with a sort of parabiblical mythology you get in both Judaism and Christianity, about angels taking human form and interbreeding with humans. There are some biblical passages that seem to support that idea, but it's not part of mainstream theology in either Judaism or Christianity. Tolkien uses the idea in the *Silmarillion*, by the way, which is what gave me the idea." (79)

Taking the opportunity to lecture through the mouthpiece of Professor Pierce, Purtill thus tells us not only which writer to read next but also how to tie together the various threads of classical myth, science, Christianity, modern fantasy, and philosophy. Myths, he suggests, are teaching stories, and what they teach is how to live an enriched life—not just the examined life favored by the Greek philosophers but a life of moral commitment and heightened awareness of nature, history, and the ritual significance of art (including bull leaping).

The myths as redacted in Purtill's fantasies are not just pretty fables; they supply danger and the possibility of personal transformation. Nor are they mere repositories of psychological symbolism, grist for the Freudian or Jungian analytical mills; they have social and philosophical, as well as psychological, applications. But they are not truly Greek anymore. The context in which the Homeric bards chanted their epics is gone. We do not know how their original listeners processed the deeds of the heroes and the squabbles of the gods. We cannot fully understand how such stories interlocked with beliefs about the universe and the self or with ritual obligations such as sacrificing to the divine and, as Jane Harrison would remind us, propitiating the dead. In place of that context, fantasy offers the mechanisms of modern fiction: plot twists and richly detailed settings and narrated thoughts of characters in whom we see ourselves. Along with those narrative conventions comes a modern worldview that emphasizes self-transformation, personal initiative, and—in a very American variation—the responsibility to resist even the gods when they demand immoral acts. The very devices that make the myths accessible also transform them—colonize them, as it were. That is not a serious issue with myths of the classical world, but it becomes increasingly problematic when writers begin to look even further afield.

Purtill's fantasies were originally marketed not as Inkling-style fantasy but as direct successors to the work of another writer, the recently (he died in 1976) deceased Thomas Burnett Swann, who is mentioned both in the jacket copy of *The Golden Gryphon Feather* and in the introduction by SF writer and classicist C. J. Cherryh. If the reader misses those clues, the design of the paperback, including drawings by the same illustrator, George Barr, clearly signals that Purtill is following in Swann's footsteps. Swann had published a number of novels set in the world of classical myth and legend, though he generally left the gods offstage and concentrated on such heroes as Aeneas, featured in *Green Phoenix* (1972), and half-human creatures such as fauns and dryads. Like Purtill, he utilized as viewpoint characters outsiders who could mediate between the mythic world and that of the reader. He similarly employed traditional motifs to explore contemporary issues of identity and justice—frequently, in Swann's case, issues of environmental responsibility and of gender and sexuality. In *How Are the Mighty Fallen* (1974), he ventured beyond the Greco-Roman world and pantheon to explore the interaction between pagan culture and a nascent monotheism. The protagonist of the novel is Jonathan, heir of the Hebrew warrior chief Saul. In this version, Jonathan is Saul's stepson, the offspring of Saul's queen Ahinoam, who is really a winged Siren from Crete passing as human. When Jonathan becomes the lover of the harpist David, worldviews clash. Swann portrays the eastern Mediterranean as a meeting place of beliefs and gods, where the Hebrew priest Samuel is in competition with Phoenician and Canaanite cults, and where Yahweh jockeys for position against Dagon and Ashtoreth. Ahinoam has brought from Crete her own set of deities, including Poseidon, whose Cyclops son Goliath is an old enemy who has likewise ended up in the Levant.

The plot and viewpoint of the story favor the pagan perspective. Whereas Yahweh, a "vengeful desert god" (128), isolates his followers from nature, the Goddess calls on hers to protect and savor the natural world. Yahweh's judgment on the love between David and Jonathan is harsh, but Ashtoreth sees it as one of many allowable variations. As Jonathan explains to David,

> "If men love men, why not let them honor the Goddess in another way. Let them affirm the order and beauty of her creation by a continual hymn of praise—your psalms, my garden, and most important, our love. To love means to link; to link means to express the continuity of life, the unity of existence." (100–101)

After Jonathan's death, the struggle between Ashtoreth and Yahweh tips her way when Jonathan's clipped wings are miraculously restored, thus allowing his soul to escape from Yahweh's Sheol and ascend to the Goddess's Celestial Vineyard (159).

By putting several mythic traditions on the same level of narrative veracity, Swann invites readers to select among them or to combine features as they will. In his fiction, it is not the heroes who must live up to divine commandments, but rather the gods who must meet the story's requirements: to validate love and honor, to provide meaning and purpose, and to offer characters a glimpse of the numinous. Roger Zelazny's various science fantasies suggest much the same thing, but in futuristic settings rather than reconstructed pasts. *Creatures of Light and Darkness* depicts the overthrow of a a corrupt and out-of-balance pantheon; *Lord of Light* pits Buddhist doubt against Hindu piety; *The Dream Master* shows how myth-inspired dreaming can either save or destroy depending on which myths one chooses; and *This Immortal* shows how human beings, or their altered offspring, might ultimately have to step into the roles we have created for our gods. Like Joseph Campbell, Zelazny invites the reader to look to myth for psychological and existential truth: he gives us permission to take on any myth and make it our own story of transformation and growth. That is what Swann and Purtill do with Greek fable, Petaja with Finnish legend, and other writers with retellings of Persian or Aztec or Babylonian myths.

But there is an important difference between castoff myth and living tradition. The Scandinavian *Eddas*, the *Kalevala*, the *Epic of Gilgamesh*, the Egyptian *Book of the Dead*, and the stories recounted by Homer or Ovid are myths of vanished civilizations or peoples converted to other religions. They no longer belong to anyone but are legitimately part of a cultural commons, available to anyone who wishes to tap into archaic mysteries. The same cannot be said of the biblical Yahweh, the Hindu gods, the *Loas* of Voudon, or the sacred stories of Australian, African, and American indigenous societies. Such stories are tempting to the writer, for unlike classical myths they are alive in oral tradition and religious practice and thus powerful, dangerous, and sacred. They are still surrounded by rituals and obligations; they demand that the listener live by their rules.

And they have owners. If I borrow Coyote from Navajo tradition for my fantasy, how can I pay for the use? Who authorizes me to turn the local spirits of coastal Australia into the equivalent of orcs and elves? The farther from European lore a fantasy writer ventures, the more complicated become the issues of belief and ownership. A number of fantasies from the 1970s and 1980s drew on Hindu or Afro-Caribbean or Australian Aboriginal traditions, responding to a sort of imaginative manifest destiny that seems to have circulated within the community of writers and readers. Panels at SF and fantasy conventions were devoted to discussing how to go beyond Celtic and Germanic tradition. New fantasies that drew on non-European motifs were greeted with excitement and awards. Among the winners and nominees of the World Fantasy Award, John Crowley's *Little, Big* (1981) is patterned after a Persian fable, R. A. MacAvoy's *Tea with the Black Dragon* (1983) draws on Chinese lore, Barry Hughart's *Bridge of Birds* (1984) reframes a specific Chinese myth, Dan Simmons's *Song of Kali* (1985) turns Hindu myth into dark fantasy, and James Morrow's *Only Begotten Daughter* (1990) works a gender shift on Christian gospels. Austrian writer Christoph Ransmayr received the Anton Wildgans Prize in 1988, the same year he published *Die letzte Welt*, a literary fantasy drawing on Ovid's *Metamorphoses* (translated as *The Last World*, 1991). The cyberpunk classic and multiple award-winner *Neuromancer* (1984), by William Gibson, mingled virtual realities and Loas. Another treatment of Voudon or Voodoo mythology, *Green Eyes* (1984), helped Lucius Shepard win the John W. Campbell Award for best new SF writer in 1985. Patricia Wrightson's *The Dark*

Bright Water, the middle part of a trilogy drawing on Aboriginal lore, was nominated for a World Fantasy Award in 1980. Michaela Roessner was nominated for a Mythopoeic Award and won the William L. Crawford Award for *Walkabout Woman* (1988), also based on Aboriginal myths. Charles de Lint's *Moonheart* (1984), another Crawford winner and Mythopoeic nominee, combines Celtic and Native Canadian myths in a modern urban setting. Pat Murphy's *The Falling Woman*, which combines contemporary archaeology with Mayan spirit-quests, won the Nebula Award in 1987. *Silk Road*, Jeanne Larsen's novel of eighth-century China incorporating a number of traditional Taoist myths, won the 1990 Crawford Award. Terri Windling's Mythopoeic Award-winning *The Wood Wife* (1996) combines a number of mythic traditions, including Native American Tricksters. Kij Johnson's *The Fox Woman* (2000), which retells a Japanese legend, was also a Crawford honoree. And this list includes only a sampling of post-1980, novel-length works, and award winners at that. Adding in all the shorter stories and less successful novels, there are hundreds of fantasies and science fantasies from the last four decades that retell, reframe, or reimagine traditional myths, legends, and tales from non-Western cultures.

Ironically, though, the more a fantasy writer seeks to validate a culture deemed backward or primitive by Westerners, the greater the risk he or she runs of condemnation on the grounds of insensitivity or exploitation. The most vital mythic traditions are found among the peoples who have suffered most from European domination, such as the tribal societies of the Americas, Africa, Polynesia, and Australia. Unlike the sacred stories of China, Persia, and India, which have already been transformed into written literature within their own cultures, and which can be ranked with the sophisticated epic traditions of Greece and Rome, oral narratives from the jungle, the outback, and the tundra have not been willingly transformed into print by their bearers. Nor are they always given the same respect as products of what Campbell calls "higher cultures." Instead, those narratives have been recorded, transcribed, and published by ethnographers and folklorists, usually without the storytellers' permission or editorial control (Foley vii-viii). Writers, in turn, have taken this publication history as an invitation to treat them as raw material to be refined and made aesthetically pleasing.

The story of this sort of (usually) well-intentioned story theft could be told about any colonial society, but the history of Australia's European settlement and its literary ambitions makes it a particularly striking example of both the desire to recreate indigenous myth as fantasy and the hazards of doing so. A number of Australian writers of European descent have used the medium of children's fantasy to explore the rich and, from a European cultural perspective, radically estranged universe of Aboriginal legend. Even as indigenous populations were decimated and their culture deliberately effaced by such tactics as the wholesale removal of Aboriginal children from their families,

Australian writers began to turn to indigenous cultures as a way of declaring cultural independence from England. A group of those writers formed the Jindyworobak movement of the 1930s and 1940s, taking a name and a set of values from what were believed to be Aboriginal traditions—though no Aboriginal writers were included in the group.

Though the Jindyworobaks came to be seen, from a Modernist perspective, as provincial and backward, their influence can be seen in a number of popular children's books based on Aboriginal legends. Fantasies such as Bill Scott's *Boori* (1979) and Jackie French's *Walking the Boundaries* (1993) introduced many Australian schoolchildren to a sanitized version of Aboriginal beliefs, traditions, and history. The best known of these writers—and for that reason the most controversial—is Patricia Wrightson. Her most ambitious work, a three-volume set that began with *The Ice Is Coming* (1977), received glowing reviews on publication and earned her many awards. In 1986 Wrightson received the highest honor in the field of children's literature, the Hans Christian Andersen Medal.

Today, however, The Song of Wirrun, as Wrightson came to call her trilogy ("Hero" 6), is out of print in Australia, and Wrightson has been criticized rather severely by critics such as Clare Bradford for her use of Aboriginal motifs. Bradford seems particularly irritated by an incident in 1978 when an Aboriginal poet named Jack Davis stood up at a conference of the International Board on Books for Young People (IBBY) and praised Wrightson's work. Far from scolding Wrightson for poaching on his cultural property, Davis instead "encouraged her to be even bolder in her writing and, far from giving up in fear, to go on" (Bradford *Reading Race* 130, quoting "Publisher's Note" to *The Wrightson List* vii). Bradford sees this incident—or at least the recounting of it by Wrightson's publisher—as a key moment in the investiture of Patricia Wrightson as a pseudo-Aboriginal elder. It is, in her view, the culmination of a long process of redefining Aboriginal traditions as white Australian property. As with similar endeavors in Canada, the United States, and other colonial locales, a goal of the project (sometimes unacknowledged, sometimes overt) was to get rid of indigenous peoples through a combination of assimilation and genocide while appropriating their songs, stories, and rituals. Sherman Alexie sums up the U.S. situation succinctly in a poem called "How to Write the Great American Indian Novel": at the end of the story, "all of the white people will be Indians and all of the Indians will be ghosts" (95). Though race relations in Australia differ from those in North America, white societies in both places share the impulse to acquire whatever is of value in indigenous culture while consigning the bearers of that culture to invisibility or extinction.

In putting Wrightson in this tradition, I believe Bradford misreads both the IBBY incident and Wrightson's work, but for the best of reasons. Although it may seem presumptuous for Bradford, a white New Zealander, to take offense on behalf of indigenous Australians who have not chosen to do so, the political point she is making is a valid one. The borrowing of one culture's traditions by another is a serious and risky business. Another incident, one that is curiously parallel to the IBBY moment, vividly illustrates the dangers.

At a set of workshops called "Reconciliation Circles," held in Queensland in 1995, a mixed audience listened to a Murri administrator named Walbira Gindin telling about her own family's experience of having children taken away in a deliberate attempt to divorce them from their culture. This official government policy went on, in some cases, for three generations, now called the "stolen generations." The result was not only broken families but also the near extinction of many traditions. As Gindin was telling her family's story, a woman in the audience stood up and said:

> I feel these waves of negativity coming from you as you speak, and I wonder why you're trying to put this negativity onto all of us here. I came here to learn about your culture and to share in your culture, but I didn't come here to be lectured at and made to feel bad about what happened in the past. Why do you feel the need to put this on us? (Grossman and Cuthbert 779)

We have here two instances of spontaneous testimony pointing in opposite directions. One is from an Aboriginal writer authorizing the white writer to go on exploring his culture; the other from a spiritual tourist demanding access to Aboriginal traditions without having to pay the accompanying fee of historical guilt for white crimes against the tradition bearers.

In the case of Wrightson, it may be possible to carve out some kind of middle ground between these two responses. Without saying that other people's traditions are fair game, we can still stop short of claiming that any crossing of cultural boundaries amounts simply to a set of "appropriating and controlling strategies" (Bradford *Reading Race* 110). Neither of these positions allows one to make fine distinctions, nor can either acknowledge the subtlety with which Wrightson has addressed these very issues through characterization, voice, and narrative frame. What is needed is a critical methodology that can, for instance, recognize Wrightson's evolution from a rather heavy-handed use of myth in *An Older Kind of Magic* (1972) and *The Nargun and the Stars* (1973) to the carefully positioned and powerful retelling of an Aboriginal ghost story in *Balyet* (1989).

Something like such a methodology has been proposed by folklore scholars, who have attempted to revise their own past practices and make amends to the field's many uncredited and unintentional contributors. I would like to adapt those folklorists' ideas as a way of reading fantasies like Wrightson's. Because fantasy so frequently borrows from oral traditions, it faces many of the same issues of power and ownership raised by the collection and study of folklore. Before any traditional tale or ballad reaches print, it must be performed, recorded, transcribed, and edited, and unless the performer is also the folklorist, that process necessarily involves collaboration. As mentioned in chapter 1, Larry Evers and Barre Toelken have explored the contradictions packed into the idea of collaboration across racial and cultural divisions. In the older model of collaborative work derived from ethnology, a native informant provides raw material for interpretation by a university-trained, usually white, scholar. Inevitably, the scholar's voice dominates the relationship, subsuming "culturally constructed metaphor, knowledge about ritual and performance proprieties, assumptions about season and occasion, [and] familiarity with context" to an externally imposed anthropological or literary framework (Evers and Toelken, "Introduction" 10).

In the case of the fantasy writer and the native myth teller, the relationship is even more problematic. The former has all the control; the latter cannot even choose whether or not to cooperate, because the myth has already been collected, transcribed, and published. The original storyteller's identity may not even have been recorded. The circumstances of the telling might have been described, but there is no way to put the entire cultural context—all those unstated assumptions and shared metaphors that Evers and Toelken speak of—into a brief written text. Stripped of context and cultural valuation, the myth becomes a sort of paper currency that the writer is free to spend any way she chooses: to buy a few shivers, a little ready-made awe, or some deeply discounted spirituality.

However, there are many sorts of collaboration within both fantasy writing and folklore collecting. Folklorists who work with Native Americans have largely moved away from an objective-observer model to one in which the scholar participates in, and may even be a product of, the cultural practices he or she is studying. One of the partnerships cited by Evers and Toelken illustrates how far the relationship between informant and scholar can differ from the older pattern:

> The story Darryl Wilson and Susan B. Park tell about their collaboration is a familiar one in many respects. An eager young student travels out from a university campus to assist a neglected elder in the preservation of traditional stories. The elder has worked for years to keep an endangered group of stories alive but has received little support [. . .]. [However,] rather than a young Euro-American university student going out to work with a Native American elder, we encounter the reverse. Darryl Wilson, a Native American university student, seeks out Susan B. Park, a Euro-American elder, to assist her with preservation and publication of the traditional stories that she recorded from his own tribal elders years before. ("Introduction" 7)

The fantasy writer, too, can choose to break from the expected pattern in working with older, printed ethnological materials. Though she cannot bring back her collaborators from archival oblivion, she can choose to represent as much as possible of their voices, identities, and values—and to mark the loss of whatever cannot be recovered and the historical reasons for that loss. She cannot restore the original context for mythic stories, but she can create new contexts—as living cultures themselves do constantly. The fantasist can use all the resources available to the contemporary novelist to fill gaps within and around the story and, at the same time, can alert the reader to the difference between being truly attuned to a cultural tradition and merely sampling a motif or two. Wrightson tries to do all of that in the Song of Wirrun, drawing on her knowledge of archival materials and her acquaintanceship with Aboriginal Australians such as Jack Davis.

I see an analogy for Wrightson's fiction in the collaboration described by Evers and Toelken. Susan Park, an anthropologist trained in the 1930s by A. L. Kroeber, found her work being completed—and redirected—by Darryl Wilson, a young Native scholar. He, in turn, discovered in Park's memories and notes a source of information otherwise lost because of subsequent disruptions in the lives of his Atsuge-Wi relatives (Wilson and Park 170). Wilson's situation represents that of many indigenous people: he has only indirect access to the traditions of his ancestors but is immersed in the culture brought by their conquerors. His ability to guide the collaboration as a trained anthropologist is directly proportional to his separation from the traditional oral culture of his people. Together, Park and Wilson create a more richly contextualized relationship to myth than either is able to achieve alone.

Though Patricia Wrightson was not a folklorist, she devoted years of careful study to written records of Aboriginal traditions, providing in *The Wrightson List* a popular compendium of traditional motifs. She tried to keep her focus on those that involve fantastic creatures and spirit beings without explicitly invoking religious ideas. As she explains, "There has been enough violation of secret and sacred beliefs. Any more of it by writers of fiction would be unpardonable" ("When Cultures" xiii). That is a distinction not always discernible from outside the culture in question, and it is likely that Wrightson inadvertently tramples on some sacred ground from time to time, as Bradford and others have suggested (Bradford "Making" 9). No amount of care could make her into a tribal elder, nor can her use of Aboriginal folklore ever be fully "authentic." However, she might have become someone rather like Susan Park—a participant in the reshaping of tradition for a modern world in which authenticity is an inaccessible ideal.

In Wrightson's trilogy, the character of Wirrun becomes her virtual collaborator. The young Aboriginal man, clanless and city-raised, is looking for what his ancestors once possessed. Like Darryl Wilson, he must function within, and sometimes in between, two cultures. Wrightson's research allowed her to give her narrator some of the knowledge that Wirrun initially lacks. Within the novels, Wirrun plays many roles: learner, skeptic, candidate for traditional manhood, mediator, hero. He sometimes takes up the burden of speaking for those who can no longer speak but sometimes, more significantly, simply indicates their absence and the tragic history behind that absence. Moreover, Wrightson's narrative devices, especially the fantastic elements, remind us throughout the trilogy that Wirrun *is* just a character. Real people cannot fly, mate with water spirits, or turn to stone, as Wirrun does. The fantasy framework makes it clear that, however realistically portrayed, he is the product of authorial research and imagination rather than an independent partner in the enterprise. Therefore, any mythic truth emerging from his story can only be conditional and limited, not the authentic vision of Aboriginal spirituality but merely one white Australian writer's reconstruction.

In order to make her case against Wrightson, Bradford focuses on everything except Wrightson's major work. An article called "The Making of an Elder" doesn't even list the volumes of the Song of Wirrun in its bibliography (although it quotes a couple of critics who praise the work), nor does Bradford's book *Reading Race: Aboriginality in Australian Children's Literature* (2001). Though I agree with everything Bradford has to say about the discourse of "aboriginality" and its abuses, I would like to take up her challenge to "reread Patricia Wrightson, without the burden of her presence as an elder" ("Making" 10). As a first step, I would suggest that we pay attention to the way Wrightson frames the relationship between Aboriginal tradition and the sympathetic but non-Aboriginal observer. She sets up the story in such a manner as to go beyond simple binaries such as outsider–insider to open up new relationships between races and cultures. In her narrative framing, she has attempted the sort of delicate negotiation and compromise that marks legal battles over copyright and trademark of indigenous motifs. As anthropologist Michael F. Brown demonstrates in his book *Who Owns Native Culture?* (2003), such solutions are never neat, never completely satisfactory. They do, however, come close to a sort of justice when they "affirm the inherently relational nature of the problem" rather than assigning ownership entirely on one side or another (Brown 10).

The Ice Is Coming opens with a satellite's-eye view of Australia:

> The old south land lies across the world like an open hand, hollowed a little at the palm. High over it tumbles the wind, and all along its margin tumbles the sea—rolling in slow sweeps on long white beaches, beating with hammers of water at headlands of rock. Under and in this tumbling of wind and water the land lies quiet like a great hand at rest, all its power unknown. (11)

This lyrical passage suits the action of the three books more fully than the reader can know at first. It sets the scene while introducing the primary player: the continent itself, which is not only shaped like a hand but also possesses the power of a hand to point and pound and shape. The natural world is primary here: on this scale, human beings are tiny and trivial, while natural forces are vast and powerful. The speaker of these words adopts a continental point of view, in more ways than one. In the same way that Wirrun will become a tool of the land, the narrator is the land's voice—but not the voice of any one component of the land.

In the next paragraphs, we are reminded that many peoples live on this land, and in many different ways. The division we expect is between native and white Australians, but Wrightson breaks up the binary. Instead of two groups, we learn of four. First there are the Happy Folk, who live along the coast. "Happy Folk" is a highly ironic term: in their pursuit of happiness, these people

> have no time to look over their shoulders at the old land behind them. Only sometimes, in their search for happiness, they make expensive little explorations into the land with cameras. (11)

The second and third groups live in the ignored interior: they are the white Inlanders and the dark-skinned People, who "belong to the land; it flows into them through their feet" (11). Finally there is a fourth race:

> born of the land itself: of red rocks and secret waters, dust-devils and far places, green jungle and copper-blue saltbush. They are sly and secret creatures. The People have known of them for a long time and said little. As for the other two races [that is, the Inlanders and the Happy Folk], if a man of them ever meets an earth-spirit he is silent for lack of a word and so no word is said. (12)

This is not just a taxonomy but a hierarchy, a ranking in terms of relationship to the primary entity, the land. It will also prove to be a ranking of great importance in the story to be told. The Happy Folk will remain almost entirely off the scene, although Wirrun is ever wary of their laws and their economics. The Inlanders will be more aware that something is going on; most will be suspicious and potentially interfering, but one of them will actually help Wirrun accomplish his task. The People will provide knowledge and support although none of them can go where Wirrun goes. As an emerging Hero, he is poised between the People and the magical creatures of the earth.

This four-part division allows Wrightson to bypass a number of conventions and expectations. She does not, for instance, separate the People into traditional and urbanized groups. Wirrun would normally be put in the latter grouping, as he lives among Happy Folk and works for one of them in a garage. He has no near kin, and the traditions of his coastal tribe are lost. Yet he knows that he should rightfully have inherited such traditions, and he honors those from other clans who have managed to carry on the old ways. Part of his quest is to establish a place for himself within traditional Aboriginal culture while living in a new reality: what is a man who has no tribal elders to *make* him a man through ritual and shared wisdom?

Wrightson also points out that, from a geologic perspective, even the People are newcomers. Earth spirits such as Mimi, Nargun, Bunyip, and Ninya are older still, and the People's claim to the land rests not on the length of their tenure but on their understanding of and respect for the forces those beings represent. One implication of this system is that there is no ownership of the land, only stewardship. Another is that groundedness is not genetic but learned. The People have learned the most, but they must work at carrying on that knowledge. The Inlanders are beginning to learn. The Happy Folk fail to learn because they don't pay attention. The narrator of the story does not ally herself with any of these groups but with the land itself. Her claim to authority depends on her ability to demonstrate awareness of and alignment with the environment and all the peoples it supports.

In order to demonstrate those qualities, she must reject yet another form of dualism. The Song of Wirrun depicts epic struggles and heroic sacrifices, but it does not divide its players into good and evil camps, as do most European-derived fantasies. In *The Ice Is Coming*, Wirrun must drive the frost creatures called Ninyas back to their rightful place in caverns beneath Australia's interior. He does not have to kill them or even defeat them in battle but rather to locate the appropriate counterforce, a fire spirit, and to bring the men from the Ninya's home territory to sing the songs that keep them in line. In *The Dark Bright Water*, a water creature called a Yungamurra kills Wirrun's friend Ularra, but Wirrun doesn't fight the Yungamurra. Instead, he falls in love with her and draws her into the human world, renaming her Murra. In the final volume, Wirrun and Murra face death in the form of a being called Wulgaru, but even death is not evil except when it gets out of place and out of proportion.

Wirrun speaks for the narrator (and, I suspect, for the author who created both narrator and character) when he is challenged by the spirit hero Ko-in. He tries to articulate his philosophy, which has to do with seeing more acutely and caring more deeply:

The hills—the sky—the sea—anyone could care for those.

He said, "There's a dung-beetle by that log. I care for that. And there's a rotten toadstool with a worm in it: I care for both of 'em. I care for that bit of fern, and the little white men by the sea, and the horse-thing in the night. I care for the ice and the fire." (*Ice* 57)

This philosophy will test Wirrun severely, requiring him to accept hardship, loss, and ultimately even death. Both the sacrifices and the caring make him a hero, which is to say, one who acts and speaks for something greater than himself.

Throughout the three books, Wirrun comes to points where the action could turn in quite different but equally plausible directions. These moments of possibility are similar to what Umberto Eco terms "inferential walks and ghost chapters": places where the reader is expected to extrapolate outcomes and fill gaps between reported scenes (214). At such moments Wrightson asks the reader not merely to wander off onto inferential byways but to recognize that Wirrun's story exists and has meaning only as a member of a set of stories, some of which are narrated and some only implied.

We might think of these moments as narrative nodes. In botany, a node is a thickening on a stem from which the plant might put forth a leaf, a blossom, another branch—or nothing at all. Wrightson's nodes are moments of thickened narrative tension and possibility. Some of them are marked by bits of personal or social history. For instance, we know that Wirrun has come to be who he is through a fairly traumatic chain of events. He and/or his parents were almost certainly among the Stolen Generations that Walbiru Gindin talks about. When we first meet him, the narrator tells us that:

> Until lately he had gone to one of the Happy Folk's schools, and now that that was finished he worked in one of their service stations. He knew the Happy Folk well, and liked to watch and think about them, for he was a young man to whom thinking came more easily than talking. He talked only to his friends. (18)

However, there is no flashback to follow this other narrative line. The narrator does not say. Not talking is a powerful trope for a number of absences in Wirrun's life. We meet no one from Wirrun's past to tell him of his tribe or his family. He never reminisces. All we have is the history encapsulated in his responses to situations. For instance, after Wirrun first goes to investigate the mysterious ice, he must return to his job and his non-Aboriginal coworkers:

> At the service station they had welcomed him back with all the
>   proper jokes.
> "Got used to living like a lord pretty quick, didn't he?"
> "Collar-proud, eh? We'll soon knock that out of you."
> Wirrun had smiled his young white smile and hosed down floors
>   and measured petrol and given change. (28)

A lot of painful history is packed into that smile, but Wrightson lets us fill it in ourselves, if we know enough to do so. The phrase "young white smile" tells us how much and how early Wirrun has had to learn about defusing tense situations. Wirrun's smile is multiply white. It is a smile of white teeth in a dark face, a smile learned by imitating white people, a smile to placate his tormentors both black and white, a smile representing his "white" self: many smiles at once, and each with a story. Those stories have been told elsewhere, by people with more direct experience than Wrightson's. For the alert reader, Wrightson has just signaled her novel's place in a network of narratives ranging from fairy tale to tragic testimony. There is more to the story than the story.

Other nodes take off into narratives of white settlement, of Aboriginal history, of traditions from Aboriginal groups other than Wirrun's, of slowly changing racial attitudes, and of resistance to any such changes. Some of them the reader may regret not following up. One of them Wrightson actually did follow up, writing a 1989 novel about the forlorn and dangerous spirit named Balyet, whom Wirrun meets only briefly. When Wrightson came back to Balyet's story, she felt the need to create another collaborator, Mrs. Willett, about whom she says in the novel's introduction, "Mrs. Willet, as an aboriginal Australian and a Clever Woman, has a better right to the story, since she inherits the laws and traditions that made it" ("Author's Note"). *Balyet* thus functions in part as an offshoot of the Song of Wirrun.

A node with particular relevance to my interpretation is the story of George Morrow, an Inlander farmer who comes to Wirrun's aid. His role is diverting the attentions of the Happy Folk from a ritual Wirrun must perform. As different groups approach Wirrun's fireside, George pretends to be, in quick succession, an anthropologist, a producer of "experimental black outdoor theater" (200), and a collector who has hired Wirrun's friends to gather poisonous snakes. It is a funny scene, and George is an appealing character, but we never see him again. Whatever he has learned from his encounter with the People's knowledge and the older magic, whatever changes he makes in his life and the world around him, we do not get to know. As Wrightson commented later, "this modern story couldn't be written as if seen through white Australian eyes" ("Hero" 6). Even an Inlander, someone whose shared hostility to the ways of the Happy Folk brings him briefly close to the People, has no further part in Wirrun's transformation into a hero.

Other nodes come after Wirrun has transformed the Yungamurra into beautiful Murra and the couple travels together through the fringes of white settlement. The narrator makes sure we know how some of those stories would go:

> He counted over the possibilities as he had done all morning while he watched her play [. . .].
>
> Take her back to the city or some country town? Leave her alone all day in a one-room flat or the yard behind a pub? Take away her play and the freedom of waters and give her instead the dirty streets, a cotton frock and an old stove? (218)

This is, of course, a story that is all too familiar: a tale of poverty, denied opportunities, abuse of Aboriginal women, violence against men. It is not Wirrun's story, but the Song of Wirrun would not be as effective or as true if it didn't link to these other stories.

Wrightson's work is, of course, not an authoritative record of indigenous beliefs and experiences. Indeed, one of its purposes is to send the reader to seek out texts that have a greater claim to authenticity. Yet all the author's good intentions were not enough to avoid the charge of appropriating another people's cultural goods, as she herself recognized. After *Balyet*, Wrightson stopped writing fantasy based in Aboriginal folklore (Murray 257), although the later *Shadows of Time* (1994) has an Aboriginal boy as one of its time-traveling protagonists. Her current status within Australian children's literature is an uneasy one: she is revered but not read (Lees 5-6). As one critic observes, "she is in the strange position of being cited in the same article as a writer who encroaches [. . .] upon the culture of Aborigines and as an example of a person sensitive to Aboriginal rights and needs" (Murray 259). She is no longer cited, as she once was, as an interpreter of Aboriginal culture and spokesperson for Aboriginal experience. That role has rightly shifted over to people like Oodgeroo Noonuccal and her successors who write from within Aboriginal society, if not from a wholly unmediated position within traditional culture.

Whatever claims have been made about her, Wrightson tried very hard not to put herself in the position of speaking for Aboriginal people, or even speaking as a scholar of Aboriginal folkways. "I'm a writer," she says, "and nothing that I say or do has more authority than that" ("When Cultures" xi). Her job as a writer was to work out in fictional form her own relationship with Australia's troubled history and haunted landscape. Her strategy was to bring in Wirrun and other characters to share the task, going where she could not go. These fictional collaborators remind readers that we too need to invite other collaborators, fictional and real, to help us extend the quest for understanding beyond the boundaries of the text itself. Rather than casting ourselves as the hero with a thousand faces, readers have had to start recognizing a thousand heroes, all different, each uniquely suited to her own quest, his own sacrifice.

After the great fantasy colonization of the 1980s, there was a retrenchment, a withdrawal back to the safety of vanished cultures and dead mythic traditions or entirely invented myths (which are never entirely invented, but rather better disguised borrowings). Though few fantasy writers were censured as harshly as Wrightson, a number of fantasy writers, including Zelazny after *Eye of Cat*, faced criticism for exploiting minorities or outsiders. The 1980s were also a time when feminism, neo-Marxism, and postcolonial theory invited readers to examine texts for reflections of real-world injustice and power imbalances, making it riskier for male writers to represent women, white writers to speak through nonwhite characters, straights to write about gays, and the privileged (which in worldwide terms includes anyone with the leisure to write) to speak for the poor. If, however, the writer has listened very carefully to what the oppressed Other has to say and writes with conviction and compassion, such writing across boundaries is generally considered to be artistically and ethically justified. And there are plenty of literary precedents: no one wants to throw out Henry James's women characters or Shakespeare's Jew and Moor (though fortunately we—i.e., the academic establishment—no longer rely on them as our sole sources of insight).

The case is a little different, though, with fantasy. What fantasy represents is not just other kinds of people but other ways of organizing and understanding the world through myth. By the end of the 1980s, it was pretty clear that some mythic traditions were going to be off limits or that writers would have to find new ways to incorporate them. The challenge was to write mythic fantasy without claiming ownership and without stripping away the myths' historical associations and personal obligations. In order for that to happen, the fantasy genre faced an ultimatum: either forego the use of living myths (which can mean falling into triviality) or change. Part of that change involves opening up the genre itself to new voices and perspectives and adopting a postmodern awareness of textual duplicity and interdependence. Some of those new voices and strategies are explored in upcoming chapters. Another part involves holding up the fantasy mirror to one's own beliefs: in Europe and especially America, where the dominant culture is Christian-based, that means drawing on Christian myths, as MacDonald and Lewis did earlier, but being willing to test those myths against modes of thought that were made available to the genre through Campbell's enthusiasms, Zelazny and Swann's explorations, and Wrightson's sympathetically portrayed and subtly differentiated perspectives.

Angels, Fantasy, and Belief

A few decades ago, my wife and I were driving in the mountains in a car that did not like to climb mountains. As we stopped by the side to let the carburetor gasp, a kindly soul stopped to see if we were all right. We explained the eccentricities of our Ford Pinto, and the gentleman suggested that perhaps the car was possessed. Had we considered exorcism? He was serious.

At that point I realized that he and I were not living in the same world—that what Kathryn Hume calls "consensus reality" is less of a consensus than it seems (21). In one world (mine) natural processes determine events, whereas in another (that of my roadside Samaritan) a host of invisible beings, helpful or malevolent, fill up space like some kind of spiritual dark matter. This discovery seems less surprising now than it did at the time. The world view that includes angels and demons has been popularized in everything from televised sermons to horror films to self-help books on how to contact your own personal guardian angel. Back in 1969, however, sociologist and theologian Peter L. Berger expressed concern over what he called "the departure of the supernatural" from the modern world (1). Berger described the situation of believers in the supernatural as that of a "cognitive minority," which he defined as a group of people whose concept of the world differs significantly from the larger society's (6). A cognitive minority must continually negotiate between its sense of reality and that contrary system upheld by those around it. Such minorities often withdraw into enclaves or cults, or they find ways to assert their views within what Berger calls "hidden nooks and crannies of the culture" (24). One of those hidden nooks is fantasy.

The term "consensus reality" comes from Hume's definition of the fantastic as deliberate violation of collective assumptions about the way the world is put together. This concept of fantasy as storytelling that knowingly departs from a shared model of reality is enormously useful. It allows us to account for cultural differences and historical changes in the boundary between the fantastic and the real without getting tangled in the thickets of epistemology. In the case of angels and demons, however, consensus reality is an illusion. My Samaritan and I might live in the same place and historical moment; we would undoubtedly use the same terms for such preternatural beings and look to the same cultural sources to understand them. Yet what we might understand from these sources is so different that consensus is a mere patch over a crack that goes right down to the foundations of the real. Fictions about angels offer a way to sort out consensus, dissensus, and any number of gradations in between. Fantasy can serve as a neutral meeting point for differing worldviews and different understandings of religious myth—but only if we agree that what we are reading is fantasy, an agreement that breaks down at exactly the same points where consensus reality fails to hold.

When a writer as conscientious as Patricia Wrightson could be charged with cultural appropriation and insensitivity, it is not surprising that a number of fantasists in the 1980s and 1990s turned to building worlds from Christian mythic materials. One way to avoid trampling on other people's sacred stories and beliefs is by using one's own instead. Inspired, as well, by the ongoing popularity of fantasies by C. S. Lewis, George MacDonald, and G. K. Chesterton, a number of writers around the turn of the millennium based their fantasy worlds on Christian doctrines, themes, and motifs. Among such motifs, the overwhelming favorites, to judge from American popular media, have to do with angels. Yet angels pose a particular definitional problem for the fantasy critic: how many people must disbelieve in a thing for its appearance in fiction to count as a violation of consensus reality?

Polls and popular media seem to show that if Americans are united in anything, it is a belief in angels, held by 75 percent, according to a 2007 Gallup poll. The Baylor Religion Survey indicates that more Americans believe in angels than in a personal God.[1] We are a nation not so much entertaining angels unawares (as Hebrews 13.2 has it) as being entertained by them. The angel fad peaked in the mid-1990s, but it is far from over. Angels are everywhere: in TV series, movies, popular songs, church windows, and comic books; on greeting cards, T-shirts, motorcycles, and knickknack shelves. A website cataloguing science fiction and fantasy about angels lists a booming 629 titles under that heading, mostly novels and most from the past two decades ("Themes"). Yet this seeming consensus is not so uniform as it appears. Fantastic narratives incorporate many conflicting conceptions of angelic nature, purpose, and metaphoric or literal status. As it does with other mythic themes, fantastic literature functions as an arena within which diverging formulations of angels—and the worldviews they imply—are negotiated.

Like the Elizabethan stage, fantasy is a space where cultural tensions can be explored with relative freedom. As Stephen Greenblatt says of the theater, fantasy may be "powerful and effective precisely to the extent that the audience believes it be to nonuseful and hence nonpractical" (18). By claiming to be all pretense, it can take on powerful themes without incurring sanction (*Harry Potter* burnings notwithstanding). In the guise of escapist entertainment, contemporary fantasy offers multiple formulations of the divine, the supernatural, prophecy, and the origins and ends of the world—all elements of traditional myth. Though fantasy denies direct application to the world of experience and faith, the stuff of which it is made—oral traditional narrative—is that which performs in nonliterate societies the work of sacred text and social compact, as well as entertainment.

Although, as evidenced by the previous chapter, it is difficult to find any body of mythology that has not been used in fantasy, writers now hesitate to exploit active beliefs, especially their own. The danger of incorporating one's own religious traditions in fantasy fiction is not the accusation of cultural exploitation, as in Wrightson's case, but a charge of blasphemy—the most notorious example being Salman Rushdie in *The Satanic Verses* (1988). Hence, in another parallel to Elizabethan theater, most fantasists up through the 1980s avoided direct representation of religious iconography, substituting, as Shakespeare did, fairies for angels and Jove for Jehovah. Even Christian writers such as Tolkien and Lewis translated their beliefs into other terms. Tolkien's world has its own thinly disguised God and Satan, its Creation and Fall, but such matters are kept in the background. Overt theology is relegated to the appendices of *The Lord of the Rings*.

Yet by the 1990s the stage was set for more explicit fantasizing of Christian myth: a solution for fantasy writers who did not want to keep recycling Tolkien yet wished to avoid cultural tourism was to look to closer to home. Anglo-American folk traditions, however, are not rich in magical or supernatural motifs in comparison with those of such places as Ireland. Some writers found usable material within minority cultures, but unless they could claim African American or Native American ancestry, their borrowings again invited questions about intellectual property and cultural appropriation. Outside of Native American tradition, there is no indigenous body of American myth, not even the rags and remnants that Tolkien was able to stitch together into a reconstructed English mythology (Shippey 220–222)—but there is Christianity. More pertinently, there is what Francis Lee Utley called the Bible of the folk: traditional beliefs and stories that surround official church teachings, including noncanonical versions of the Garden of Eden, Noah and the Ark, Jonah in the Whale, and a trickster Devil. Among such folk-religious motifs, those most readily available for transplanting into American fantasy concern angels.

Not only are angels powerful beings poised between the human and the divine, but they also have the advantage of being both scriptural and local. Unlike, say, Noah's Ark, angels are not identified with a single biblical event or a distant setting like Mount Ararat. If the same archangel could appear to Daniel in the Old Testament and Mary in the New, then he might well show up in New York or Arkansas. Additionally, angels are less abstract than God and their roles less clearly defined than those of Satan or Christ, leaving room for the writer's imagination. On biblical authority, angels can misbehave, even fall from grace. They can pass as human but have formidable powers, which can be used to destroy or to comfort. They don't have to be explained. Everyone knows what an angel is—except that what "everyone knows" is not the same from one person to the next.

Angelic Beliefs

At least four strands of angel belief can be distinguished within American popular culture. I call these the Archaeological, the Thomistic, the Hallmarkian, and the New Age. Each has its partisans, who are not shy about condemning the other versions as heretical. Each has been used as a basis for fantastic narratives, though these narratives are not always packaged as fantasy.

The Archaeological view of angels is archaeological in two senses. First, it draws on the physical remnants of civilizations whose oral traditions parallel biblical accounts. Clay tablets describing Sumerian demigods, Babylonian carvings of winged messengers, Egyptian tomb paintings of spirit guides, Zoroastrian texts cataloguing *yazatas* and other spiritual beings—all testify to the wealth of sacred and supernatural motifs adapted by Jews and early Christians. Each angelic image derives from a different era and mythology and thus represents a different way of seeing the world. The angels of Genesis are not the same as those of Revelation; nor are cherubim, seraphim, or half-human nephilim the same as messenger angels (Hebrew *malakhim*). Therefore, second, the Archaeological perspective attempts to keep this intricate cultural layering separate, rather than constructing a single historical narrative. In Foucauldian fashion, it emphasizes context over continuity. It peels back layers of meanings the way Heinrich Schliemann excavated the various Troys. Furthermore, the Archaeological site that is angeldom was not complete with the compiling of the Christian Bible: new layers were added by Augustine in the fifth century, Pseudo-Dionysius in the sixth, Thomas Aquinas in the thirteenth, and John Milton in the seventeenth.

Archaeological angels come in different shapes and sizes depending on which era a writer chooses to unearth. They are powerful, alarming beings, each race with its own history and agenda. Some are chimaeras: part man and part beast like the cherubim of Ezekiel, with four wings and the faces of a man, a lion, an ox, and an eagle. Others are immaterial spirits, akin to demons and djinns. Perhaps because of the influence of sculpture, they often have a stony quality: beautiful, pale, hard, and unchanging, like marble statues—or vampires, with which they converge in contemporary narratives.

In contrast with the Archaeological treatment of angels, the Thomistic approach attempts to find unity over time: to construct a single theologically valid, biblically supported truth about the origin, nature, and purpose of angelic beings. Out of the preceding list of angel shapers, I picked Thomas Aquinas as the namesake for this approach because his disquisitions are a model of magisterial pronouncement on the subject. Thomas is both cited and imitated by religious scholars such as Hugh Pope, author of the entry on "Angel" in the 1907 *Catholic Encyclopedia*. Pope describes the Thomistic approach (without naming it as such) at the end of his entry, when he acknowledges apparent contradictions within, and multiple influences on, Hebrew writings but nevertheless perceives in the various accounts of angels "a most natural and harmonious progression" (481).

Thomas's angels are God's emissaries, conveying messages from the unseen Divine and carrying out His orders. Though immaterial, they can take on virtual bodies, which can even mimic sexuality, just as they can mime ingesting food when the occasion requires: "not a true eating, but figurative of spiritual eating" (267). Though most Thomistic angels are masculine in form and appearance, Thomas hints that they may assume either sex. His discussion on the issue of angelic reproduction slips over to demons, angels' fallen kin, which he says can impregnate women by gender shifting: "it is not from the seed of such demons, nor from their assumed bodies, but from the seed of men taken for the purpose; as when the demon assumes first the form of a woman, and afterwards of a man; just as they take the seed of other things for other generating purposes [...] so that the person born is not the child of a demon but of a man" (267). Here, as elsewhere, he resembles a science fiction writer working out the implications of a set of narrative motifs taken as logical premises. If Genesis says *this* about angels but Ezekiel says *that*, how do we reconcile them? Angels, says Thomas, are a vast army of eternal beings, each with a place in the heavenly hierarchy, from the highest Principalities and Thrones to the lowliest guardian angels.

One of the biggest differences between the Thomistic conception and the Hallmarkian is that, though both are biblically based and consider themselves orthodox, the Hallmarkian view humanizes and individualizes angels. This softening results from a change in the principal validation for belief, for the Hallmarkian model combines scriptural sources with personal testimony and the Bible of the folk. Alongside quotations from Revelation, Hallmarkian writers cite memorates: anecdotes of angel sightings and averted disasters, stories of missed flights that turned out to be doomed, warnings not to invest in a fraudulent stock, or telephone conversations with an aunt who had actually died hours before.

As discussed in chapter 4, memorates share motifs with, and are frequently recounted alongside, traditional religious or supernatural legends. Such legends include stories of fairies and alien abductions, as well as more explicitly religious narratives about the Holy Ghost, the Three Nephites of Mormon lore, and so on.[2] Fantasies based on any of these legend cycles can serve as the print analogue of oral memorates: a narrative space in which supernatural motifs and human characters are on the same footing.

One major difference between biblical narratives and memorates about angelic messengers is that the former are part of a cosmological cycle. Angels play important parts in the Creation and Fall, the Annunciation and Incarnation, and, ultimately, the Apocalypse and Last Judgment. If they intervene in individual lives, wrestling with Jacob or feeding Elijah, it is because those individuals play key roles in the struggle between good and evil. Biblical angels are, more often than not, terrifying, especially when the divine message is death: "So Jehovah sent a pestilence upon Israel from the morning even to the time appointed; and there died of the people from Dan even to Beer-sheba seventy thousand men." (2 Sam. 24.15). The gentler angels of personal testimony, on the other hand, are more concerned with the state of the soul than the fate of the cosmos, and sometimes not so much the soul as the body. Rather than waging war in Heaven, the angels of memorates devote themselves to keeping us safe from fire and flood or even to ensuring our financial security. Whereas Thomistic angels carry out Divine judgments, their Hallmarkian counterparts carry personal messages of comfort and advice—not unlike greeting cards from the company whose name I have attached to them. Unlike Thomistic angels, they are usually feminine, in accordance with their perceived role as guides and spiritual nurturers.

Peter Gardella has explored the relationship between the Hallmark corporation and the recent popularity of angels. Cable television's Hallmark Channel, for instance, perpetually rebroadcasts the CBS series *Touched by an Angel* (1994–2003). In Hallmark stores nationwide, one can buy not only angel greeting cards but also angel statuettes ranging from wide-eyed children to "Mrs. Fries, the Guardian Angel of waitresses" (Gardella 19). Visual representations have an advantage over verbal texts in that they need not specify a particular theological slant. As Gardella notes, "The generic spirituality of angels enables them to take every form and to enter every setting in American society without giving offense [. . .]" (18).

It is more difficult to stay theologically generic in narratives. Martha Williamson, producer of *Touched by an Angel*, often found herself defending the show's humanized angels and its deemphasizing of redemption through Christ (Clark 218). She responded that the network's mandate was to entertain the largest possible audience, and so, though she "shares your personal beliefs," she was forced to compromise on doctrine (218). It is not clear from this statement exactly whose beliefs she shares—again, a necessary strategy to appeal to a consensus that may be more apparent than real. The characterization of guardian angels as emotional and fallible, their embodiment by appealing actors (glamorized by Hollywood lighting), and, most particularly, the genre within which most of the stories were cast—a form of supernatural fantasy that has been termed *film blanc* (Valenti)—all combine to offer an alternative construction of angelic existence.

Part of Williamson's show's success was its ability to temporize over which sort of angels it invoked: Hallmarkian or New Age. As with Hallmarkian angels, New Age belief is communicated primarily by memorate and legend; unlike the former, New Age angels are largely freed from scriptural validation. Though not completely divorced from biblical texts, New Age angels draw on an eclectic mix of beliefs and sacred narratives. They are explicitly associated with guiding spirits from many traditions: Hindu bodhisattvas, Shinto ancestors, Native American totemic animals, and especially spirits of the virtuous dead. This last association now appears in the blandest of mainstream Christian references, such as the newspaper comic *The Family Circus*, in which dead Grandpa is a recurring character, lurking ghostlike around the family or hanging out on clouds in Heaven. It is difficult to pin down the origin of this formerly heretical belief, which seems to have arisen spontaneously within American folk religion. Gardella suggests Emanuel Swedenborg as a source: his visionary and revisionary cosmology, laid out in 1758's *Heaven and Hell*, included an assertion that "all angels were former human beings who continued to grow spiritually" (61). Swedenborg's ideas, and his books, were distributed across America by none other than John Chapman, Johnny Appleseed, who turns out to have been something of a Johnny Angelseed as well.

If Swedenborg's conception took root in America, it did so because the ground was already prepared. The transformation from death's heads to cherubs on New England gravestones, for instance, signaled an eighteenth-century revolt against Calvinist teachings on death; this shift in iconography is one of the first signs of a blurring of the divide between divine messengers and human souls. Certainly by the end of the Civil War, the notion of angelhood as afterlife was widespread, reinforced by Spiritualism, Mormon theology, and the flood of consolation literature that followed the war's devastation (Long 782). Barton St. Armand discusses the change as an aspect of a "sentimental love religion" (77). He identifies the new religious formulation with women's more active participation in spiritual debates and locates its fullest expression in Elizabeth Stuart Phelps's best-selling novel *The Gates Ajar* (1868). In this book-length dialogue, Phelps's mouthpiece character, Aunt Winnifred, reassures readers that their dead loved ones are indeed angels and outlines an afterlife that translates American middle-class existence into eternity, complete with pets, potatoes, and pianos, arguing that most people would be miserable in the Heaven described in church.

Mark Twain satirized Phelps in his *Extract from Captain Stormfield's Visit to Heaven* (1907–1909), and yet his conclusions about the afterlife surprisingly converge with those of Aunt Winnifred:

> People take the figurative language of the Bible and the allegories for literal, and the first thing they ask for when they get here is a halo and a harp, and so on. [. . .] They go and sing and play just about one day, and that's the last you'll ever see them in the choir. They don't need anybody to tell them that

that sort of thing wouldn't make a heaven—at least not a heaven that a sane
man could stand a week and remain sane. (40–41)

Twain argues for an eclectic heaven of the sort later envisioned by many New
Agers. In Will Vinton's animated film of Twain's story (a segment of *The Adventures of Mark Twain*, 1985), Heaven becomes a vast multicultural party, a
grander and more peaceful version of the spaceman's bar found in George
Lucas's *Star Wars* and a host of science fiction stories.

Though Twain and Phelps agree on the absurdity of the popular image of
Heaven, they disagree on the literality of their alternatives and hence on the
genres of their respective texts. Phelps's novel is presented as realism; Twain's
story as fantasy. This generic disagreement runs throughout the history of
American angel narratives. Each of the four conceptions outlined earlier has
generated a substantial body of fantastic fiction, but the framework varies.
New Age angels can typically be found in supernatural romances and fantasies
in the magic realist mode. Hallmarkian angels are rare in fiction but predomi-
nant in film and television dramas, usually in stories of love and personal redemption such as the Christmastime perennial *It's a Wonderful Life* (1946).
Thomistic angels, with their eschatological associations, show up most frequently in fantasies about apocalyptic predictions either fulfilled (if the writer
is an evangelical Christian) or averted (if the writer is a skeptic). The latter are
labeled fantasy; the former are usually not. The characteristic genre for Archaeological angels is science fantasy, the hybrid form that fuses traditional
magical motifs and materialistic rationality.

Writers choose genres for many reasons, from market demands to aesthetic
imperatives. They also resist genres, deliberately violating conventions or creating interstitial forms. Once chosen, however, a particular genre brings with it a
logic of plot and symbol, a cast of character types, and a distinctive way of constructing narrative time-space (Bakhtin's *chronotope*). The broader fantastic
mode, characterized by any deliberate violation of consensus reality, includes
all of the genres named in the preceding paragraph, as well as the kind of fantasy most people think of when they hear the term: heroic adventure or quest
narrative set in a magical Other World. Each genre of the fantastic constitutes
not only a chronotope but also a statement about reality and belief. The cultural
work of fantasy differs from that of the supernatural romance or the apocalyptic
thriller. It is not surprising, therefore, that the four categories of angels outlined
before, each representing a different way of adapting religious tradition to the
conditions of contemporary existence, tend to cluster within different genres.

New Age Angels in Fiction

The most recent variant, New Age angels, show up most often in nonfictional
self-help books such as Teresa Moorey's *Working with Spirit Guides: How to*

Make Contact with Angels, Fairies, and Power Animals (2008) or self-styled "angel intuitive" Chantel Lysette's *Azrael Loves Chocolate, Michael's a Jock: An Insider's Guide to What Your Angels Are Really Like* (2008). These titles indicate the basic concept: angels are one kind of magical creature among many, they are powerful but approachable, and they exist primarily to guide and protect humans. This view can be found among the teenagers Lynn Schofield Clark categorizes as "mysticals": those who put *Touched by an Angel* on the same level as such other series as *Charmed, Buffy the Vampire Slayer,* and *The X-Files,* constructing from them a generalized notion of supernatural Others:

> they would have no difficulty believing that a witch could be a guardian angel. As far as they were concerned, an angel could be a ghost and vice versa, or a ghost could be an ancestor. Stories and symbols might be drawn from religious sources or from places like family stories of good fortune, "legend trips," the entertainment media, or popularized African traditions of ancestors. (112)

Memorates recounted by such mysticals resemble those of more orthodox Christians in imagery and narrative form but not in interpretation. One young man described to Clark an experience after attending a Bible camp: "I turned around to say something to my brother, and then I looked up on the top of the chapel, and an angel's standing there. I grabbed my brother. 'Do you see that?' 'No.' 'There's an angel standing there.'" (85). Yet the same teller also offered a memorate about glimpsing a demon (after a wild party) and claimed that neither vision "changed him much. This was because he was not convinced that these events had actually occurred" (86).

This combination of skepticism and eclectic dabbling with the supernatural characterizes a number of fictional texts, especially paranormal romances, a recent publishing category that harkens back to the TV series and *films blancs* mentioned earlier, to Anne Rice's vampire novels, to supernatural Gothics by Barbara Michaels and Mary Stewart, fantasies by Sanders Anne Laubenthal and Diana Paxon, and ultimately to folk narratives about elfin knights and other unnatural lovers. The first of many paranormal romances focusing specifically on an angelic love interest was Margaret St. George's *The Renegade,* 1996).[3] St. George combines the romance formula with cinematic angel fantasy and detective story, acknowledging the latter by naming one of the secondary angel characters Dashiell (a play on the -el endings of angel names). Having an angel for a hero—with strict rules for interactions between angels and humans—allows St. George to keep her lovers at arms' length until the final pages, when the Avenging Angel Samuel is reborn into the body of a human and can be paired with Brett, the heroine. The narrative focus alternates between Brett's peril and Samuel's unearthly attractiveness. Theological considerations are carefully shunted aside. When asked about God, Samuel replies, "There are things—mysteries—that I'm not permitted to discuss" (86). The few hints we are given about angels' nature and cosmic role leave them poised between the New Age and Hallmarkian categories, with a push toward the former in the fact that Samuel was once a mortal and is reincarnated as one at the end.[4]

A recent and best-selling example of paranormal romance is Nalini Singh's *Angel's Blood* (2009), which incorporates many figures from American popular culture: not only angels but also vampires, zombies, and the vampire hunter heroine (read Buffy-esque slayer). According to the cover blurb:

> Vampire hunter Elena Deveraux knows she is the best—but she does not know if even she is good enough for this job. Hired by the dangerously beautiful archangel Raphael, a being so lethal that no mortal wants his attention, Elena knows failure is not an option—even if the task is impossible.
>
> Because this time, it's not a wayward vamp she has to track. It's an archangel gone bad.

As this description indicates, the plot is a mix of hard-boiled thriller, magical fantasy, and steamy romance. Angels serve more as a new erotic sensation than as signifiers of any cosmological master narrative, let alone a Christian worldview. Yet the choice of angels over other supernatural beings as objects of desire is related to their religious associations. Gothic heroes must be dangerous and off-limits; hence, the very proximity of angels to God adds to their erotic charge. No less an authority on the fetishized supernatural than Anne Rice has commented that the popularity of vampires is a deflected expression of a longing for "a loving supernatural presence that will save us from the perils and disasters of ordinary life" (9). Rice does not mention the parallel longing for a sexual expression of religious impulse, largely unacknowledged in Christianity, though prominent in other traditions. Angels combine the eternal beauty and danger of the vampire with a hint of divinity—and sexy wings.

A very different use of angels can be found in Nancy Willard's *Things Invisible to See*, which takes the New Age angel back to its visionary roots. Willard's elegant novel combines baseball, World War II, folk belief, and a Swedenborgian vision of the divine manifesting through the mundane. There are angels throughout, but mostly in disguise: as birds, ghosts, paintings on the inside of a teacup, a spirit guide called the Ancestress, and the destroying angel Death. Willard, who has elsewhere retold *Paradise Lost* for children, is aware of the many traditions of angelology, and in this novel she gives several of them equal weight. The opening sentences of the book invoke a vision of

> Paradise, on the banks of the River of Time, [where] the Lord of the Universe is playing ball with His archangels. Hundreds of spheres rest like white stones on the bottom of the river, and hundreds rise like bubbles from the water and fly to His hand that alone brings things to pass and gives them their true colors. (1)

Those divine playthings show up throughout the book as baseballs, coins, the laws of chance, and the invisible particles that the heroine Clare learns to see as she leaves her injured body to travel with the Ancestress:

> In the chair, Clare's mother slept on, still as a snowbank. Through the carnations on the nightstand flowed streams of light, the spawning grounds of a million tiny stars.
> *Molecules*, said the old woman. (12)

The language of her vision suggests Carl Sagan's apostrophes to science more than any Christian faith. Later, an African American conjurer named Cold Friday combats death in a holy and hilarious exorcism. The fantasy framework thus allows Bible stories to coexist with scientific terms, poetic references to alternate with comic misunderstandings, and Christian beliefs to sit comfortably next to ancestor worship and voodoo. If none of it is literally true, all routes to insight are open, and souls can be redeemed in a baseball game against the dead as easily as in a revival meeting.

Hallmarkian Angels in Fiction

Hallmarkian angels have not had the benefit of attention from a poet such as Willard, but a series that attempts a similar magical-realist rendering of angels in ordinary life is Mignon F. Ballard's set of mysteries. Ballard's recurring detective is a guardian angel named Augusta Goodnight, modeled on the *film blanc* angels of *Here Comes Mr. Jordan* (1941) and *It's A Wonderful Life* but even more on *The Bishop's Wife* (1947), *One Magic Christmas* (1985), and *Michael* (1996). The angels of the first two are heavenly bureaucrats; in the latter three angels mingle on earth with human beings and alter their lives for the better. The Christmas angel Gideon in *One Magic Christmas* and the title character in *Michael* are fully humanized, the former a craggy-faced cowboy and the latter a beer-drinking slob. Embodying the proximity of New Age and Hallmarkian angels, Michael is an eternal spirit temporarily in human form, while Gideon is a former human who drowned in the Snake River saving a child. Yet both play the same role: issuing spiritual wake-up calls to skeptical and jaded individuals.

Augusta Goodnight offers a similar service to people she assists while uncovering villainy and bringing perpetrators to justice. She is a guardian angel temp—normally assigned to tending the heavenly strawberry fields rather than safeguarding mortals. Because she has been away from Earth since the 1940s, the narrator can explicitly signal Augusta's indebtedness to older examples of *film blanc* ("She sat on the stairs looking as if she'd just stepped out of an old movie [. . .]"), complete with movie-star lighting ("The woman pulled off her hat to smooth her glorious hair, and for a moment I thought I saw a flicker of a glow") and musical underscoring ("The old forties song, 'Coming in on a Wing and a Prayer,' was playing over the jukebox, and no one seemed to have noticed it but me") (Ballard 2, 5, 43).

Because no one but the narrator notices the guardian angel, the story, though fantastic, can remain within the generic boundaries of the cozy detective story. Augusta stays offstage while the heroine investigates. Augusta's interventions are exactly the sort of happy accident that one finds in legends and personal experience stories. Indeed, if the reader already believes in guiding angels, then there is nothing fantastic about the narrative at all. This reader-provided megatext[5] explains why there is so little need for angelology—or even overt religion—in the novels. Ballard reinforces beliefs for a believing audience by leaving them tacit. The few details about Heaven are familiar not only to moviegoers but also to heirs of the sentimental love religion. Anything further in the way of backstory or a larger supernatural scheme would call too much attention to the fantastic nature of the narrative.

Perhaps this is why it is difficult to name any truly Hallmarkian fiction that is labeled as fantasy. The generic demands of fantasy call for systematically developed mythic content. Though not completely Hallmarkian, Nancy Springer's *Metal Angel* offers enough points of overlap with Ballard's novels to demonstrate the contrast between their respective forms. Both utilize the *film blanc* convention of angels coming to Earth to change mortal lives. Both draw on angel legends and memorates combined with motifs from popular culture. Both humanize their angel characters—but whereas Ballard offers a few minor foibles to render her angel more approachable and endearing, Springer's angel is trying to be evil. He has a made a deliberate choice to fall into humanity, and that decision governs much of the novel's plot and underlies its thematic complexity. Volos, the Metal Angel of the title, adopts the persona of a rock star as an act of rebellion against God. Unlike Augusta Goodnight, he is not only the catalyst of the story but also its central focus, which means that the narrative must touch on his past, his heavenly ranking, and his desires. To fill these out, Springer moves away from the Hallmarkian view of angels and approaches the Thomistic.

God is left offstage and is understood variously by the different characters. Volos sees God as an abusive father: "The Supreme Being has been known to destroy whole choirs if their chanting does not please him" (44). He thinks God has interfered with his plans to become human by sticking large, very material wings on the human frame he has imagined for himself. Those wings make him an object of desire for some characters and a freak to others, they become his signature image, they render him physically vulnerable, and they ultimately lead to his and others' redemption. Religious ideas are not tacitly assumed in this novel; instead, they are brought forward, debated by the characters, and dramatized as a conflict between rigid fundamentalism and open-minded charity. Volos denies he has come to earth to be a Hallmarkian angel: "Not to be anybody's bloody savior, that is for certain! Not to help or guard or deliver or ransom or redeem. If you have any good-angel thoughts of me, give them up" (43). Naturally this means he will end up helping, guarding, delivering, ransoming, and redeeming, though without giving up his self-created persona of the dangerous, sexualized and sexually ambiguous Byronic rock star.

Thomistic Angels in Fiction

Springer's novel acknowledges that it is fantasy: the spine of the paperback labels it as such. Some implications of this generic label include placement in bookstores or libraries next to (and thus on a par with) fantasies based on other mythic traditions, an expectation that supernatural elements will be foregrounded in the text and their underlying principles examined systematically, and an agreement between writer and reader that any truth value claimed for the work as a whole will be symbolic or metaphoric rather than literal.

A number of other fantasies go beyond Springer's in their exploration of the mythic framework surrounding Thomistic angels. Genre fantasy writers typically look for complex systems of magic rather than occasional touches of the supernatural, and they are more likely to find these in scripture than in the local legends and memorates that authorize Hallmarkian and New Age angels. Fantastic uses of the Thomistic tradition range from comic to elegiac. Among the former, Suzette Haden Elgin's short story "Magic Granny Says Don't Meddle" (1984) is a satiric bagatelle reminiscent of Twain's "Captain Stormfield," whereas James Morrow's *Towing Jehovah* (1994) attacks religious orthodoxy with Swiftian savagery and wit. In Elgin's story, a woman in Arkansas accidentally discovers a pesticide effective against ticks; removing ticks from the ecosystem turns out, by some system of cosmic weights and balances, to trigger an infestation of angels:

> Their snow-white wings were folded, and all about their faces played touches of golden light. Walking under the trees in grave discussion, sitting in dignified clusters along the creekbanks, they were all the glorious colors of heaven. Stained-glass scarlet and emerald and royal blue and silver and gold and purple, blazing with all the colors of the great cathedrals of Europe. And, thought Mary B, totally unsuitable for the modest farmhouses and ramshackle barns round which they gathered. (87)

The description clearly distinguishes these from Hallmarkian or New Age angels. Neither human nor comforting, they belong in European cathedrals rather than Arkansas farmhouses. Elgin's comic tone disguises the fact that angels are a threat to ordinary existence; their "little fuddy-duddy-looking harps" and "skinny trumpets" (89) are the same instruments that will ultimately call forth the apocalypse unless the "Divine Constraint" can be reimposed by finding and restoring the tick population.

In Morrow's novel, the end of the world comes even closer. God has died; his mile-long corpse is found floating in the north Atlantic. Angels are still around, but they are in sad shape:

> "I'm dying," the angel corrected Anthony. Indeed. His halo, previously as red as the Texaco logo, now flickered an anemic pink. His once-bright feathers emitted a sallow, sickly aura, as if infested with aging fireflies. Tiny scarlet veins entwined his eyeballs. "The entire heavenly host is dying. Such is the depth of our sorrow." (13)

With God dead and angels moribund, it is up to the human characters to take charge, first of the enormous body and then, in the final book of the trilogy, of the world. Apocalypse is threatened but averted: life goes on without the Big Man in the sky—or his messengers. This pattern of Apocalypse-averted is one of two recurring fantasy scenarios identified by Thomas Doyle in a study of popular apocalyptic fantasy. The other is "premillennialist apocalyptic fiction" that fuses the techno-thriller formula of Tom Clancy with literalized scenes from Revelation. Nontheist writers such as Morrow tend to favor the former, whereas fundamentalist Christians such as Tim LaHaye and Jerry B. Jenkins (in the Left Behind series, 1995–2007), Larry Burkett (in *The Illuminati*, 1991), and Hal Lindsay (in *Blood Moon*, 1996), write the latter. Many of the second group moved from writing straightforward prophecy to fiction, the advantage of which is, as Doyle points out, that it need not set a specific timeline for the Final Days (1:12). Instead of predicting the Apocalypse—and risking being proven wrong—one can describe it in a novel as having already happened.

In contrast with Hallmarkian angels, who work to maintain the status quo, the angels of Thomistic fiction often stand for a radical transformation of the world. Perfect themselves, they cannot tolerate the imperfections and compromises that characterize human society. Hence they desire to end it all, to go back to the conditions before Creation. Sometimes this desire is ascribed only to Lucifer and the fallen angels, as in Lyda Morehouse's quartet of novels starting with *Archangel Protocol* (2001); other times it is shared by their unfallen kin, as in Tony Kushner's *Angels in America* plays (1991–1992). In either case, it is up to humans, or humans plus a subgroup of the angels, to keep the world going with or without God's blessing.

This turn toward the apocalyptic governs not just fictions of the present or near future. Roberta MacAvoy's Damiano trilogy (1984) places Thomistic angels in a Thomistic world: Italy and France in the fourteenth century. Hints of apocalyptic imagery appear in the second volume, *Damiano's Lute*, when the characters are confronted by an outbreak of plague. This plague is Satan's doing; his motivation is tempting mankind, and especially Damiano himself, to sin as a step toward bringing the world closer to its ultimate end. Damiano

is a particular target because he is an innocent who believes church pronouncements that powers like his are wicked. He would rather be a simple
musician than a wizard, yet through his magical powers he has invoked the
angel Raphael to be his instructor on the lute and thereby invited Satan's
enmity. The fallen angel resents his unfallen brother, and his efforts against
Damiano are part of a larger plan to bring Raphael down.

MacAvoy stays within the Thomistic framework for both angels and demons
so long as Damiano remains her viewpoint character. However, when Damiano meets the Lappish witch Saara, the literal truth of church teachings comes
into question. Saara is not a Christian. When she meets Raphael, she sees not
a Catholic archangel but a spirit of the air whom she names Chief of Eagles.
Where Damiano sees a winged man, Saara sees Raphael as

> "An eagle," she contradicted. "With human face and hands."
> Damiano recoiled from the idea. "Monstrous! Why would he look like
> that when the angel form is higher and more beautiful, and he himself is by
> nature high and beautiful?"
> She snickered. "Evidently you think the body of a man is more beautiful
> than that of an eagle. There are two ways of thinking about that." (*Damiano's
> Lute* 90)

MacAvoy uses the fantasy framework to point out that there are two—or more
than two—ways of thinking about just about everything to do with belief and
the sacred. Her meticulous reconstruction of early modern Europe and its beliefs is a starting point for a larger investigation of sin, power, suffering, and
sacrifice. Christian beliefs are tested against Saara's pagan ones and later those
held by a Muslim Berber and a Chinese dragon. An interesting issue is what
Raphael's own beliefs might be. In interactions with Damiano, he does not directly contradict church teachings, but he sometimes calls them into question.
When the Berber Djoura asks Raphael (whom she sees as a great Djinn) to
teach her how to pass for a Christian, he begs off, "Because I myself don't know
how. There are so many dogmas AND sacraments, and one need only do or say
one word wrong to get into a great deal of trouble" (*Raphael* 190).

MacAvoy's angels are thus both rigorously Thomistic and something else.
One might classify them as New Age, because of the implied turn toward eclectic spirituality, but a more accurate designation is Archaeological. The Thomistic conception becomes one layer of a more complex whole. Raphael is variously Djinn, air elemental, Buddhist teacher, angelic warrior, instructor in lute,
and even, at one point, mortal slave, but he is not all these things at once, or to
all perceivers. His identity depends on context, and the various historical and
cultural contexts are scrupulously defined by the narrative. This attention to
perspective is less typical of fantasy than of science fiction, in which clashes
between worldviews are common and prominent. What MacAvoy sets up

by arranging meetings between Christians and pagans, East and West, and medieval and modern perspectives, SF writers explore in terms of alien contact, time travel, or forgotten technology.

Archaeological Angels in Fiction

Science fantasy hovers between categories, setting up rival belief systems within a narrative that not only allows for but demands multiple reading strategies (like the situated fantasies that are explored in chapter 8). Using such a setup, a number of science fantasies incorporate angelic figures. Examples include Sheri S. Tepper's *A Plague of Angels* (1993), Sharon Shinn's *Archangel* (1997), John Crowley's *The Deep* (1975), Gene Wolfe's *The Shadow of the Torturer* (1980), Sean Stewart's *Resurrection Man* (1995), and Madeleine L'Engle's *Time Quintet* (1962–1989). With the notable exception of L'Engle's, the angels in these works are rarely benign and never safe. They may be aliens who accidentally resemble the angels of tradition, artificial constructs that mimic those traditional figures, or futuristic humans who have transformed themselves technologically into the forms we have always imagined. They are always powerful, dangerous beings who must be avoided, placated, or fought. Both science fiction and secondary-world fantasy encourage systematic working out of principles and implications of each departure from consensus reality. Science fictional discourse requires that there be rational, material explanations for wings, glowing auras, agelessness, ability to kill at a distance, and messages from a higher power. Such explanations often invoke archaeological knowledge: either it is posited that such creatures once existed and were documented in folk legend and temple art, or the collective unconscious as expressed in earlier traditions is seen as a key to some undiscovered truth about the universe.

Tepper's novel is a fair representative of the form. In it, the titular angels don't appear until most of the way through a typically convoluted Tepper plot involving a postapocalyptic setting, hidden pockets of technology, gang-dominated cities, man-hunting androids, and "archetypal villages" where citizens play the parts of Hero, Witch, Fool, Orphan, and so on. These villages are a bit of cultural engineering designed both to protect surviving humans and to restrict their actions and movement. The shadowy figures manipulating the whole situation are the angels, or, more precisely, thrones. Tepper makes her Archaeological orientation quite explicit. One character explains:

> "[. . .] thrones is a name for an order of angels. When one thinks of angels, one gets sidetracked with old pictures, feathery wings, trumpets and harps, all that. But if you consider what an angel really might be, you get a different idea. A creature dreadfully powerful and awesomely old, for example. A creature not necessarily at all manlike. A terrible creature, perhaps." (415)

These thrones are both human and alien. They are literally thrones—great platforms in a shadowy place of power reminiscent of both ancient temples and the throne room of the Wizard of Oz. Their origin is mysterious, but their purpose is clear: to bring humanity back from complete catastrophe by letting loose the lesser disasters of hunger, war, and sickness. Tepper's plot is more coherent than it first may appear. This future Earth is itself an archetypal village with angels as archetypal figures of the divine. In a move typical of science fantasy, the heroes of the story simultaneously fulfill the thrones' prophecies and break their control. Tepper is suggesting that we need archetypes but should not worship them or the stasis they impose. By literalizing the Archaeological angel, Tepper and other science fantasy writers call attention to the darker implications of literal belief. The one exception, L'Engle, constructs a positive version of the Archaeological angel by insisting on its figurative nature.

In her science fantasies, L'Engle introduces a variety of angelic guides for her child heroes. The first is the witchlike Mrs. Whatsit, who looks like a vagrant with "several scarves of assorted colors [. . .] tied about the head, and man's felt hat perched atop" (*Wrinkle* 16) but later transforms into a winged centaur with "a nobly formed torso, arms, and a head resembling a man's but a man with a perfection of dignity and virtue, an exaltation of joy such as Meg had never before seen" (64). In *A Wind in the Door* (1973), a being of multiple eyes, wings, and flames (first mistaken for a group of dragons) is called a *cherubim*. L'Engle deliberately uses the Hebrew plural to represent the entity's biblically authentic complexity and contrasts it with less Archaeological renderings of the (singular) *cherub*. As the cherubim comments snippishly, "I suppose you think I ought to be a golden-haired babyface with no body and two useless little wings?" (*Wind* 57). *Many Waters* (1986) sends two characters into a version of the ancient world populated with undersized humans and mammoths along with unicorns, manticores, seraphim, and nephilim. The last two are, like many mythic creatures, both human- and beast-formed. The seraph Adnarel is sometimes a scarab beetle and the nephil Eblis a great lizard, but both appear as beautiful winged men as well. The angel of *A Swiftly Tilting Planet* (1978) is a young unicorn, and in *An Acceptable Time* (1989), a snake named Louise the Larger serves as *malakh*, or messenger.

L'Engle's willingness to include beetles and snakes among heavenly messengers, along with her angels' metamorphoses, indicates that she is reading biblical sources in both historicized and metaphoric fashion. The original template for seraphs might have been a winged serpent, and an angelic snake is all the more authentic for being alarming. One of L'Engle's mouthpiece characters, commenting on a Hallmarkian angel trinket, reinforces this contextualized reading and uses science to validate it: "Hierarchy was the word used by Dionysius the Aeropagite to refer to the arrangement of angels into three divisions, each consisting of three orders. Today the physicist arranges the fundamental interactions of matter into hierarchies instead. But it does go to show you that at least they've heard of angels" (169). Such angels, though, are un-likely to

> "look like that beautiful angel in your icon: there is a reason that the first thing they say in scriptural appearances is '*Fear not!*'" (169).

Some Christian commentators fault L'Engle for being too New Age-y, too broadly accepting of different spiritual paths, but looking at her angels, she is clearly more Archaeological than New Age. She offers many routes to enlight-enment, and many angelic guides, but she distinguishes them by place, time, and language of origin rather than blurring them together. Her modern pro-tagonists have access to multiple religious traditions, but they are continually reminded of the need to remember historical contexts and to look beyond the messenger's form to a transcendent content.

A Fifth Element?

L'Engle's novels begin to suggest a fifth version of the angel emerging within fantasy: one that builds on Archaeological knowledge but commits fully to none of the strands of belief. Because this version incorporates and critiques the other four, an appropriate term for it is the Meta-Angel (not to be confused with Springer's Metal Angel). A Meta-Angel is historically grounded, self-aware, per-petually shifting. It foregrounds its own narrativity and metaphoricity, under-cutting any attempts to impose literal readings or specific dogmas. This Meta-Angel finds its fullest expression in the metafantasies of John Crowley.

Angels are scattered throughout Crowley's work, reflecting both his Cath-olic upbringing and his awareness of the power of conventional symbols. Crowley's angels are figurations of narrative itself: signs indicating the power of signs. In *Engine Summer* (1979), the story of a saint is recounted by an angel, but neither saint nor angel is defined in religious terms. *Saints* are those who lived their lives in such a truthful way that their stories continue to be told, whereas *angels* are the powerful and arrogant people of the past whose down-fall led to a diminished, posttechnological world. *Ægypt* (1987) opens with a vision of angels, "two four six many of them, each one shuffling into his place like an alderman at the Lord Mayor's show"(5). This vision, delivered to Eliza-bethan astrologer John Dee's assistant Edward Talbot, is multiply embedded in narratives. Talbot tells his vision to Dee; Dee writes it; both are characters in an unpublished historical novel by Fellowes Kraft; Kraft is a character in Crow-ley's tale; his manuscript is being read by another character, a failed historian named Pierce Moffett. These characters and their nested stories are part of a four-volume meditation on history, knowledge, obsession, and the changing realities brought about by changing perceptions of reality. Angels fit variously into that reality, their role at any time depending on characters' beliefs.

Crowley's most recent angel appears—or more precisely, is glimpsed, hinted at—in *The Translator* (2002). Though less obviously fantastic than its predecessors, *The Translator* is the most innovative in its use of angels. Borrowing from the Russian philosopher Nicolai Berdyayev (*Translator* 138), Crowley posits national angels somewhat like those in *Angels in America*. These angels are getting ready to destroy the world: the year is 1962, and the Cold War is heating up with the Cuban missile crisis: "They should have been keeping us from harm, and maybe that was what they thought they were doing, each in its own way. But the power they had together, the power put in our own hands, was too much, and in the end they . . . they let it go. Mutual assured destruction" (286). Or so it might have gone, if not for Crowley's twist. He imagines not one but two angels for each nation, a greater and a lesser: a Throne and a Dominion, perhaps, or a Principality and a Power. The lesser angel of each nation embodies countercurrents to the dominant culture: whimsy instead of anger, poetry instead of war. One of the characters, the emigré poet Innokenti Falin, seems to be the lesser angel of Russia. He sacrifices himself to divert the greater angels from their destructive course. All this is presented as an undercurrent beneath a realistic surface of coming of age, love, betrayal, and the writing and translation of poetry. Though much of the plot has to do with the protagonist Kit Malone translating Falin's poems into English, an important clue near the end of the book is the suggestion that it is Falin, rather than Kit, who is the translator. He translates himself; he transmits his poetic gift to Kit. Crowley makes use of fantasy's power of concretizing metaphors to construct his plot and his message, but at the same time he metafictionally reveals the technique of redoubling and reinventing symbols such as angels in order to make of them bridges into the unknown.

Meta-Angels are open-ended signs. Unconstrained by belief, they resonate among the semiotic categories of icon, index, and symbol, freely exploiting and combining metaphoric resemblances, causal links, and mythic allusions. Crowley does not ask his readers to accept Berdyayev's idea literally, nor does any strain of Christianity endorse it. As signs, Meta-Angels are equally available to those who believe and those who don't. Self-conscious, metafictional narrative can point in both directions at once, using the same motifs to call out to believers and skeptics alike.

In my opening anecdote, which I used as a sort of antimemorate to undercut, rather than reinforce, belief in the supernatural, it is not clear which of us represents the cognitive minority and which the majority. Perhaps my roadside helper went off afterward to tell the same story with a different message: listen to this experience of automotive demonic possession and be warned! Though I interpret the experience through a materialist lens, the anecdote testifies to the existence of powerfully held supernatural beliefs that were to become ever more mainstream throughout the 1980s and the 1990s, until cognitive minority and majority switched places. If we were to put the issue to a vote—is the car mechanically defective or possessed?—I could well have gone, in the space of a couple of decades, from the winning to the losing side. Within the cultural cranny that is fantastic literature, though, nobody need lose such cultural battles. If I were to construct the memorate differently, using its narrative framework to call attention to our overlapping but incompatible ways of reading the situation, majority and minority could speak with equal authority, trading off like Crowley's greater and lesser angels. *The Translator* comments on its own generic ambiguity by embedding alternative visions into the plot. When America's greater angel endorses materialistic common sense, its lesser angel reminds us of visions and mysteries. When the greater angel argues loudly about orthodoxy and apocalypse, the lesser angel whispers of doubt, even of a world in which angels are unneeded.

Crowley's and other metafantasies fit less comfortably within the George MacDonald/C. S. Lewis brand of religious fantasy than in the tradition represented by Ursula K. Le Guin, whose fictions tend to encourage self-critical doubt over faith. Le Guin uses no angels in her fiction, with the possible exception of a race of beautiful, winged, mindless predators in her early science fantasy *Rocannon's World* (1966). Yet she found them useful for describing nature in an early poem called "Wild Angels," in which she addresses the spirits of the Western landscape as "Angels of the shadowed ancient land/ That lies yet unenvisioned, without myth [. . .]" ("Legends" 4). Le Guin once showed that poem to her father, the anthropologist A. L. Kroeber. She says she did not think about the fact that she was calling the West a land "unenvisioned, without myth" to a man who had spent the past five decades recording the rich mythic traditions of coastal Indians. Here is how she remembers their exchange:

> "It's fine," my father said. "But what do you need angels for?"
> "To mediate," I said. I had been reading [the novels of] Charles Morgan, and was really up on angels.
> "Why?" said my father. "Mediate what? You're *here*—it's *here*."
> The man had spent too much time, you see, with Indians. ("Legends" 4)

Like Kroeber's angel-free friends, contemporary fantasy seems to be striving toward a recognition that consensus reality is not a settled condition but a continual debate among cognitive minorities. Native American storytellers, voodoo priests, Mexican American curanderos, Buddhist monks, Pentecostal healers, and atheists may have little in common with regard to belief, but they can send messages to one another. Fantasy itself can be the *malakh* that hails us from another world.

Literalist Interlude: Burning Harry Potter

Genres rarely make the headlines. Fantasy did so in 1989, when a Muslim cleric issued a death sentence on Salman Rushdie for, among other sins, creating a fantasmagoric version of the Prophet in his novel *The Satanic Verses* (1988). Then, beginning in 2001, various conservative Christian groups cashed in on the popularity of J. K. Rowling's Harry Potter series by staging public book burnings. In both cases, the reaction seems entirely out of proportion to the cause. Something more than literary taste is at stake—or at the stake. Though I said earlier that fantasy can function as a safe zone for exploring controversial beliefs because of its inconsequentiality, the book burners would argue that it is not so trivial after all. The issue is myth: how and by whom it can be invoked and interpreted. Fantasy's way of linking us to myth is not merely wrong but dangerous, according to those who allow only a single, literal interpretation of any sacred text.

Fantasy and the Pillars of Faith

All, then, stand or fall together—the divinity of Christ, and the divinity of the Bible and its religion, all, rest on this threefold argument. All, it is claimed, are attested and proved by a threefold display of divine power, manifested—

1. By the performance of various acts, transcending human power and the laws of nature, called Miracles.
2. By the discernment of events lying in the future which no human sagacity or prescience could have foreseen, unless aided by Omniscience; the display of such power being called Prophecy.
3. By the enunciation of Moral Precepts beyond the mental capacity of human beings to originate.

These three propositions cover the whole ground. They constitute the three grand pillars of the Christian faith [. . . .] (Graves, chapter xxxiv)

In this summary of the foundations of faith from Kersey Graves's *The World's Sixteen Crucified Saviors* (1875), we can see why religious authorities might find mythopoeic literature so alarming. Fantasy comes under attack not because it questions articles of faith but because it depicts exactly the sorts of events on which Graves says belief is based: miracles, prophecies, and revelations of a hidden moral order and divine plan. To see why that is so threatening, we must look more closely at the rationales offered for rejecting specific works or the entire genre of fantasy.

It is not only "pagan" elements such as Harry Potter's spell books and, earlier, *The Wizard of Oz's* good witches that makes fantasy a target for book burners. Even when a work of fantasy expresses its author's avowed faith and rests on biblical authority, there is no guarantee that some religious commentator or preacher will not take offense. Many of the writers of angelic fantasies mentioned in chapter 6 would consider themselves to be devout, and all acknowledge the impact of a Judeo-Christian heritage on the moral vision enacted within their stories. Yet, just as C. S. Lewis felt obliged to correct George MacDonald's theology, contemporary commentators scold fantasists for departing from orthodoxy and thereby leading readers—especially young readers—astray. These commentators, weighing in online, in print, or from the pulpit, speak with complete assurance that theirs are the sensibilities that must be considered, their religious perspective the only one that counts. So their religious communities tell them, and the media, at least the ones to which they subscribe, confirm the fact.

C. S. Lewis himself rarely rouses the ire of even the most fundamentalist of critics, perhaps because of his other writings about Christianity. Just about any other writer of fantasy, though, has been condemned by or forbidden to the faithful. Some of those who approve of Lewis view his friend Tolkien's work as un-Christian, despite his lifelong commitment to Catholicism. The deeply spiritual Madeleine L'Engle, like MacDonald, comes dangerously close to a form of Univeralism, threatening the exclusive claims of salvation through Christ or the church. J. K. Rowling's Church of Scotland affiliation does not prevent her from being condemned as a Satanist because of her depiction of non-evil magic.[1]

Some of this acrimony is territorial, reflecting doctrinal divisions within Christianity itself. Just as heretics have historically received harsher treatment than unbelievers, fantasists who do not even claim to be Christian are less likely to be viewed as a threat unless, like Philip Pullman, they challenge dogma directly. Pullman wrote his Northern Lights trilogy as a sort of anti-Narnia, counting himself among those "who detest the supernaturalism, the reactionary sneering, the misogyny, the racism, and the sheer dishonesty of

[Lewis's] narrative method" ("Darkside"). Pullman's fantasy stayed under the fundamentalist radar for several years despite the provocative use of the word "daemon" for his fantasy world's externalized, beast-formed souls (not to mention an unfallen alien Eden, usurping angels, and a God gone AWOL). Eventually, however, the books were noted by people like the group of ministers in my community who took it on themselves to warn the local school district that Pullman's stories "are definitely trying to introduce children to a spiritual experience which would be very contrary to a Biblical Christian world view" (Santee A10). The key here is the type of "spiritual experience," not the lack of it.

Ursula K. Le Guin, whose nontheism is as deeply engrained as Pullman's, is praised by some Christian commentators for her message of responsibility toward the Earth and respect for those different from oneself. For others, however, like Michael D. O'Brien, Le Guin's "intelligence and creative power" (108) nearly make her work acceptable, but ultimately the virtues of her work are a honeyed trap because

> Earthsea presents the universe as a dynamic system in which magic, science, and religion are merged into what is called the Great Balance or the Equilibrium. In the great balance between good and evil, all supernatural powers are merely naturalized. The resulting effect in the reader is a lowering of vigilance against the occult. By marvelous sleight of hand, Le Guin achieves this by appearing to be a moralist. (109)

Even more than Pullman, she commits the sin of depicting a spiritual experience without biblical authority, which is more dangerous than imagining no spirituality at all.

O'Brien represents a sizable readership for whom no morality is possible outside of religious, and specifically evangelical Christian, belief. Furthermore, his worldview and theirs includes the existence of a nonmetaphorical occult. Sorcery is real, they say, and always demonic. No amount of scientific evidence against any such real-world magic would ever convince these readers, because their model of reality, like their morality, is not based on science but on a reading of scripture. O'Brien finds a number of fantasies acceptable: specifically those that employ symbols within a traditionally Christian interpretive framework. Dragons, for instance, must represent evil: "Actual dragons may or may not have existed, but that is not our main concern here. What is important is that the Christian 'myth' of the dragon refers to a being who actually exists and who becomes very much more dangerous to us the less we believe he exists" (32). Of particular interest in his statement, besides his hedging on the possible existence of dragons, is the attempt to control interpretation. Stories can only refer in a certain way; they must be read, if not entirely literally, then at least emblematically, according to an established system of assigned meanings. Dragons are not merely evil, but Evil: they are a traditional signifier for the Devil. There is no room in this reading system for ambiguous or wise Chinese-style dragons, any more than there can be good witches.

But O'Brien finds Tolkien, Lewis, and MacDonald to be more than merely acceptable: "Each of these authors labors in a different part of the vineyard, and each fulfills a task that is irreplaceable" (158). He believes in the value of the right kind of literature, as he defines rightness, and he respects the symbol-making power of the imagination. The same cannot be said of all who view fantasy from a religious perspective. For some commentators, no fantasy is acceptable, no matter how orthodox its worldview or how devout its writer. Why would fantasy as a mode of storytelling (or as a vehicle for speculation about the nature of things) come under such fire? Berit Kjos, an amateur theological watchdog, makes the following frequently-quoted comment:[. . .] today's culture trains children to see reality through a global, earth-centered filter. This "new" mental framework distorts truth, stretches the meaning of familiar words, and promotes spiritual "insights" that are incompatible with Christianity. Packaged as entertainment, this message usually bypasses rational resistance, desensitizes opened minds, and fuels general acceptance of pagan spirituality. ("Spirit")

Stretching meanings and promoting insights do not seem to be bad things in themselves. Make a few minor changes, such as altering *distorts* to *explores*, and you have a reasonable summary of fantasy's potential for offering new, eclectic perspectives on religious experience. This potential has been noted by Christian commentators such as Connie Neal (*The Gospel According to Harry Potter*, 2008), John Granger (*Looking for God in Harry Potter*, 2006), and Danielle Elizabeth Tumminio (*God and Harry Potter at Yale: Teaching Faith and Fantasy Fiction in an Ivy League Classroom*, 2010), as well as many a minister casting about for a topic for next Sunday's sermon.

But Kjos makes another comment that gets at the heart of the matter. She says that "the most deceptive spiritual counterfeits look most similar to God's truth" ("Spirit"). In other words, fantasy (even Lewis's) is deceptive because it speaks in the language of the spirit—that is, of myth, though evangelical Christians do not like to use that word to describe biblical narratives. All the debate over the acceptability of Tolkien and Rowling and L'Engle and Pullman, all the book burnings and library challenges, all the sermons for and against fantasy suggest that there is an important debate going on, not over individual texts but over interpretation. How should we read fantasy? Who has the authority to decide what a myth means?

Many of the discussions of Harry Potter and Narnia take place in the same venues and with the same arguments that are employed in debates over such vexed topics as the identity of the Beast of the Apocalypse or Paul's views on homosexuality. In both cases, the opposing viewpoints come down to the question of how to make meaning from a text in which simple referentiality is neither possible or sufficient. Neither the Bible nor Pullman's trilogy simply means what it says, nor does either direct the reader to a nonproblematic extratextual reality. We cannot read them as we do the daily newspaper or an account of the Civil War. The same is true of all mythic texts. They invite applications beyond their boundaries—to explain creation and death, to guide moral decisions, to justify social institutions—and yet at the same time they defy rational comprehension of their symbols and transformations. Myths are disturbing and inexplicably comforting; they never seem the same from reading to reading. It is no wonder that there is disagreement about their meaning and use, or that people have fought to the death over the right to interpret them one way or another.

From Pillar to Post

Many people cannot live with such indeterminacy. Hence the literal school fights to hold on to certainties such as the inerrancy of scripture, whereas skeptics like Kersey Graves, quoted previously, deny those very foundational beliefs, the pillars, he says, of Christian faith. Yet fantasy—whether explicitly antitheological like Pullman's or apologetically instructive like Lewis's—can never claim to be inerrant. Indeed, the quality that makes fantasy fantastic is its untruth. Like fairy tales but unlike scriptural narratives, fantasy proclaims itself to be an account of what never was nor ever could be. If fantasy means anything at all, that meaning must come indirectly, through analogies and symbols whose meanings are unstable and dependent on the reader's experience and circumstances. Fantasy thus falls in line with various postmodern and poststructuralist schools of interpretation: its very structure suggests that proclaiming truth may be more deceitful than outright lying. The danger in fantasy, for biblical literalists, is that it gives its readers practice at reading complexly and symbolically.

A fantastic symbol is like a mooring rope tossed from a boat. Some symbols catch hold in the individual reader's imagination, whereas others slip back into the water. As George MacDonald said of fairy tale, "It is there not so much to convey a meaning as to wake a meaning. If it do not even wake an interest, throw it aside. A meaning may be there, but it is not for you" ("Fantastic"). Neither skeptic not fundamentalist, MacDonald was a sort of proto-deconstructionist, glorying in the indeterminacy of meaning, as when he compared fairy tale exegesis to the act of boiling roses. The final product may be unambiguous, but it is no longer a rose. By implication, the same could be said of interpretations of overtly religious symbolism: the more explicit and invariant the reading, the less true.

But MacDonald was never a skeptic. He saw no contradiction between the fantastic imagination and his version of Christianity, any more than he saw conflict between faith and science. MacDonald envisioned the realm of magic as neither good nor evil in itself but a route toward self-understanding. Like Thomas the Rhymer's vision, in the ballad of "True Thomas," of a "bonny road/ Which winds about the fernie brae" toward Elfland and which lies between the roads to Heaven and Hell, symbolic fantasy becomes in MacDonald's work another route to heaven, less direct than the path of righteousness but no less wondrous. Versions of that path appear in many of MacDonald's fantasies, including "The Golden Key." Those who take the path through fairyland always end up closer to heaven—even the demonic Lilith. In this spiritual optimism he resembles Madeleine L'Engle, whom O'Brien condemns as a neo-pagan, more closely than he does Lewis, with whom O'Brien groups him.

R. Scott Bakker, self-proclaimed skeptic and writer of dark, philosophical fantasies, points out that the fantasy readers he meets are more often literalist Christians than scholars trained in observation and interpretation, ambiguity and irony. Yet fantasy, he says, is the product of a scholarly, even scientific worldview: only when science transforms the magical beliefs and anthropomorphisms of myth into literal untruths do those become the stuff of fantasy. Science changes the consensus about—and thereby the nature of—the reality that fantasy bypasses. Like science fiction, fantasy is

> an attempt to use narrative to compensate for an ever more isolated "cognitive present." The worlds depicted in fantasy fiction typically operate on principles long since discredited by our contemporary scientific worldview. In terms of basic structure, very little separates Middle-earth from prescientific worlds like Biblical Israel or Vedic India or Homeric Greece. (34)

Yet, says Bakker, we all have a need to tell stories in which the universe cares about us: "some kind of innate 'anthropomorphic imperative'" (35). The problem is not that we still construct fantasies but that too many of us have not learned how to read them conditionally, literarily rather than literally. Bakker sees this battle over literal and symbolic readings of fantasy—and hence of myth—as a teaching opportunity: "Fantasy fiction, and genre fiction in general, represents an opportunity to communicate in the most profound sense, which is to say, to negotiate common ground between drastically different perspectives" (38).

Before any such negotiation can take place, however, both sides must agree to declare the fantastic to be neutral ground, and that means suspending the sureties of faith at least for the span of reading. In contrast with what Bakker calls the "magical belief in how words work" required for biblical literalism (33), readers must adopt something like MacDonald's willingness to let symbolic narratives remain untranslatable into simple propositions about the universe. They must also let go, at least while immersed within a fantastic narrative, of what Christian tradition terms the "solas"—the "onlies"—of doctrine: *sola fides*, justification only through faith; *sola gratia*, salvation only by grace; *solo christo*, redemption only through Christ; *soli deo gloria*, glory only to God; and above all, *sola scriptura*, truth only to be found within the Bible, the inerrant and transparently significant word of God. In a work of fantasy, all of these become, instead, *not only . . . but also.*

Bakker's own Prince of Nothing trilogy (2003–2006) depicts a holy war over clashing dogmas, none of which fully account for the imagined world's complexities. No such "only" works in his universe. Le Guin's Earthsea series likewise undercuts attempts to read the stories for sola-like truths: even propositions about magic and balance that underlie the first books are called into question by the final volume. As the series develops, new voices are introduced, and the wisdom of wizards is challenged and enriched by the perspectives of women, "barbarians," and dragons. In many fantasies, the Christian or Muslim "only one God" is replaced by, for instance, a trickster Goddess, as in Diane Duane's Tale of the Five (1979–1992), or a pantheon of five deities of varying gender, as in Lois McMaster Bujold's *The Curse of Chalion* (2001). The angel fictions of MacAvoy, L'Engle, and Crowley school readers in the art of reading religious icons multiply and conditionally.

In place of invariant scriptures, fantasies frequently depict fragmentary or ambiguous prophetic texts within their secondary worlds. Many of these are oral texts, like the traditional narratives that preceded the written Genesis. Tolkien's Middle-earth has no official scripture, only the ballads and elvish hymns that document the Creation, Fall, and historical record of the First and Second Ages. Patricia McKillip's fantasy plots often revolve around the characters' attempts—never completely successful—to reconstruct the past from riddles and other hints in oral tradition, as in her Riddle-Master trilogy (1976–1979) and *The Bards of Bone Plain* (2010). Le Guin's *A Wizard of Earthsea* ends by casting doubt on the reliability of traditions on which the narrative itself is presumably based: the song of Ged's great deed "has been lost," though "there is a tale" that may hold some of the truth; "in Iffish they say" one thing about his journey, while "in Tok" they say another, and both are contradicted by storytellers "in Holp"; "so of the song of the Shadow there remain only a few scraps of legend, carried like driftwood from isle to isle over the long years" (205). The message is not that there is no truth, but that listeners (and readers) must construct that truth for themselves; that history, like magic, is both conditional and dynamic, changing according to the understanding and needs of its users.

In contrast, G. P. Taylor's *Shadowmancer* (2003), a novel written as a reply to Rowling and Pullman, takes great pains not only to make its supernatural framework conform to evangelical Christian doctrine but also to instruct its readers in the single right way to interpret fantasy. Magic in the novel is carefully distinguished from miracle: "I am not a witch, or a warlock, or a sorcerer. They are filled with wickedness. All I have is that which is given to me by Riathamus" (27). Despite the name-change for God ("Riathamus" translates as a ruler of kings), Taylor clearly intends us to take the distinction between evil sorcery and divine intervention as operative in the real world, rather than simply in his imagined universe. In interviews, Taylor mentions his own pre-conversion dabbling in the occult (a term which seems to cover every spiritual tradition other than Christianity) and expresses his ongoing belief in the existence of supernatural forces:

> if you get involved in the occult, then you are going to invite all sorts of very negative spiritual forces into your house and sometimes into yourself, or to attach themselves to you. And I firmly believe there's no other way of getting rid of these things other than by the name of Jesus. (Interview)

Throughout the novel, characters encounter similar unambiguous declarations about good, evil, God, and the devil (a.k.a. Pyratheon). Those declarations come from angelic characters—the speaker just quoted is a "Keruvim," a barely disguised version of cherubim—or from the sacred Book of Life or direct from God himself. An episode late in the book has the heroes meet a mysterious shepherd who offers them fishes and loaves, knows everything about them, and finally introduces himself as "I AM WHO I AM" (239). Most of these pronouncements are direct quotations or close paraphrases from Biblical passages. The good characters have no doubts about what to believe or how to proceed. The language of the text is full of phrases like "Thomas suddenly knew" (45) and "it was so real, so true" (51). In contrast, the evil characters say things like "What is truth? It is all relative" (87). The lesson is clear: fantasy's truth claims are the same as, and dependent on, church teachings. As many readers have noted, the unfortunate result is that the fantasy falls flat: at moments where one would like to see a some character depth or an ambiguous and multivalent symbol, one gets, instead, a Sunday-school lesson.

Ironically, none of this was enough to guarantee a favorable reception from Christian reviewers. Though many approved the book as a non-Satanic alternative to Potter, the ever-vigilant Berit Kjos warns that "such a story can't be trusted as a Christian book! A 'Christian book' can't deviate from the truth. It can't reinvent God and spiritual warfare without misleading readers and distorting their understanding of our Lord and His Word ("Shadowmancer"). Even the more imaginative Christian reviewers found the book untrustworthy as an entry into true belief. It emphasizes the occult too much, takes its biblical quotations out of context, recombines them freely, and may even be covertly pro-Islamic: "It should be pointed out that Taylor believes the Muslim God is the same as the Jewish and Christian God" (Montenegro). The most serious problem is that "the gospel does not appear, nor is there any mention of Christ. The 'God' character is called Riathamus and the 'devil' character is called Pyratheon, so it is not clear whether these are meant to be the Christian figures or just some fictional characters" (Thomas).

In other words, the book fails the literal-reading test. The very elements designed to make it appeal to believers are the grounds for rejection: direct reference to the Bible, generous dollops of doctrine, divine miracles, and a barely masked God and devil, but all of these occurring in a displaced fantasy universe where their truth value becomes problematic.

Even the most faithful transcription of faith language into a work of fantasy has the effect of setting religion adrift. The pillars of Christianity become mere pontoons as readers are invited to test the story's message not against scriptural authority or historical precedent but rather against their own experience. Fantasy's re-rigged ships of myth are tethered only by symbols, anchored only in the reader's heart. Each imagined world must compete with others of its kind, not on the basis of prior conviction but rather of internal consistency and imaginative richness. And in this postcolonial world, there are plenty of choices, including fantasies derived from other, non-Christian mythic traditions or even, like Bakker's novels, incorporating the dissonance that arises from the meeting of rival beliefs.

The Postcolonial Fantastic

At the same time that fantasy came under increasing pressure to conform to a strict theological and ideological standard, the genre was opening up to experimentation, indeterminacy, and a global perspective. These two trends represent two ways of reading and two ways of living in a postmodern world. Though they may seem unrelated, attempts by religious conservatives to ban fantasy and the recent emergence of fantasy into the cultural and literary mainstream are part of the same historical shift, which has to do with a general awareness of the constructedness and contingency of all cultural narratives, including myth. One response to this awareness is to embrace it; the other is to insist all the more strongly on literal and singular truth even within a form that claims no fidelity to the real world.

Just as the new science of comparative mythology forced reevaluation of biblical narratives in the eighteenth and nineteenth centuries, a shifting literary landscape in the late twentieth century demanded that Westerners rethink their self-appointed role as emissaries of Modernity and arbiters of truth. Between the 1970s and the 1990s, to paraphrase Salman Rushdie, the Empire wrote back. On one hand, a rich array of poems, plays, essays, and novels began pouring forth from African, Caribbean, south Asian, and indigenous North American and Australian writers. On the other, critics such as Edward Said, Ngugi wa Thiong'o, Paula Gunn Allen, and Gayatri Spivak taught the world how to listen to those voices and why the most important explorations of power and most eloquent expressions of resistance might be coming from formerly marginalized groups. Fantasy no less than other literary modes was radically altered by this decentering. The genre's relationship to sacred traditions and oral entertainments made it a natural platform for new cultural formulations and critiques. One of the most eloquent of postcolonial fantasists is Nalo Hopkinson, who describes her own deliberate remythicizing of scientific discourse in novels such as *Midnight Robber* (2000):

Part of what I set out to do was to imagine what paradigms for technology a society might develop without the all-pervasive influence of American technology and the way it references Greek and Roman mythology (we talk about the "Apollo missions"; we've named planets after Greek and Roman gods; we call our cities "metropolises"). But a diasporic Caribbean culture might name its computer operating systems after a West African deity with the power to go anywhere, see anything. Its concepts of stewardship of its planet might be based in Taino values (the Taino are the indigenous people who were living in the Caribbean when Columbus stumbled on that part of the world). ("Essay")

Hopkinson thus reconfigures technological language in such a way that the wielder of the machine is no longer science fiction's boy genius, heir to Tom Edison, Jr., of dime novel fame—pale, privileged, and immersed in Western culture. The person sitting in front of the computer screen might be a young Caribbean or African woman. On the screen is Eshu, an operating system named for the Yoruba god of crossroads. Though Audre Lord famously declared that the master's tools cannot dismantle the master's house, they might do so if rebaptized—not simply renamed but washed clean and born anew into another mythic universe. Science fiction, as a form of fantastic literature, offers an opportunity to return to a time when myth and science were indistinguishable from one another and to let them grow into whatever configuration a reimagined history might allow.

As literary fantasy, like other European-derived cultural institutions, spreads around the world, its practices and potentialities becomes available to writers who can claim mythic traditions other than those of the Bible or Homer. The most powerful claims have traditionally been based on blood: both the blood-ties of ancestry and the blood shed as one civilization encroaches on or enslaves another. Yet upbringing can also be a source of authority, giving resonance and depth to the creative use of the memories, beliefs, and narrative structures of a writer's own family and earliest teachers and allowing the writer to use those beliefs and motifs to challenge Western mythology. Some critical schools transform *authority* into *authenticity*, maintaining that no one without an authentic claim to a particular mythic tradition is allowed to invoke it. The difference is subtle: one perspective invites us to look for added value in the work of writers with particular experiences and background, and the other tells us to dismiss the work of those without that background. Authenticity can become another sort of *sola* like those of religious orthodoxy: true myth *only* by right of birth.

Nalo Hopkinson, quoted previously, does not claim to be the authentic spokesperson for any mythic tradition. She draws on a complex ancestry and a multicultural personal history in a number of fantasy and science fiction stories, starting with *Brown Girl in the Ring* (1998). Reflecting Hopkinson's

own background, the novel is both Canadian and Caribbean; it juxtaposes futuristic technology with belief in *duppies*, or disembodied spirits of the dead,
and in *obeah*, the practice of healing through guiding spirits. In the introduction to her anthology *Mojo: Conjure Stories* (2003), Hopkinson emphasizes the
persistence of such traditional beliefs despite, or even in response to, brutal
transplantation from Africa. Her title, for instance, refers to *mojo*, "a magic
imbued with African flavor and with the need of indentured peoples to take
some control over their lives" (vii). And in the introduction to *Whispers from
the Cotton-Tree Root: Caribbean Fabulist Fiction* (2000), she describes the further wanderings of those African emigrés and their magical traditions: "I look
over the stories I've chosen for this anthology and realize that although all
twenty of the writers are of Caribbean background, most of them currently live
outside the Caribbean. That's no surprise from a region where many have
found it necessary to leave in order to pursue their goals" (xi). Hopkinson herself has lived in Jamaica, Trinidad, Guyana, Canada, and the United States. She
draws freely on the languages and traditions of all these places, while at the
same time claiming allegiance to the imagined worlds of fantasy and science
fiction and the critical perspectives of science and history. It is significant that
she titles her collection "fabulist fiction" rather than "magical realism," a term
that can imply a religious or superstitious worldview unable to distinguish between the real and the unreal. In the usage of many critics, Modern writers
knowingly write fantasy; those who live outside the circle of Modernity write
(charmingly naive) magical realism.

But Hopkinson and a number of other contemporary non-European writers write fantasy. Hopkinson explains:

> I grew up in a milieu of Caribbean writers and writing. I bring that sensi-
> bility to my own work, but I write within a particularly northern tradition of
> speculative and fantastical fiction. There, plot and content are equally im-
> portant and the speculative or fantastical elements of a story must be 'real':
> Duppies and jumbies must exist outside the imaginations of the characters;
> any scientific extrapolation should seem convincingly based in the possible.
> [. . .] Northern science fiction and fantasy come out of a rational and skep-
> tical approach to the world: That which cannot be explained must be proven
> to exist, either through scientific method or independent corroboration.
> (*Whispers* xiii)

As she worked with writers who stayed within Caribbean culture, Hopkinson
developed an appreciation for another way of using magical traditions to comprehend the world:

> But the Caribbean, much like the rest of the world, tends to have a different
> worldview. The irrational, the inexplicable, and the mysterious exist side
> by each with the daily events of life. Questioning the irrational overmuch is

unlikely to yield a rational answer, and may prove dangerous. Best instead to find ways to incorporate both the logical and the illogical into one's approach to the world, because you never know when life will just drop you down in that hole, into a ceiba space where none of the rules you know operate. (*Whispers* xiii).

Thus Hopkinson speaks as a border crosser, someone who moves freely among cultures and whose fictions frequently transgress genre boundaries. There are a number of such border crossers working within the contemporary fantastic. They reserve the right to combine metafictional techniques with postcolonial politics in a way that reveals the critical power of traditional worldviews. They deliberately juxtapose the capitalist postindustrial landscapes of Toronto or London or Tokyo with other realities, other perspectives. These perspectives incorporate myths, folktales, and legends from places other than Europe and belief systems other than Christianity, but they do so with self-awareness and sophistication. The border-crossing writers reflect the experience of groups that have managed to survive colonialism and cultures that in many cases have leapfrogged over the Modern entirely (or, *vide* Bruno Latour, the illusion of modernity). One way to be postmodern is to challenge the master narratives that construct the modern world, including the Christian narrative of sinful nature and divine redemption and the historical narrative of Western dominance that positions everyone else as the savage past.

Many of the border-crossing fantasists have, like Hopkinson, relocated across literal borders. It is impossible to tie them to a single location; instead, each writes from a trajectory. Salman Rushdie's trajectory goes from Mumbai, India, where he was born, to England, where he studied at Cambridge University and worked as an advertising copywriter while starting his literary career. Now, on the strength of fantasies such as *Midnight's Children* (1981) and after the uproar caused by his use of Islamic myth in *The Satanic Verses* (1988), he is an international celebrity. The trajectory of Nega Mezlekia, author of the historical fantasy *The God Who Begat a Jackal* (2002), extends from Ethiopia to the Netherlands to Canada. Amitav Ghosh, winner of the Arthur C. Clarke Award for the genre-blending novel *The Calcutta Chromosome* (1995), moved from India to England to the United States. One narrative thread of Vikram Chandra's *Red Earth and Pouring Rain* (1995) mythologizes its author's own journey from India to the United States and, temporarily, conditionally, back again. Karen Lord, author of the Crawford Award-winning *Redemption in Indigo* (2010), a fantasy that combines West Indian tales and African legends with a touch of science fiction, was born in Barbados, studied science at the University of Toronto, and received a doctorate in the sociology of religion from Bangor University in Wales before returning to Barbados to teach. Nnedi Okorafor, born in the United States, grew up with an awareness of Nigeria, from which her parents had emigrated and to which she occasionally made family visits. Okorafor incorporates West African narrative elements and perspectives in fantasies such as the World Fantasy Award-winning *Who Fears Death* (2010).

Each of these novels similarly moves between cognitive worlds. As does Hopkinson with her Caribbean and Canadian heritage, Okorafor credits her double perspective for the ability to transform African experience into fantasy: "the categories of fantasy or science fiction aren't in Nigerian vocabulary. I feel like part of why I'm able to write it is because I was born and raised in the United States. Thus I've been exposed to this specific style of writing *along with* African literature with fantastical elements" ("Between Cultures" 78). All the writers mentioned previously similarly use this sort of cultural parallax to call into question the great narrative structures through which institutions justify their existence and with which historical subjects—that is, all of us—attempt to make sense of injustice and intimidation and desire and death.

By incorporating elements of the fantastic borrowed from non-Western mythic traditions, these writers challenge readers to find new patterns, new motivations, and new outcomes in the master narratives. *The Calcutta Chromosome*, for instance, retraces the history of the discovery of malaria in India by Sir Ronald Ross—a classic instance of the inscription of colonial rule within the narrative of science. Ghosh revises the story so that the real discovery is made, not by the English doctor but by his Indian assistant Mangala, who is also an incarnation of the Goddess. Ghosh has historical evidence to back up his revisionist version of the discovery, including, despite some interesting silences, Ross's own memoirs: "There are several intriguing moments in the *Memoirs* when it is possible to divine that laboratory assistants played a more significant part in the malaria work than Ross would care to admit" (Chambers 62). Mangala, aided by Ross's servant Lutchman (who in real life doubled as Ross's guinea pig), manipulates him into making his discoveries so that she can use the fast-mutating malaria "bug" to alter the human genome. Says one of the characters who is trying to piece together the real story:

> "It's my guess that by about 1897 Mangala had run into a dead end, and she'd come to the conclusion that the existent strains of malaria wouldn't let her go any further. That's why she was so desperate to have Ronnie figure the whole thing out and publish it. Because she actually believed that the link between the bug and the human mind was so close that once its life cycle had been figured out it would spontaneously mutate in directions that would take her work to the next step." (*Calcutta* 249)

The story inverts all hierarchies: the servant is the real master, the scientist is the naive assistant, a woman holds power over men, a disease becomes a cure, the outsider is the secret center, and myth takes on the power of reason. By setting his novel both in the near future and in the colonial past, Ghosh reveals that both past and future are narrative constructs and can therefore be rewritten, using myth and the fantastic to challenge the hidden assumptions that transform ideology into destiny.

These postcolonial fantasies share a number of qualities, including a breadth of setting that mirrors their authors' peripatetic lives. They are witty, exuberant, sprawling, and impassioned—books that one can get lost in. Most are intricately plotted, rife with secret connections and hidden histories. And all of them offer perspectives on the contemporary world that are enhanced by, if not completely dependent on, their authors' double positioning as Westerners and non-Westerners, insiders and outsiders, immigrants and emigrés who are always leaving and always arriving. These qualities also mark the works of another group not usually considered postcolonial in the same way. It is possible to cross a cultural divide without stepping across any national boundaries. A number of First Nations, Native American, and Aboriginal writers become internal border crossers whenever they draw on indigenous cultures while at the same time taking part in the international, technologized, highly mediated world of modernity and postmodernity.

Participation in the technologized world is not a choice. It may be possible to live in relative isolation from television, brand names, and social media, but not if one is a writer. What the writer can do is create a dialogue between the dominant culture and various alternative viewpoints, as Hopkinson does, without letting the majority voices drown out all others. As in the case of the angel fantasies discussed in chapter 6, a single text can represent one thing to a cognitive majority and quite another to a cognitive minority. One reader's literal truth is another's symbolic fiction. Yet writers who speak from the position of a cognitive minority are more aware of the majority than the other way around—another variation on the principle that the oppressed are obliged to understand oppressors better than they themselves are understood. And writers of fantasy who incorporate alternative worldviews derived from direct experience of non-Western traditions are among the most sophisticated critics of simple literality and the single message.

Making Contact in the Fantasy Zone

One of the best models for understanding what goes on in postcolonial fantasy was developed by Mary Louise Pratt in response to quite another genre: historical narrative. Pratt looked at an unusual chronicle:

> dated in the city of Cuzco in Peru, in the year 1613, some forty years after the final fall of the Inca empire to the Spanish and signed with an unmistakably Andean indigenous name: Felipe Guaman Poma de Ayala. Written in a mixture of Quechua and ungrammatical, expressive Spanish, the manuscript was a letter addressed by an unknown but apparently literate Andean to King Philip III of Spain. ("Arts" 1)

In this massive missive (1200 pages in manuscript), the author "took over the official Spanish genre for his own ends. Those ends were, roughly, to construct a new picture of the world, a picture of a Christian world with Andean rather than European peoples at the center of it—Cuzco, not Jerusalem" ("Arts" 2). Guaman Poma adopts the conquerors' language, their religion (his history of the New World starts with Adam and Eve), and their genre, but his text subverts the system within which those operate. It subtly critiques the invasion and reverses hierarchies even while seeming to praise the Spanish rulers and the works of missionaries. Pratt suggests that the text offers two quite disparate messages to native and European readers.

This doubleness is typical, says Pratt, of art produced within a zone of cultural contact, such as the postinvasion Andes. The "verbal arts of the contact zone" include "[a]utoethnography, transculturation, critique, collaboration, bilingualism, mediation, parody, denunciation, imaginary dialogue, vernacular expression" ("Arts" 4)—all involving some sort of doubling of form, message, and audience. Each of these strategies of indirection and redirection allows the writer to bridge a cultural divide while still maintaining a degree of autonomy. Each involves appropriating the forms of the dominant society in order to critique its structures of power and meaning. In a sense, genre itself becomes a meeting place, a contact zone, and that is true not only of historical chronicles but also of fantastic fictions. The arts Pratt describes, such as autoethnography, parody, and imaginary dialogue, can all be found in the fantastic novels of transnational writers such as Ghosh, Rushdie, and Hopkinson and also in the works of internal border crossers such as Leslie Marmon Silko, Thomas King, Archie Weller, and Sam Watson.

King's *Green Grass, Running Water* (1993) is not usually classified as fantasy, but Greg Bechtel makes a case for using that term and for grouping such works with "genre fantasies" such as Charles de Lint's *Moonheart* (1984). Bechtel observes that the usual interpretive horizon for writers such as King is not a form but an identity: Native literature. One could add to his Canadian examples U.S. writers such as Leslie Marmon Silko, Sherman Alexie, and Louise Erdrich, and certainly it makes sense to read their works together, looking for common themes and techniques. However, as with any genre issue, the useful question to ask of a text is not "Does it belong in this genre?" but rather "What happens when I read it in terms of this genre?" Bechtel suggests that *Green Grass, Running Water* can be read in more than one way and that a reading that pays particular attention to impossible elements, irruptions of the supernatural, and the interpretive protocols of fantasy is justified by the results. He calls the resulting fusion *syncretic fantasy* "because it posits alternative realities that coexist, interpenetrate, and interact with the everyday real in which we (i.e. most North Americans) profess to live our lives" (4).[1]

Such works, among which he also includes Hopkinson's *Brown Girl in a Ring* and Eden Robinson's *Monkey Beach* (2000), not only depict colliding worldviews but also offer a framework for interactions between seemingly incompatible cognitive systems. Fantasy, he suggests, becomes a metacognitive form when its imagined worlds encourage readers to look beyond "the dominant 'reality' of the culture in which it exists" (Bechtel, Dissertation 29). This outward look is, of course, exactly the opposite of the blinkered viewpoint of the biblical literalists discussed in the Literalist Interlude preceding this chapter. It requires, rather than forbids, alternative interpretations. Though most definitions of fantasy focus on the impossibility of the narrated events and imagined worlds, Bechtel's concept of syncretism emphasizes their believability, which is based in such qualities as internal consistency and subjective— which is to say symbolic—truth. The primary source and model for both world-building consistency and symbolism is mythic narrative, meaning that every well-imagined fantasy gestures toward someone's traditional beliefs, either now or in the past. Implicitly, the fantastic narrative is, when seen from another perspective, a realistic one, though that perspective is held by a minority or by a lost culture or by no one outside the fiction. Syncretic fantasy might therefore be seen by some readers as not fantasy at all. Its genre depends on who is reading.

Like *Green Grass, Running Water*, Silko's *Ceremony* (1977) responds to more than one generic reading practice. It tells the story of Tayo, a half-Pueblo man who comes back from World War II psychologically damaged by violence and prejudice, only to find his family broken and his community divided and unable to maintain its own traditions. Much of the novel documents the dark history and present devastation found on reservations such as Tayo's. Yet Silko shows that Native life is more than just poverty, deculturation, and alcoholism. From his grandmother, his Uncle Josiah, and his cousin Rocky, Tayo knows what it is to have love and support. Grandma, the only one of the three alive after the War, insists that the healer Ku'oosh be brought in to help her shell-shocked grandson, and Ku'oosh offers Tayo traditional cures: Indian tea, cornmeal, and stories. Some of those stories are interpolated throughout the novel: Pueblo creation myths, ceremonial chants, stories of witchcraft, and stories of rain and renewal. Yet Ku'oosh is not confident that these stories are remedy enough for Tayo or for the ills of the modern world: "'There are some things we can't cure like we used to,' he said. 'not since the white people came. The others who had the Scalp Ceremony, some of them are not better either'"(38). Ku'oosh sends Tayo to an unconventional Navajo healer, Betonie, whose ceremonial objects come from many cultures:

> Hard shrunken skin pouches and black leather purses trimmed with hammered silver buttons were things he could understand. They were a medicine man's paraphernalia, laid beside the painted gourd rattles and deer-hoof clackers of the ceremony. But with this old man it did not end there; under the medicine bags and bundles of rawhide on the walls, he saw layers of old

calendars, the sequences of years confused and lost as if occasionally the oldest calendars had fallen or been taken out from under the others and then had been replaced on top of the most recent years. (120).

Betonie's explanation is that "'In the old days it was simple. A medicine person could get by without all these things. But nowadays . . .' He let his voice trail off and nodded to let Tayo complete the thought for him" (121). Similarly, he starts Tayo on a healing path but leaves it up to Tayo to find the ending of the ritual, a new ceremony to fit a new world.

Tayo's ceremony fuses Pueblo and Navajo ritual with bits of Anglo and Mexican culture. It takes him from the fringes of Gallup, New Mexico, to the half-wilderness of Mount Taylor, where he meets figures from myth: a hunter who might be Orion; a mountain lion; and a woman who seems to be one of the Pleiades, or an embodiment of the mountain, or both. With their help he completes a search for his uncle's stolen cattle that is also a vision quest. In the process, he finds the strength to overcome his emotional scars and to oppose the destructive witchcraft to which even some of his own people have turned.

Tayo's ceremony is his life, and both are blends of identities and traditions. The ceremony and the novel named for it are both instances of Pratt's arts of the contact zone. The former takes a Native American cultural form and incorporates bits of contemporary history and culture, just as Betonie's magic incorporates Anglo-American images and English words (122). The latter is an American novel as realistic as Faulkner's or Hemingway's but at the same time fantastic, full of spells and witches and shape-shifters that gradually reveal their true power. Seemingly incompatible realities are syncretized in both narrative and the ritual, with mixed-blood characters such as Tayo and Betonie leading the way. For an insider audience, those who share Tayo's Pueblo heritage, Silko's narrative offers a way to recognize and reconnect with the sacred in a transformed world. For an outsider audience, synecdochically represented by Tayo's unknown paternity, the story proffers not so much recognition as *re-cognition:* a new way of thinking through the problems of identity and faith. For the majority of American readers, schooled in Eurocentric history and Judeo-Christian symbols, Silko's fantastic narrative opens up a contact zone within which each of the pillars of faith can be compared with, and perhaps replaced by, alternative versions of the miraculous and prophetic and an expanded and revised moral code.

Constructing a Postcolonial Zone: The Example of Australia

In Australia, where the oppression of native peoples and cultures was, if anything, even more severe than in North America, it has been harder to create contact zones, and, as discussed in chapter 5, attempts by white writers such as

Patricia Wrightson to blend their traditions with those of indigenous Australians have been met with suspicion or hostility. Non-Aboriginal writers from Australia have generated such a collection of ignorant, patronizing, and demeaning texts about Aborigines that some of the latter want to call a halt to any further attempts. As the novelist Melissa Lucashenko says, "Who asked you to write about Aboriginal people? If it wasn't Aboriginal people themselves, I suggest you go away and look at your own lives instead of ours. We are tired of being the freak show of Australian popular culture" (quoted in Heiss 10).

Whereas American writers often treated native cultures as noble, if doomed, and Indian characters as heroic adversaries or guides to the white hero (as in James Fenimore Cooper's Leatherstocking series), early depictions of Aboriginal people at best treat them as part of the landscape and at worst—and there is a pretty clear worst in Austyn Granville's lost-world romance *The Fallen Race* (1892)—as subhuman. Representations of Aboriginals improved during the first half of the twentieth century, but only to the extent of reimagining them as doomed and childlike innocents, comic caricatures, or savage shamans: exotic repositories of mystic knowledge. Not until the 1970s did a serious challenge to such representations arise. That decade marked the emergence of the first generation of Aboriginal writers and the appearance of a number of children's books derived from Aboriginal lore, including Patricia Wrightson's early work and Bill Scott's *Boori* (1978), a hero-tale that takes place when "The Dreamtime had ended in Australia, and no white man had yet found the great land of the south" (1). Kath Walker's *Stradbroke Dreamtime* (1972) differs from Scott's and Wrightson's books in being based in her own experience as a member of the Noonuccal clan of coastal Queensland and in combining autobiography with retellings of myth. With these volumes and others that followed, Aboriginal history and storytelling became familiar to Australian schoolchildren, something they were now encouraged to see as part of Our National Heritage rather than distant and primitive.

Though few Aboriginal voices were heard, Aboriginality was becoming a standard part of the Australian fantastic. One of the most important venues for debating the direction of white-Aboriginal interaction was science fiction or, more precisely, science fantasy, rather than straight fantasy such as Wrightson's. Mid-twentieth-century SF writers such as Frank Bryning, A. Bertram Chandler, George Turner, Damien Broderick, and Terry Dowling made attempts to open up a dialogue between cultures in stories of alien contact and a multicultural future.[2] Dowling's Tom Tyson stories, for instance, depict a future Australia dominated by Aboriginal political and religious traditions after the white community's collapse into barbarism. *Rynosseros* (1990) and subsequent collections focus on the adventures of a non-Aboriginal, or "National," hero operating within this cultural sphere. Unlike most of his predecessors, Dowling does not equate Aboriginality with either tradition or nature—he is just as likely to pit advanced Aboriginal technology against National attempts at resurgence or to frame the conflict between tradition and novelty as a struggle between tribal factions. By adapting the science fantasy tradition of Cordwainer Smith and Jack Vance—characterized by distant futures, radically altered humanity, technological effects that resemble magic, and exuberant, even baroque language—to the Australian scene, Dowling thoroughly reboots Eurocentric SF conventions, down to their mythic base (Dowling, "Dancing"). Though he has received many honors for his evocative fiction, Dowling did not please all early readers with his imagined future. To some it seemed to be an example of cultural appropriation and to others yet another instance of an Australia-equals-convicts-plus-Aborigines habit that irked fan critic Graham Stone. By the time *Rynosseros* appeared, however, other factors besides fan resentment of such "national obsessions" (Stone 10) were operating. Even as Australian SF writers began to realize the possibilities offered by incorporating traditional Aboriginal voices and motifs, those possibilities were starting to close off, just as they were to do in fantasy. The 1970s were characterized not only by the emergence of writing by Aboriginal authors but also by the first stirrings of political activity by Aboriginal activists—many of them the same individuals. Kath Walker, for instance, not only wrote poems of protest but also led a campaign for full citizenship rights for Aboriginal people. In a very short time the intellectual climate shifted from dismissal of Aboriginal culture to extolling its richness and thence to condemning the exploitation of Aboriginal traditions by anyone not born to them.

And, indeed, Aboriginal ideas of the sacred have all too often been invoked by people who have no notion either of the discipline that traditionally accompanies the myths or of the historical forces that have repeatedly threatened their transmission. Joseph Campbell and other myth popularizers have made the Dreamtime a byword among pop psychologists and New Age religionists. One literary equivalent of such New Age religious tourism is the transforming of Aboriginal myths into fantasy stories with white protagonists (Charles Hulley's 1994 novel *The Fire Crystal* is a blatant example). Another is the use of Aboriginal characters as mystical commentators on technological societies. The 1983 film *The Right Stuff*, for instance, cuts away from its high-tech settings to show an astronaut helping to set up tracking sites in Western Australia, where he meets a group of Aboriginal men who find nothing odd in the notion of flying out into space: "See that old bloke there? He know. He know the moon. He know the star, an' he know the Milky Way. He'll give you a hand, he know" (quoted in Muecke 2). And, sure enough, later in the story, an Aboriginal ceremony provides magical sparks that help protect John Glenn's space capsule. As Stephen Muecke points out, the script uses "Aboriginality [as] a representation or emblem of 'the primitive'—[to] set up against space travel as the ultimate achievement of Western modernity" (2).

Simply condemning all such references to Aboriginal beliefs by outsiders as inauthentic does not allow readers to distinguish between cultural appropriation and cross-cultural communication. Criticisms of Dowling's work fail to note how differently he constructs the relationship between the traditional and the modern. In the Tyson stories, mysticism is not separated from scientific knowledge. Either worldview, or both in conjunction, can be found among characters of any race. As Dowling's series developed, culminating in *Rynemonn* (2007), he worked very hard to create an alternative vision of racial and tribal identities, to provide a genuinely new concept to go with the estranged term, but it is not an easy task for an outsider to imagine a new form of selfhood for a group that has been so strongly Othered. Most white Australian writers have simply chosen to avoid such controversy. Grai Hughes's alien-artifact story "Twenty-First Century Dreamtime" first appeared in a fanzine in 1989 and was popular enough to reprint in the professional magazine *Aurealis*. There, however, the editor commented that "the author had intended to expand the story to novella length, but in his research discovered that aspects of the extended version would offend certain taboos of the Aboriginal people" (Strasser 4). Instead of a contact zone, science fiction was in danger of becoming a no-contact zone.

One way to keep lines of communication open is to address the difficulty directly. SF writer Rosaleen Love deals with the problem of writing across cultural and racial lines by focusing on the fallibility of the human sciences. Her story "Trickster"(1993) starts out looking like a problem story using paleontology to solve a fossil riddle but turns out to be about the unknowability of other people's pasts. An ancient skull found near Melbourne defies categorization, even to the extent of shifting its form:

> At night in the skull room the bones rearrange themselves, a little, not much. The indentations in the skull from Cow Swamp deepen. The orbital ridges thicken. Scratches in the teeth enamel sink in, just a fraction.
>
> Soon there will be a new theory of the origins of the human race.
>
> The workers in the skull room assume the bones remain the same and it is their theories which change. But that is not the case.
>
> The bones know. It amuses them. (159)

Love's story goes about as far as one can go in refusing to claim ownership of the cultural Other, and it manages to do so in a witty and thought-provoking way. It reminds us that contact often involves not only dialogue but also "miscommunication, frustration, and even mutual incomprehensibility" (Bechtel, e-mail). Its silence invites others to speak, to open up a contact zone of the sort represented by Sam Watson's *The Kadaitcha Sung* (1990) and Archie Weller's *Land of the Golden Clouds* (1998). These two novels might be said to alter the meaning of earlier texts, such as Terry Dowling's early Tom Tyson stories, just as Rosaleen Love's trickster skull retroactively changes the origins of the human race.

The Kadaitcha Sung contains a heady mix of storytelling tropes that led reviewers to label it variously as science fiction, myth, horror, fantasy, and magic realism (Watson, "I Say" 591). The novel compresses the whole history of white-Aboriginal relations into the family story of the creator god Biamee, his twin sons Booka and Koobara, and his present-day descendent Tommy Gubba. Tommy is a half-white, urban social worker, but he is also a supernatural hero who talks to spirits, makes himself invisible, and goes in quest of the powerful stone that is the heart of the Rainbow Serpent. Initiated as a Kadaitcha, or tribal enforcer/shaman, he must maintain his double identity and function in both worlds, magical and mundane, in order to defeat the evil Booka, who has possessed the body of a white politician. Tommy's clan is the Biri, but he has to reach outside his own family connections and traditions in order to achieve his quest. His initiation takes place in a cave in sacred Uluru, half a continent away from his home (and well outside the traditional stewardship of either Tommy's tribe or Sam Watson's). Beating Booka at his own magical game requires assembling allies among Aborigines, whites, and spirits and also acquiring an amulet brought from Africa by his white girlfriend's parents—it requires, in other words, all the resources of his own culture and an infusion from other cultures as well. Tommy's final triumph comes only after a great deal of violence (including sexual violence) and at great emotional expense. Though offered privileges "beyond price" by Biamee (251), he forfeits his reward and his life when he chooses to disobey tribal law and let a member of another clan go unpunished for her clan's past treachery. Instead of killing Jelda, a young woman of the black possum people, as he is instructed, Tommy sends her away from Brisbane bearing his child. For this disobedience, he must die, but he was already doomed because the Kadaitcha tradition he represents is too wild, too powerful, and too violent to live on in the new social reality of the Aboriginal people.

The Kadaitcha Sung startled many readers when it first appeared. It did not fit into the accepted forms of discourse for Aboriginal writers—it was not a retold folktale or a tragic autobiography or a piece of mystical wisdom. Even a commentator as knowledgeable as Stephen Muecke, collaborator on and editor of many Aboriginal texts, found the book "virtually unreadable" (Gelder and Jacobs 108)—much as the Spanish found Guaman Poma's Quecha-inflected history in Pratt's account. Yet what Watson was doing in the novel was what another novelist and essayist, Mudrooroo Narogin, said Aboriginal writers should do: "The Aboriginal writer is a Janus-type figure with one face turned to the past and the other to the future while existing in a postmodern, multicultural Australia in which he or she must fight for cultural space" (24). Turning to the past is acceptable; staking a claim to the future by using modes such as SF is more controversial. Watson's book functions within the contact zone of European-style fantastic fiction. It also reasserts the points of contact between urban Aborigines and those who live more traditional lives. As Watson reminds us:

> white economists and white administrators have tried to separate the so-called true Aboriginal person, the so-called full-blooded tribal person, who

is essentially a hunter-gatherer, from the urban blacks who were agitating
for such bullshit things as land rights and that sort of thing. I wanted to re-
dress that and say, not only to white Australia but also for my own brothers
and sisters, that even though we live in a land of concrete and bitumen, and
even though we speak in the language of the conqueror, wear the clothes of
the conqueror, deal in the currency of the conqueror and essentially earn a
living within the camp of the conqueror, we are still very much a tribalized,
fully cultural people and we still have, even through that boundary of concrete and bitumen, we still have a very strong link to the land. So I constructed a story about the Kadaitcha figure within traditional Australia.
(Watson, "I Say" 590)

The Kadaitcha Sung functions within the contact zone of genre fiction; it is
itself an arena for negotiation among different traditions of narrative and characterization; and its central figure Tommy Gubba, whose name, occupation,
and mixed blood all represent cultural interactions, asserts the continuity of
Aboriginal tradition within modern urban Australia.

An article in the *The MUP Encyclopaedia of Australian Science Fiction and
Fantasy* acknowledges Watson's originality: "There are many wonderful books,
most of them for young readers, with elements of Creation stories in them.
But only one book so far by an Aboriginal author delves into the fantasy range;
this is *The Kadaitcha Sung* by Sam Watson [. . .]" (Weller, "Indigenous Mythology" 97). The author of this article, Archie Weller, has himself written
a novel that straddles the line between fantasy and science fiction. Weller
was acclaimed as an Aboriginal writer of distinction for his realist novel *The
Day of the Dog* (1981), but he has also had his claims to Aboriginal ancestry
challenged. Similar questions have been raised about the racial identity of
Mudrooroo Narogin and a number of other writers identified as Aboriginal.
Rather than scrutinizing writers' family trees, we might note the significance
of the fact that Australians of mixed or unknown race would self-identify with
the most visible and most oppressed racial Other. In the *MUP Encyclopaedia*
article, Weller seems not to be numbering himself among Aboriginal writers,
simply pointing out that "A novel by Archie Weller, *The Land of the Golden
Clouds* (Allen & Unwin 1998), has two Nyoongah, or Southwest Aboriginal
characters, among those who go on a quest in an Australia three thousand
years in the future" (97).

What Weller does in his futuristic setting is to offer a broad range of racial
and cultural possibilities. His questing characters interact with several groups:
pale city-dwellers who rule by psychic powers, even paler Nightstalkers who
live in caves and prey on the above-ground races, Gypsies moving within and
between different groups, Caribbean visitors who have preserved a higher
level of technology than any of the Australians, and even a society whose religion is based on the game of cricket. The central characters Red Mond Star

Light and his kin, though, represent perhaps the most interesting version of racial identity. They belong to a tribe of hunter-gatherers of mixed descent, but mostly European, called the Ilkari. Their myths and rituals reflect the influence of their Aboriginal neighbors, whom they call the Keepers of the Trees. Some of them have Aboriginal ancestry: "Sometimes, though it was strictly forbidden by the Keepers' laws, an Ilkari woman would give herself to one of the Keeper men and thus there were Ilkari who had a Keeper ancestor. But never would a dark Keeper woman give herself to a white man. Their race was much too pure and regal for that" (5).

In the post-Holocaust world of the novel, dark skin is both a mark of honor and a survival advantage: many of the Ilkari suffer from skin cancer because of exposure to the sun. The palest people are also the least trusted: the cave-dwelling Nightstalkers. In the course of the story, many cultural boundaries are breached. Red Mond shelters and falls in love with a Nightstalker woman, and one of the Keeper warriors falls in love with a Caribbean visitor. Like Sam Watson's Kadaitcha warrior, the Ilkari not only draw on indigenous Australian traditions but also ally themselves with other non-European powers. Red Mond and his fellow wayfarers survive by pooling several sorts of knowledge: forgotten technology, traditional stories, and newly developed psychic abilities. As they travel, they shake up the societies with which they interact, giving a boost to dissident factions within each. By the end, a relatively stable but fragmented world is giving way to a new cultural dynamic that may result in a new and less destructive civilization.

Weller offers two different visions of Aboriginal futures. On the one hand, the Keepers of the Trees remain apart, preserving the myths and disciplines of nomadic life that have kept their ancestors alive for millennia. On the other hand, descendants of Aboriginal people and the stories those descendants tell provide the basis for a new hybrid humanity. Neither cultural pattern is marked within the narrative as the right or only way to be Aboriginal. Weller and Watson are able to use SF and fantasy to explore and reinvent Aboriginality not in spite of but because of those genres' racist origins. A storytelling form that has been used to depict racial and cultural interactions, even in the most outrageously biased fashion, can be redirected to present other points of view. Once the Other has been invoked, there is no way to post "Keep Out" signs on the genre. It has become a contact zone, as becomes evident when one reads *The Kadaitcha Sung* and *Land of the Golden Clouds* alongside Dowling's most recent Tom Tyson stories. Even the earlier Tyson stories change their meaning when they are read with Watson's and Weller's novels. No longer do they bear the burden of speaking for Aboriginal points of view, if they ever did so. Instead, they can be about what it might be like to live among Aboriginal neighbors in a radically altered future, one in which science and myth go hand in hand and white Australians must reinvent themselves, with the help of those neighbors, after bringing on ecological and other disasters.

In the first collection, *Rynosseros*, Tyson was a hero in the H. Rider Haggard romance tradition: the white colonial who acquires power from native peoples and finds a love interest hidden among them but not one of them—another pagan princess. He was opposed by Aboriginal Kurdaitcha men (an alternative spelling of Watson's Kadaitcha) who resented his acquisition of a tribal ship and tribal spiritual gifts. More recent stories, though, have changed the impression of who Tyson is and what might be at stake in his search for his own identity. Tyson, it seems, may be an artificial creation made by the Aboriginal Clever Men as part of their own exploration of life and spirituality. He, like various artificial intelligences he meets in his adventures, is a product of their superior technical ability, and his frequent frustrations have more to do with differing scientific goals among Aboriginal factions than with any personal vendetta.

Tyson does not acquire power from the Aborigines but rather is allowed by them to make his own discoveries to supplement their own—so long as he abides by their social rules. What he discovers has do with his own origins, with the land itself, with hidden forces and intelligences at work in that land, and with the organizing of all those factors into myth-like narratives. His is a quest for pattern, and his dispatchers on that quest are the Aborigines, "as changed, changing and changeless as they now are, who have always had the soul-map of the songlines to keep intact this vital, pivotal connection between self and place, reality and dream, identity and the infinite, are caught between amusement and grudging approval at this growing habit among Nationals" (*Rynemonn* 6). The patterns he finds have to do with three images that were planted in his unconscious by his Aboriginal creators: a star, a woman's face, and a ship. Each of these seems to have had a purpose that events in Tyson's life have redirected. His own personal archetypes, these images signal many things, some of them contradictory. It is up to Tyson, finally, to decide what story they will combine to form, which will be the story of his life.

And it is up to other writers, Aboriginal and "National," to decide what to make of the contact zone that is fantastic fiction. The zone has been broadened repeatedly by Dowling, Love, Weller, Watson, and others. By writing in genres such as fantasy and SF, Aboriginal writers remind us that they too participate in contemporary world culture and have a claim on all forms of literary discourse. For non-Aboriginal writers, working within science fantasy may be less perilous than attempting to describe the Aboriginal past and present from an outsider's perspective, for such attempts all too often come across as "patronising, misconstrued, preconceived, and abused" (Jackie Huggins, quoted in Heiss 198). Within the zone of SF, abuse and misconstruction may continue, but there is no excuse to carry preconceptions over into the future. Dowling's complex future is best read not as an appropriation of Aboriginal themes but as an invitation to other writers, especially Aboriginal writers, to take part in a dialogue about possible futures and new ways of being human. One of the most important functions of science fantasy such as Dowling's and Weller's is to show us our own preconceptions and offer ways to bypass them.

Giving Up Authenticity for Contact

In the postcolonial world, only those who deliberately ignore the existence of mythic traditions other than their own can assert, as fundamentalists of all faiths do, that theirs is the sole path to the sacred. A cognitive majority generally seeks to impose its way of understanding the world on minorities and outsiders, or at least to hush them up—hence the efforts of Christian commentators to make fantasy literature forswear all "pagan" myths and to enforce a particular interpretation and use of Christian ones. Writers of fantasy who wish to speak for other cognitive and mythic traditions have the opposite problem. For an indigenous culture struggling to maintain its identity in the face of the many mechanisms of colonization—including economic, cultural, and religious sanctions—the complex task is to remind outsiders of its heritage and its ongoing vitality without giving away the things that properly belong to the group.

Different placements within power structures create different interpretive challenges. For the fantasist who works within Christian traditions but does not subscribe to a fundamentalist ideology, the challenge is to broaden the mythic base and to shake up orthodox interpretations. For Native American or Aboriginal Australian fantasists, or for writers who move from one cognitive world to another, there is no sole truth, no singleness of any kind. Such writers are learning to redirect cultural forms such as genres and to make them carry multiple messages. In the end, these tasks are not so different. The end product in both cases is a new kind of fantasy, one that asks readers to appreciate cognitive and narrative complexity, to find their own resolutions to spiritual issues without falling back on received interpretations. Contemporary mythic fantasy can learn from Hopkinson and Ghosh and Silko and Watson, as well as Tolkien and Lewis. At its best, it incorporates all kinds of "post-ness": postcolonial, post-Christian (in the sense of that it functions in a world of many belief systems), post-human, postmodern. In order to do that, it must create narrative structures that reflect all these sorts of disruptions and doublings. The next chapter takes up some of the fantastic narratives that call particular attention to our inescapably postmodern condition.

Coyote's Eyes: Situated Fantasy

I. Seeing

Ursula K. Le Guin's story "Buffalo Gals" tells of a young girl who survives the crash of a small airplane in the Western desert. The girl, Myra, is alone; the pilot is dead, and one of her eyes is injured, gone. She wakes to find a coyote looking at her, seemingly ordinary though "a big one, in good condition, its coat silvery and thick" (17). But the coyote also speaks: "There was a burned place in the sky, up there alongside the rimrock," she tells Myra, "and then you fell out of it" (17). A couple of pages later, the coyote looks entirely different:

> She saw a tawny skinned woman kneeling by a campfire, sprinkling something into a conical pot [. . .] The woman's hair was yellow and grey, bound back with a string. Her feet were bare. The upturned soles looked as dark and hard as shoe soles, but the arch of the foot was high, and the toes made two neat curving rows. She wore bluejeans and an old white shirt. (20)

Her rescuer is no longer a coyote but Coyote. Coyote knows about missing eyes. At their first meeting, she tells Myra about her own experience of throwing her eyes up into a tree and then whistling to call them back, "But that goddam bluejay stole them, and when I whistled nothing came. So I had to stick lumps of pine pitch into my head so I could see anything" (18). Eventually Myra too gets an eye made of pitch. Jay makes it for her, but the story is Coyote's, so it is really Coyote's eye. With two eyes, Myra regains depth perception: "if she shut the hurting eye and looked with the other, everything was clear and flat; if she used them both, things were blurry and yellowish, but deep" (28).

It takes Myra a while to acquire a second eye, but the narrator employs two from the beginning of the story. The furred coyote seen through one eye is the wise, foolish, barefoot Coyote seen through the other. Her animal lair is also "a ramshackle cabin on the high edge of town" with a crooked sign over the door that says "BIDE-A-WEE" (30). (Coyote is wise but not tasteful.) Coyote's friends are Jay, Jackrabbit, Young Owl, Doe. They dress and live, though the narrator never tells us so explicitly, somewhat like contemporary Native Americans. They dwell lightly on the land, making impermanent and permeable homes and eating what is at hand. Though they have few belongings, they share a strong sense of hospitality, extending even to alien Myra. Their rituals emerge from daily life: the dancing ceremony that heals Myra's eye starts out seeming like a neighborhood party. Versions of Coyote's eye-juggling story are told by Klamath, Paiute, and Navajo narrators, among others (Jones and Ramsey 121–122, Toelken 125–128).[1]

Coyote explains that there are two kinds of people, but the two kinds are not humans and animals but rather the "First People" and newer residents. The latter are "The others. The new people. The ones who came" and messed things up even more than Coyote at her most foolish (32). Since their arrival there have been holes in the world, and Myra is finally taken by Horse (a relative newcomer himself) to one of these. At first she strains to see, and then, though "she felt as if her left eye were not seeing at all" (40), she makes out a blurred streak:

> Something moved there—"It's cattle!" she said. Horse stood silent, uneasy. Chickadee was coming back towards them.
>
> "It's a ranch," the child said. "That's a fence. There's a lot of Herefords." The words tasted like iron, like salt in her mouth. The things she named wavered in her sight and faded, leaving nothing—a hole in the world, a burned place like a cigarette burn. (40).

The narrator sees both sides of the barrier and has words—"iron," "cigarette"— to describe the other side. Coyote also sees and can enter into the burned places. Tricksters can cross all barriers, although they usually pay for the privilege. Coyote steals a salmon from the New People that turns out to be poisoned bait. She dies painfully, but, as Grandmother Spider tells Myra before sending her home across the barrier, "Oh, don't worry about Coyote! [. . .] She gets killed all the time" (50).

"Buffalo Gals" is many kinds of story at once: a fairy captivity narrative (a common motif in such stories is the touch of fairy ointment in one eye that allows the captive to see through illusion), an Indian adoption story, a parable about history, a beast fable, and a story about myth. It is also a fictional memorate: imaginary Myra's account of coming into contact with the sacred beings of Native American myth. What holds all these disparate kinds of narrative together is the metaphor of seeing. As Coyote says, in answer to Myra's question about where there might be "people like me, humans": "Resemblance is in the eye" (31). One eye sees animals, the other people; both together see something like truth.

This sort of three-dimensional vision corresponds to what Donna Haraway calls "situated knowledge."[2] Haraway is talking about science here, staking out a middle position between a disembodied and ethically neutral empiricism and a social-constructivist view of knowledge that acknowledges responsibility but leaves us with no sort of objective truth. The goal is to "have *simultaneously* an account of radical historical contingency for all knowledge claims and knowing subjects, a critical practice for recognizing our own 'semiotic technologies' for making meanings, *and* a no-nonsense commitment to faithful accounts of a 'real world' [. . .]" (187). However, science is not the only knowledge system that could benefit from such a middle ground. History too searches for truth but inevitably sees that truth from a limited and culturally determined perspective. So does myth. What one sees is determined by one's culture, but one need not be constrained to a single cultural system: it is possible to look simultaneously through one's own natural eye and through Coyote's eye.

II. Saying

Haraway arrives at this model of situated science via feminism, which questions the notion of a disembodied (i.e., in practice, male-bodied) intelligence: "Feminists don't need a doctrine of objectivity that promises transcendence, a story that loses track of its mediations just where someone might be held responsible for something, and unlimited instrumental power" (187). She suggests that one of its benefits is the ability to speak across cultural barriers: "the ability partially to translate knowledge among very different—and power-differentiated—communities" (187). Both of these statements address the relationship of knowledge to power. Le Guin's story touches lightly on issues of power and its abuse, but she provides a more explicit rendering of that theme in a scene from her 1985 novel *Always Coming Home*. That novel is usually grouped with utopian, rather than fantastic, fictions, but one of Le Guin's aims in writing it was to bring utopia back to its mythic origins, to erase the line dividing the rational utopia from the mythic Golden Age, which is, as she points out, "on all the evidence of myth and mysticism, and the assurance of every participatory religion [. . .] to those with the gift or discipline to perceive it, right here, right now" ("Non-Euclidean" 81). The difference between the Golden Age and the dystopian present is a matter of perspective and will: the ability to see what the natural world offers and the will to turn away from destruction. *Always Coming Home* takes place in a postcatastrophic future, among people who have taken up a way of life similar to most preindustrial societies around the world: small communities, sustainable agriculture combined with hunting and gathering, considerable leisure, appropriate and largely handmade technology (but with a railroad and a computer system), and lives enriched by oral literature and guided by daily and seasonal rituals. The fictional society resembles that of the animal people in "Buffalo Gals" because both have the same model: the Indian tribes of the Pacific coast and the inland West.

Whereas in "Buffalo Gals" two realities are depicted as being seen through different eyes, in *Always Coming Home* the two ways of existing are more like modes of speech. Both stories rely on female mediators: just as Myra, the focalizing character, crosses over from the world of ranches and airplanes to that of talking animals and gods, the narrator of *Always Coming Home*, who calls herself Pandora, is able to move between present-day northern California and a postcatastrophic utopia. Pandora speaks of this forward projection as "an archaeology of the future" (3); it involves close study of the landscape, science fictional extrapolation, desire for a better way of life, guilt over present and past devastation, and a sort of cultural triangulation among ethnological descriptions of similar societies around the world. One thing it does not include is direct access to the pre-Columbian societies of the same coastal region. Some early readers of the novel thought it a nostalgic exercise in reconstruction: a sort of imaginary vacation among the early California Indians. However, Le Guin forestalls that reading early on by letting us know that no such cultural tourism is possible. The people who once actually lived, rather than "might be going to have lived" (*Always Coming Home*, xi) in her Valley of the Na, were wiped out by white settlers. "One may listen," says Pandora, "but all the words of their language are gone, gone utterly" (4).[3] She says the same thing more strongly in a 1988 address to the Mythopoeic Society:

> The people who live in the Valley now, in the 20th century, I know well enough: they are my own people. I wanted to know also about the humans who used to live there, the ones the Spanish called the Brave, the Wappo; I wanted to learn how they lived there, how they were part of that patterns of springs, rocks, trees, animals, and all the other kinds of people. And what they thought, what they said, what songs they sang. — But there was nothing to learn. Nothing to hear. Nothing to know. Not one song. Not one word.
>
> "What did she carry? What did she wear?"
>
> Genocide is a terrible word, which we use freely. What about murder of the word—of a culture—of what makes us human? We don't talk about that, or we call it progress and the pioneer spirit, this desertification of human versatility, variety, and beauty.
>
> The people who lived in the Valley are silent, now and forever. We did not listen to them. We—my people—killed them without hearing one word they said. (10)

Power, unequally distributed and terribly misused, has blocked cross-cultural communication of the sort Haraway values and Le Guin seeks to recreate. There is no going back, only forward.

Yet *Always Coming Home* is in every detail a three-way conversation among past, present, and future, with one voice eloquent in its silence. To describe it in the visual terms of "Buffalo Gals," one would have to invoke a third eye, perhaps a mystical third eye as in some Hindu traditions. With three eyes, one can see not merely three but four dimensions, the fourth being, of course, time. In one section of the novel, called "Time and the City," Pandora recounts two stories that represent the way her future people, the Kesh, look back at our time. One is a mythologized history of the advent of a terrible being called Little Man, who cuts down trees, poisons water, and flattens mountains to make room for himself and his myriad copies. Little Man's destruction is only halted when a few human people ask Coyote for help, and:

> Coyote came. Where she walked she made the wilderness. She dug canyons, she shat mountains. Under the buzzard's wings, the forest grew. Where the worm was in the dirt, the spring ran. Things went on, people went on. Only Little Man didn't go on. He was dead. He died of fear. (159)

This version of Coyote is close kin to the trickster-helper from "Buffalo Gals," only instead of being killed by the New People, she undoes their damage. Also linked to the "Buffalo Gals" is the second vision of the time of civilization. In the section of the novel titled"A Hole in the Air," an unlucky man of the Kesh finds a gap like the one through which Myra sees the ranch. He goes through to find a road, on which "a four-wheeled motor hit him at great speed and went over him and went on" (154). Because he is only partly in this world, he is able to get up and go on to find houses full of "backward-head people" along with their electrical noise and toxic food (155–156). Returning via another death to his own time, he recounts what he has seen and then expires again, but this time, "he died wholly. He died of grief and poison" (157). Unlike the child Myra, who is given special dispensation to pass between the worlds without harm (and with the boon of a new eye), the adult visitor to our time is given nothing but terror and pain.

This bleak tale stands out as exceptional within a mostly hopeful extrapolation of future possibilities, but the form of this novel allows for many contraries and paradoxes. Fragmented, experimental, visionary, multigeneric (including poems, songs, drawings, recipes, dramatic scenes, and oral and written tales from the Kesh), metafictional, open-ended, and encyclopedic (literally so, in the section called "The Back of the Book"), *Always Coming Home* is a major work of postmodern fiction, although Le Guin is not usually listed among the usual postmodern suspects. One reason that the book is not read as the postmodern achievement it is might be Le Guin's reputation as a writer of integrative stories rather than disruptive and ironic ones, a reputation that she has earned by utilizing the romance conventions of fantasy and science fiction. The darker elements in her work are nearly always counterpointed by utopian impulses, as the devastation of the backward-head people is countered by the quiet endurance of the Kesh and the wily inventiveness of Coyote. In much of her fiction, myth becomes a critical tool, as it is here. That critical function extends even to the narrator's mythic name, which invokes the ambiguous legacy of Western civilization: Pandora the booby-trapped gift of the gods, the bringer of ills and hope, the spouse of Epimetheus or Hindsight. Le Guin recasts Pandora from victim to trickster, ally of the Native American Coyote. Her version of Pandora also suggests other mythic allusions: she is Cassandra, who warns without being heeded, and Sybil, speaking for the dead. Linguistic anthropologist M. J. Hardman identifies a central technique in *Always Coming Home* as denaturalizing assumptions built into our language and culture, what she calls Linguistics Postulates. Le Guin, she says, allows readers to "become participants in a culture where the postulates are the unity of all living beings, where number is not an issue, where competition and violence is for children, and where the Linguistics Postulates of their own language are not used, but rather English is used beautifully and creatively to step aside from such structures and create others" (54). Fantastic mythmaking is one of the tools for making such postulates visible and thereby calling them into question.

Though *Always Coming Home* demonstrates many of the formal characteristics of postmodern literature, such as metafictional frame breaking, "Buffalo Gals" mostly sticks to straightforward storytelling, although Coyote lobs a few remarks to the reader over Myra's head. Both stories construct and maintain alternative points of view reflecting different mythic and linguistic systems; both depict truth as something situated in the viewer's identity and culture. As I have argued elsewhere, much contemporary fantasy shares with postmodernism its skepticism about totalizing systems of thought and narrative constructions of reality, but fantasy has other means of depicting the breakdown of such cultural masterplots (*Strategies* 46). It does so at the level of story rather than discourse. Instead of unreliable storytellers, it offers unlocatable worlds. Where a postmodern novel might deliberately withhold narrative closure, a fantasy can provide such closure and yet leave it on the other side of an impenetrable barrier. The happy ending takes place in another reality or on another psychic dimension, as in Garner's *The Owl Service*. The very romance structure that sends a hero through a portal to achieve a quest (Mendlesohn 1) can double as a metafictional critique of heroic hierarchies and colonializing quests. Often the only boon the hero attains is the experience of having been through the portal and seen through the hole in the world: the hero returns, as Myra does, wearing one of Coyote's eyes.

Haraway alerts us to the significance of technologies of seeing: the many kinds of scope (tele-, micro-, etc.) that allow us to peer at the universe. She reminds us that "all eyes, including our own organic ones, are active perceptual systems, building in translations and specific ways of seeing, that is, ways of life" (190). The eye constructs its object. It turns the thing it looks at *into* an object, and that is an exercise not only in perception but also in power: "Vision is always a question of the power to see—and perhaps of the violence implicit in our visualizing practices. With whose blood were my eyes crafted?" (192). Her suggestion is for a science that acknowledges its own complicity and privilege—which could well be an eye made of pitch rather than one crafted from someone else's blood. Such a science emulates myth: "the myth not of what escapes human agency and responsibility in a realm above the fray, but rather of accountability and responsibility for translations and solidarities linking the cacophonous visions and visionary voices that characterize the knowledges of the subjugated" (196).

In Le Guin's fiction, myth also emulates science. The traditional narratives of the Kesh are empirically validated and precisely calibrated to their way of life. They claim no universal applicability, no truth beyond what can be observed here and now. The nearest thing to outright villainy in the novel is the attempt by a neighboring people, the Condor, to impose their own systems of governance and meaning upon the Kesh. As soon as the Condor mythos becomes grounds for invasion, it becomes false, because the thing that made it true—its rootedness in the lives of its people—is gone. It is no longer situated.

These stories by Le Guin demonstrate two of the forms of what we can call situated myth. One employs science fictional and metafictional techniques to create multiple perspectives; the other brings different ways of seeing into its plot, drawing on traditional motifs from fairy tale and legend, such as the enchanted eye. A number of other contemporary writers have similarly combined romance forms with postmodern techniques to produce fantasies of framed or situated myth. Many of these, writers as diverse as John Crowley, Michael Bishop, Elizabeth Hand, Karen Joy Fowler, China Miéville, Kim Stanley Robinson, Delia Sherman, Neil Gaiman, Michael Chabon, Andrea Hairston, and Kelly Link, have been directly influenced or inspired by Le Guin's example. However, Le Guin is not the only model for the situated fantastic; she stands alongside other genre-blending codiscoverers such as Jorge Luis Borges, Angela Carter, Italo Calvino, Alan Garner, Samuel Delany, and Gene Wolfe in making fantasy into a powerful critical and epistemological tool.

What these writers all have in common is the use of narrative structures that mimic the disjunction of two or more worldviews. In their fiction, different mythic systems meet and clash. Each demonstrates an awareness of the incompleteness of any one source of vision and the inability of any one writer to claim complete ownership even of his or her own mythic traditions. Much the same could be claimed of the postcolonial fantasists discussed in the previous chapter, and indeed there is considerable interaction and overlap between the two groups. Writers of situated fantasy share with postcolonial fantasists an awareness of power imbalances and past and present injustices. Postcolonial fantasy, like situated fantasy, is always framed within a discourse of the Other—it is always a contact zone. The nature of that zone differs, however, according to the direction from which one enters it. It can be a way of laying claim to a more privileged cultural position, or it can be a way of re-nouncing that privilege, of relinquishing the role of supposedly neutral ob-server and arbiter.

III. Knowing

Where Le Guin emphasizes seeing and saying, other situated fantasies inter-rogate interpretation: the active processes of reading and listening to stories. Jeanne Larsen's Chinese historical fantasy *Silk Road* (1989) offers a scene well along in the story in which the main characters cross a marketplace. On the other side of the square they notice a barbarian storyteller:

> a remarkably tall woman, her hair the color of dirty copper, [who] spun some wild tale for a crowd of yokels come into town for the day. As we passed, I noticed that her skin was virtually colorless; its freakish pallor re-vealed the blue web of a storyteller's forking veins [. . . .] (205)

They decide this figure is of no importance to their quest and pass on. Yet the attentive reader might note that the red-haired storyteller is one of the author's many appearances in the novel. She also appears as a pedantic scholar, author of *The Thousand Insect Classic,* named Jin Luo-Sun—a phonetic rendering of "Jeanne Larsen" (165); as a chronicler named Lan Jen-Yi (93); as Ji Ni-Lu, the seventh-century author of a compendium of women's erotic secrets, as well as the translator of that text, Lars Jensen (118); as the author of some of the first deliberate fictions, or "Esoteric Transmitted Records of the Bizarre," within Chi-nese culture, one Lha Er-Sun (182–187); and as compiler of tales named Mi Tu (381). These appearances are not mere postmodern jokes, winks to the audience. Rather they are reminders that the world we are reading about is a look through alien eyes and an interpretation into an alien tongue. They acknowledge that the world of eighth-century China, or Great Tang, is gone, represented now only by mute objects and textual fragments, some of which may be forgeries:

> The above is a selection from a spurious scroll sold to that remarkable figure (explorer, imperialist, archaeologist, thief, as you will) Sir M. Aurel Stein. Purportedly a relic of one of the cave libraries at Dun-huang, the text has now been discovered to be a pastiche based chiefly on a corrupt version of the splendid eighteenth-century collectaneus, the *Gu-jin tu-shu ji-cheng.* (*Silk Road* 167)

Even contemporary Chinese scholars and translators have to fill in temporal and cultural gaps, and the North American novelist must draw on their reconstruc-tions to mediate between her readers' world and the storied reality in which her characters speak and act and suffer. It is precisely a storied reality: to bring the world to fictional life, Larsen must revive its beliefs and the mythic narratives through which those beliefs are transmitted. Alongside the human characters are ghosts, dragons, and various higher and lower deities from a number of traditions: Confucian, Buddhist, Taoist, and rural folk practice. Because of their presence, Larsen's China, unlike many such fictional reconstructions, is neither static nor uniform.

Furthermore, the story Larsen wishes to tell is that of a woman artist, and neither women's lives nor their forms of artistic expression are as well documented as the doings of male politicians and warriors. Like the native peoples of California whose silence fills the empty spaces in *Always Coming Home*, the wives, craftswomen, and nuns of ancient China have left little of themselves in the textual record. One group of women, however, speaks directly to us from the past: courtesan poets such as Xue Tao, on whom Larsen wrote her dissertation (Larsen, "Tale" 306). The hero of *Silk Road*, Greenpearl, also known as Parrot, becomes such a poet. But poetry, and especially courtly Chinese poetry, is an extremely high-context verbal artifact: much of its meaning is dependent on a shared knowledge of a social milieu, philosophy, and aesthetic system that outsiders can only approximate through study of nonpoetic texts and other cultural evidence. When Larsen shows how Greenpearl, stolen from her family and sold into a brothel, can find her poetic voice and take charge of her own story, she is providing a new context within which readers can make sense of poetic images and metaphoric systems modeled on—but never identical to—the work and milieu of the Tang poets.

Silk Road and its successor novels *Bronze Mirror* (1991) and *Manchu Palaces* (1996) take up different eras in Chinese history and different forms of artistic expression open to women in those eras. Filled with historical detail and metafictional play, they are stories about the past but also about interpreting—which is to say, constructing—the past. Rather than hiding the uncertainties and interpretive choices that any historian confronts, Larsen uses the devices of fantasy to show the reader how to build a world out of bits and pieces. By letting us into the novelist's workshop, she makes us partly responsible for what emerges. In one chapter, called "In the Realm of Transformations," a narrator invites the reader to participate in the making of a fiction—"*ficcioun* they'll say in English four hundred years beyond the Great Tang's fall" (333):

> Right now, in the Tang, the people say these lights are the cleanest lanterns of the foothill villagers, come to pay respects to the temple of The Enlightened One. More and more lights gather, and if the ground were crisp with snow (but it is the year's fourth month, remember?), you would hear their quiet hissing as they extinguished themselves and fell. Try to grasp one—ah, impossible. Try, then, (the monks will urge you to it; success is a sign of the heart's purity), to pull one toward you with a cedar branch. But wait. First invent a sturdy railing on the cliff's edge. And having done that, if you are certain you will pass the test, reach forward, out over the void. Draw in one of these wonders, and never mind if it is real or not. (334)

It becomes impossible to tell whether one is reading one of what the tale calls "fictive histories" (426) or "verisimilar romances" (433). Both must be constructed; neither is a straightforward representation of reality. By foregrounding the process of imaginative (re)creation, Larsen offers a corrective to too-easy assimilation of other cultures and other pasts to the narrative patterns of the contemporary Western world. Those narrative patterns include both history and popular fiction. Though, as she says, "cross-cultural literary appropriation is [. . .] inevitable" ("Tales" 309), it is possible to acknowledge one's own complicity and thereby alert readers to other such acts of appropriation and thus to their responsibilities toward the past and the cultural other. "I share the contempt," says Larsen,

> for the poorly-researched, condescending (for what's more condescending than superficial research?), stereotype-laden, anachronism-ridden, blooper-fraught, *quipao*-rippers that have constituted "China" for too many Western readers. Those very books spurred me to try to do the job better, using both primary and—my debt to other Sinologists is great—the best of secondary sources. ("Tales" 309)

However, it is not enough merely to do a better job of hiding the seams. Larsen turns the fictional garment inside out, showing the reader how it is made:

> So the trilogy includes (for aesthetic and epistemological reasons as well as political and didactic ones) careful imitations—fake translations, bald-faced forgeries—of such Chinese literary genres as the ballad, formal *shi*-poems, song-lyrics, literary tales, commonplace books, the anecdotes called "records of the fantastic," storytellers' promptbooks, memoires, and biographies. In the last book, I turn more attention to my Western predecessors, writing a British opium addict's diary of his trip to China, and the like: partly—as always—for the fun of it, but partly as a further signal that these novels can, after all, be placed in a long tradition of travelers' self-interested, ideology-riddled, altogether questionable accounts. ("Tales" 309)

Thus postmodern play and fantastic trickery can be ways of writing more responsible history, especially when that history crosses gulfs of time, space, language, and identity—and what history does not? But there is one additional kind of gulf that Larsen is interested in: her novels build imaginative bridges that simultaneously span and reveal the gaps between belief systems. By translating myths into fiction, they reveal that much of our understanding of any mythic text is likewise a fiction. The many realms of the supernatural that impinge on Tang society reflect and reveal the structures of that society; thus the Jade Emperor of Taoist belief governs a comically bureaucratic Heaven resembling the court structure of the capital city of Chang-an, whereas the Western Motherqueen rules over a monastic retreat in the mountains of Kunlun. Other deities take note of Greenpearl's adventures from the perspective of their various domains: in the sky, the Moon Goddess presides over poetic inspiration; in a terrifying underworld, Yama, the Hindu god of death (for the world of the novel includes beliefs from both ends of the Silk Road) judges souls such as that of Greenpearl's murdered nanny; Greenpearl's mother implores the Buddhist Guan-yin to take a maternal interest in her; the minor Kitchen God in Mama Chen's house, where Greenpearl is being trained as a musician and companion to wealthy men, ascends to heaven to make his annual report to the Jade Emperor and is grilled on Greenpearl's progress. The primordial dragon Nu Wa rules over all: the world and the story within which all characters, both human and divine, have their being. At the end of the story, Nu Wa, linking beginning and ending like another mythic serpent, the tail-biting Worm Ouroboros, "considers how the next tale might begin. My name is, for the moment, Parrot, she thinks. And wonders how it will all come out this time around" (434).

Larsen's novels are thus exercises in resituating knowledge, both historical knowledge and literary knowledge. Their postmodernity is part of the tale: as Greenpearl travels the Silk Road from barbarian west to settled east, and as she learns, endures, and finds companions along the way, she also learns—and shows the reader—how to interpret her own story. Early in the novel she acquires a tiny scroll covered with unreadable writing. This scroll, a secret gift from the Western Motherqueen, is another kind of silk road: "its slick silk wrenched itself from my fingers, or seemed to, and the whole length of the writing unrolled itself before me, a white road marked with black signs through the dusk of the room" (66). Greenpearl only begins to understand its message as she makes her literal and figurative journey. Greenpearl's quest is a double one. She is looking for her own voice (that is, her identity and the right to express it), and she is looking for her mother. Fulfilling the latter task requires that Greenpearl must, like any good epic hero, travel through heaven and hell and all the known world. Just before leaving the mortal world, she visits the household of a silkworm farmer, the Widow Chian, whose daughters-in-law teach Greenpearl not only the art of silkmaking but also an unusual form of writing:

> Many women south of the central Yangzi, we discovered, know a written language not used by men [. . . .] in form, the words resemble the oldest Chinese writing, not the Soghdian or Indic scripts I'd seen along the Silk Road. Spring-gauze once whispered to me that she'd heard some of them had been preserved long ago when an emperor forbade any written symbols save those he chose as standard; many of the outlawed variant forms become women's words. Even the order of the words in a sentence, and their relationships to one another, are not like the language these women speak to their menfolk every day. But perhaps I tell more than I ought. (392–393)

Such women's writing actually exists, a script called *nüshu* discovered by Western scholars only in the 1980s but in circulation among the women of

Hunan Province for perhaps a thousand years. In Larsen's novel, the scroll Greenpearl carries throughout her journey turns out to be written in women's script. Once she has learned to read it, Greenpearl can meet her mother and find a new role as the Dragon Monarch's Minister of Verisimilar Romances— in other words, as a writer of works like *Silk Road*. This is literally the case: she is commanded by the Dragon Monarch to read from the scroll, but the words have been washed away. She has no recourse except to write them herself: "'Daughter, if the Monarch commands you to read her what's written on the scroll,' Seagem continues, 'and there is nothing written on it, what must you do?'" (433). All the quests come together in the act of composition of the story we have just read, written by its protagonist in women's script on a silken scroll woven by women, a scroll which is also the road on which silk is carried from eastern China to the West. This is an elegant conclusion to an intricate, engaging, and richly poetic tale, but it is also an object lesson. Says Larsen, "I repeatedly invite readers to look askance not only at a chapter's narrator but also at the cultural and chronological outsider who wrote it" ("Tale" 315). To do so, she uses not only the resources of postmodern narrative and poststructuralist theory (there are call-outs, for those who recognize them, to Lévi-Strauss, Derrida, and Cixous) but also those of traditional storytelling, especially the many oral sources and written forms of fantasy. Fantasy becomes, because of its denial of its own truth claims, a more accurate form of history:

> My aim, then, has been to present tales uttered by wild-haired, long-armed, pale-skinned storytellers speaking with forked tongues, texts so inter-laced with pseudonyms and various winking foreign eyes, that it should become impossible to forget that the books are indeed stories and not some "real thing." Comments by the various narrators, translators, and editors, serve, I hope, as signals that the text at hand is not a perfect transcription of a world out there (for surely no text is, whatever you may tell yourself about the realness of the world), but a flawed and impure artifice, joyously recursive and— yes—possibly perverse. One that keeps glancing (*oh I know this, it's just like me, what am I to do?*) in the mirror (*see? There I go again*) to check if it (*or I*) might not be looking a tad too (*shall I say it?*) narcissistic (*perhaps if it does something different with its hair?*). ("Tale" 316).

Rereading *Silk Road* two decades after its first appearance, I do not find it easy to remember how experimental it once seemed: we now live in a world where Lyotard's master narratives are routinely disrupted and Baudrillardian simulacra are old friends. Now what stands out in the novel is its vividly imagined setting and emotional truth: we care about Greenpearl and her friends, and we find their world all the more convincing for its conditionality and fantastic exuberance. The novel stands alongside *Always Coming Home* and such other late-twentieth-century metafantasies as Samuel R. Delany's *Tales of Neverÿon* (1979), Angela Carter's *Nights at the Circus* (1984), Robert Holdstock's *Mythago Wood* (1984), John Crowley's *Ægypt* (1987; revised and retitled *The Solitudes*, 2007), and Geoff Ryman's *Was* (1992) as a groundbreaking and deeply satisfying work—but also as a product of its era. It is not a coincidence that all these works appeared in or around the 1980s, which critic Brian McHale identifies, retrospectively, as "the peak decade of postmodernism." The very aspects of such texts that once seemed most groundbreaking now mark them as artifacts of a specific cultural moment. If they are to survive that moment, they will have to be redefined as classics, which involves rereading in light of historical contexts, as well as subsequent textual interactions and continuing cultural relevance, as I am attempting to do here. That ongoing relevance has something to do with situated knowledge, which means that the very metafictional devices and Pynchonesque disruptions that once seemed to reveal the impossibility of knowing the universe now seem instead to point toward a more sophisticated way to understand the knowing, perceiving, and speaking self.

Nowadays metafiction is everywhere. Television series include recursive episodes in which the characters meet the actors playing their fictional analogues. Movies that are remakes of remakes incorporate bits of fan discussion about previous incarnations into the dialogue. In graphic novels such as Brian Lee O'Malley's *Scott Pilgrim* series (2004–2010), stories are embedded within stories and characters comment on their own fictionality. Picture books such as David Wiesner's *The Three Pigs* (2001) introduce very young readers to the delights of intertextuality and frame breaking (in this case, literal, as the three little pigs discover and cross the frame around the illustration, changing the outcome of their story). For older children, self-conscious fictions such as Chris Van Allsburg's *The Mysteries of Harris Burdick* (1984), Diana Wynne Jones's *The Game* (2007), and Roderick Townley's *The Great Good Thing* (2001) demand close attention and active participation from their readers by continually changing the fictional rules and withholding narrative closure. Though none of this is unique to the postmodern era, its ubiquity from the 1980s onward does suggest a contemporary fascination with the mechanisms of the fantastic imagination and a worry about the constructedness of reality.

All this metafiction makes it nearly impossible to read *any* tale without seeing the half-transformed sources, the untold backstories, the sleight-of-hand diversions that produce both realism and fantasy. Every story becomes its own metacommentary, every text an interactive and unbounded hypertext. As audiences are educated in postmodernity, the need for individual texts to deconstruct themselves grows less urgent: we have already been there and undone that. Granted the indeterminacy and self-reflexivity and ideological complicity of every text, what cultural work should contemporary fantasy seek to accomplish?

IV. Owning Up

The other function of Haraway's situated knowledge, besides acknowledging its own limitations and location within specific identities and cultural positions, is to take responsibility for what it knows and what it does with that knowledge. A situated science is an accountable science. The same is true of other forms of knowledge, including history and myth. A strong sense of responsibility toward the things one knows pervades Le Guin's work and emerges gradually in Larsen's. Both incur accountability by emphasizing myth's surroundings; locating the mythic pattern in past history in one case, future history in the other. In two other situated fantasies, Alan Garner's *Strandloper* (1996) and Molly Gloss's *Wild Life* (2000), the obligations that have always accompanied myth but that are forgotten by many fantasy writers become the central focus of the narrative.

Fantasy can allow the reader to escape, briefly, from history: that is one of its great sources of pleasure. In place of history's ambiguities and cascading changes, fantasy typically offers changelessness and clear divisions of good and evil. For those of us who live within history and who thus seek to understand the past by arranging written documents into linear narratives, fantasy reminds us that in societies without writing, time is instead shaped by myth and ritual into recurring cycles of death and renewal. The spells and transformations invoked by fantasy writers are only a small part of a complex mythic world view that challenges historical narrative tropes such as progress. Lazy and derivative fantasy neglects that challenge. Too many fantasy worlds reproduce political structures from the past—or drastically simplified models of those structures—without examining their inner workings or pointing out their inequities. At the same time, they invoke powerful mythic symbols with no notion of their human cost: the tragedy and sacrifice that make renewal possible. Garner's and Gloss's stories, however, invoke the mythic worldview in all its danger and mystery. They do so by having protagonists fall out of history into a fantastic dreamtime and then return as renewers of myth.

Both novels can be read in many ways: as studies in character, voice, history, cultural clash, and survival. Neither one looks much like fantasy. *Strandloper* retells a true story about an English farmer/bricklayer, William Buckley, transported to Australia in the beginning of the nineteenth century. In *Wild Life*, Gloss creates a character, Charlotte Bridger Drummond, who is a composite of several real women writers and places her in a carefully reconstructed turn-of-the-century Pacific Northwest. Both books deal with major historical changes. For Gloss, it is the displacement of human communities and the disruption of ecological systems by the westward movement of European Americans. For Garner, it is postindustrial class struggle in Britain, as well as the devastating effect of European colonization on the native population and cultures of Australia. Neither writer lets you forget what is at stake in the world of events even as you are swept along with the characters into another way of perceiving time, change, and humanity. Both books also function as criticism of fantasy's ways of using or abusing mythic sources.

Strandloper is organized into five sections, each corresponding to a major shift in the life of William Buckley. Each section is named for an identity he acquires along the way. First he is chosen to be Shick-Shack, or Oak-Apple Man, at the start of his village's annual fertility festival. As Shick-Shack, William must make the ritual sacrifice of swallowing a burned loaf; his sacrifice becomes more literal as he is hauled away from church ceremonies in chains for the crime of copying out sentences from a seditious text lent him by his upper-class friend Edward. During the long voyage to Australia, alliances among the convicts signal the beginnings of a new social organization. William's name in this new society is Crank Cuffin, underworld slang for "crazy fellow." Part of his craziness is his insistence that he will make his way back to England even if it means walking the whole way. He knows the direction: north to China and then turn left.

Landing on the Australian shore, William and two other convicts make a break, but only William gets past the guards. He marches toward China singing "Owd Cob and Young Cob/And Young Cob's son;/Young Cob's Owd Cob/When Owd Cob's done" (109). As he struggles on, he loses his compass, making a new one by marking a letter N on a piece of bark; loses his squeamishness by eating snails and carrion and drinking his own urine; loses his clothing in a flash fire; sheds his old identity—Owd Cob—to make way for another new self. In the longest section, William is Murrangurk of the Beingalite tribe, who believe him to be one of their own, dead and reborn (and thus white-skinned, like the dead). The historical Buckley lived among the Aborigines for more than thirty years, but accounts of his life often skip that episode, picking up the story with his reappearance in 1835, as a Crusoe-like "wild white man." For one eyewitness, "During the whole course of his residence, and amidst all his wanderings there were no interesting events [. . .]" (Wedge 167–168). For Garner, though, William's life as Murrangurk is the time when his life takes on form and meaning. Murrangurk is a visionary. He learns to weave his lifelong migraine-induced visions, bits of Cheshire folklore, and the Aboriginal tales that he inherits from his namesake into a single mythic narrative. This narrative is about change: how the coming of Europeans to Australia disrupts age-old traditions that have maintained the land and held up the sky.

When William returns to England, he becomes Strandloper, named for the plover that runs back and forth between sea and shore. He sees himself as part of the mechanism of time: "I'm sort of like a governor, making folks shape [. . .] crossing back and to; there's always summat wants fettling [. . .]" (190). To the Beingalite tribe, stones are alive; rainbows create the world; dreams prophesy; bees dance the turning of earth toward dawn. This is all magic, but it is not easy magic. To take part in it, William must lose everything he has had, and he must learn the disciplines outlined in myths. At the center of the Murrangurk section, one incident distinguishes Garner's fantasy from easier sorts of magical tourism. Garner has never been one to let his heroes off easily; in *Elidor* and *The Owl Service*, the protagonists risk madness and isolation in their quests for magical insight and beauty. But in *Strandloper*, the penalty is both simpler and devastatingly concrete. When his beloved adopted nephew violates a mythic stricture, Murrangurk must hold the boy for a killing blow:

> Brairnumin stood, and put his arms out behind him for Murrangurk to take. He bowed his head, and, with the blow of a konnung club, Bungerim smashed his skull.
>
> Murrangurk caught the body as it fell, and cradled it. (154)

This is an excruciating scene, one of many William must endure and the reader witness. His participation in the act of violence—harder than having violence inflicted on oneself—is the penalty for taking the myth in. In return, he gets no wishing ring, no enchanted sword, no crown; only a greater resolve and a glimpse of something holy. Coming back at the end of the story to the English oak where he was named Shick-Shack, he discovers that the pebbles in its hollow trunk are "blades of flint. The People had made them: Yambeetch and Warrowil. The People had known the oak. One tree was all, and all the world one Dreaming" (198).

On the surface, Molly Gloss's *Wild Life* is not much like *Strandloper*. Garner's language is bone-bare, often obscure (packed with archaic criminal argot and Cheshire dialect), and mostly dialogue, like a radio play. Gloss's language is sensible and precise, growing more elusive and poetic as her narrator-protagonist undergoes a change of perspective. Garner's hero is solitary; Gloss's is a woman embedded in obligations. William Buckley is stoic and archaic, whereas Charlotte Bridger Drummond is funny and opinionated and modern. But *Wild Life* can be retold in almost exactly the same terms as *Strandloper*. It, too, involves shifting identities, a harrowing journey, and the catching up of familiar experiences into a new and more mysterious pattern of story.

At the beginning of *Wild Life*, Charlotte is at home with her five sons. In the diary that forms the bulk of the novel, she records her reading; her opinions on progress, feminism, and popular literature; and her conversations with her sons and her housekeeper Melba. Like William, she is suddenly called away from home. Unlike him, Charlotte goes voluntarily, to look for a missing child. Melba's granddaughter has vanished from the logging camp where her son-in-law is working, and he suggests that some large two-footed creature might have carried her off.

Charlotte's journey corresponds to William's sea voyage. Traveling by ferry, rail, and footpath, she enters a different world, of smoke and stumps and looming old-growth evergreens. It is a world almost without women. Rather than changing her name, as William does, Charlotte changes her voice. From the

self-confident rebel of the opening, she transforms into the self-doubting re-
corder of somber scenes and disturbing events. Among the latter is an attempt
by a member of the search party to molest her in her tent. This incident indirectly leads to her getting separated from the group and lost in the deep woods.
She loses her way, her supplies, her boots, and her identity as a member of a
civilized society. By the end of this section, Owd Cob, or Owd Charlotte, is
gone. She is ready to meet the Others.

An exact parallel with Garner's story would have Charlotte, at this point,
being taken in by a band of Klickitat or Kwakiutl Indians. Instead, figures out
of Northwest legend gradually emerge from the forest background: a band of
giant anthropoids. Charlotte is reluctant to report what she sees. The first entry
in which she mentions them is also the last to which she can attach a tentative
date, and all she is willing to say is, "Cold. Very poor. Beasts in the shadows.
How much longer?" (178). At this point her writing alters again, losing its reasonable connectedness but recording in a vivid, unpunctuated rush the jumble
of sensory experience:

> being so afraid to go on alone and to suffer alone the cold nights so densely
> black in which my eyes strain and strain to see emptiness I must welcome
> the company even of monsters or ghosts though I don't get close but watch
> them watch for them and follow their great bare tracks (cannot be made
> by weightless phantoms but impressed deep in the moss the mud individ-
> ual toes distinct) and tonight they lie together in the crevice of a rock an
> undercut. (179)

As she follows the creatures, they gradually shift in her mind from monsters to
dumb gentle beasts to people, albeit not human people. Surviving by imitating
their browsing of plant life and insects, she moves closer and closer until she is
accepted as one of their band and begins to understand something of their
musical language. At the same time, she ceases to see their activities as mindless foraging and begins to sense purpose, tradition, and even spirituality in
their movements and utterances.

Charlotte does not live with the Sasquatches as long as Buckley does with
his tribe, nor is she inducted into an articulated set of rituals and mythic texts.
However, in the few weeks she travels with them, she does share their way of
living in an endless present. The headings of her entries change from "12 April"
to a dateless "Evening, cool" or "Morning clouds breaking through to a fair
afternoon" (187, 189). In this reckoning, time does not pass so much as recur:
every morning is the same morning reborn. Yet this time outside of time holds
powerful experiences: joy of reunion when two groups meet, tragedy when
one of the children is shot by humans, communion (in every sense of the
word) in the solemn consuming of the dead child's flesh. Like Murrangurk,
Charlotte does not so much learn the myths of her adopted people as live
them, including their sometimes painful strictures.

In the last section of the book, Charlotte is separated from her band and rescued by a party of naturalists on the slopes of Mount Saint Helens. Unlike Buckley, she still has a place among friends and family. Like him, she is altered almost beyond recognition and has a new role to play in the world. Both characters bring back the gift of story, a gift which is also a warning and a reminder of duties neglected.

Interspersed among Charlotte's diary entries are other sorts of textual fragments, including excerpts from two of her own fictional works. One of these is the lost-world romance about Bigfoot she was beginning to write before her adventure: *Tatoosh of the See-Ah-Tiks*. Instead of finishing this rollicking adventure novel, she came home to write a very different kind of fiction, which is stripped down, intense, eerie, and elusive—indeed, rather like Garner's. Several of the stories share a setting and themes with both the diary and the abandoned romance. One, called "Dark Things," merges Charlotte's own adventure with the ultimately disclosed fate of Melba's grandchild—killed and buried by her own father—to make a haunting new story shape:

> After her death, the child lived for a time in the tops of the old trees, among owls and woodpeckers.[. . .] A man glimpsing the child one day, believed he had seen a night jar or a crow; but on another occasion a woman's eye caught a flashing of white high up in the trees, which she understood to be a ghost, translucent and insubstantial as a child's bones, lifting and turning above her[. . .]. Of course, the child, by then, had been dead for days. (217)

This is magic of a sort, but hardly wish fulfillment or escape. The child is reborn as a ghost, like Buckley/Murrangurk. The cost is the loss of everything from her previous life, including her humanity. She lives on in a way, with the forest birds, but she does not get to go home, intact except for a new eye, like Myra in "Buffalo Gals."

Coming back home and back into history, Charlotte muses not on her own hardships but on what has been lost to the world: "I had meant not to think about such things, but here it came: no secret dark hiding places for giants along this part of the river, none for many years. And I stood there wondering how long before the whole of this country was tamed and hedged about, emptied of the last of its mysteries, and the connection between ourselves and the wild world irrevocably broken" (245). The mystery whose loss she mourns can only be found in her own words. Like Greenpearl, she has to write her own path from here on out.

In both *Wild Life* and *Strandloper*, history has impinged on myth. The life William Buckley lived as Murrangurk is about to vanish, at least along the Australian coast. Remnant bands of Sasquatch will dwindle away. The cycles of nature are disrupted, and people are increasingly dissociated from them and from the myths that enact them. Yet having lived for a time within a mythic worldview, both characters can view history critically. Both novels suggest that historical forces are real but that the narratives we construct to explain them are more mythic than we acknowledge. Progress, class struggle, manifest destiny—anything that imposes direction and a purpose on historical change is a story concocted by humans. Some of these stories are destructive; none are inevitable. The best counter is an alternative story. The problem is where to find these alternatives. Myths don't just lie around waiting to be picked up. They belong to specific cultures and to the people who maintain those cultures. Both writers address this problem, Gloss more explicitly.

By choosing the case of William Buckley, Garner authorizes the transfer of Aboriginal myths to an Englishman: after all, Buckley was actually adopted by the Beingalites and given their secrets. Furthermore, Garner draws on his own extensive knowledge of rural English traditions to provide Buckley with a comparable background of custom and belief—if he is already Shick-Shack and Young Cob, then the transition to Murrangurk is eased considerably. The narrative establishes multiple parallels between Cheshire village life and Aboriginal practice. The fictional Buckley is aware that these connections make it possible for him to move between cultures as Strandloper, the shorebird stitching together realms as disparate as land and sea. But Buckley cannot really communicate his sense of mythic continuity to his fellow Englishmen. He tries to explain why it is important that his tribe continue to endure, or "thole," on their lands:

> "If we're shifted, we'll not thole. And if we don't thole, land dies. It needs walking, and it's us must walk it. Do you not see? We're all one, and have been since I don't know when, since Beginning. It's same as, like, whatsitsname, whatd'ye'call'em. Church!" (168)

But the only response he gets is "This is sentimental nonsense" (168). So William remains only an exception to whom the forces of history need not listen. The novel itself becomes the culmination of Buckley's efforts, making Garner verge on cultural appropriation when he has the ancestral spirit Bunjil reassign Buckley's role and privileges to himself: "The Dreaming will wait until another singer comes, because of you, and he will travel as you have travelled, but he will sing in another Time" (182). Why should this other English singer—Garner or his narrative stand-in—speak for the vanished tribes? Who elected him Murrangurk? As in the case of Patricia Wrightson's legend-based fantasies, writing this novel risks being labeled a pseudo-elder, an Aboriginal wannabe. Does the novel's narrative sophistication and linguistic sensitivity justify crossing boundaries and speaking for the other, as I believe Wrightson's careful framing and redirecting of the stories ameliorates her borrowings?

Garner has discussed this question in essays about his work, revealing his awareness of the rights of indigenous peoples to their own religious traditions: Speaking elsewhere of an anthropologist's decision to print a Winnebago Sioux Trickster myth, he says it should probably not have been set down on paper: "Exposed to an unprepared world, his published text cannot be interpreted aright. It becomes [. . .] pabulum for such as the New Age mystics, who act as though knowledge does not have to be won but can be scavenged" ("The Voice in the Shadow" 154–155). Garner's knowledge of Murrangurk is the hard-won product of years of historical and ethnological research, investment of his considerable empathy and painful introspection, transference of his own family's lore and language to Buckley, and study with an Aboriginal elder ("The Voice That Thunders" 237). His powerful storytelling testifies to these efforts, although the author's doubts about his enterprise are not acknowledged within the book itself—the novel might benefit from a few of Larsen's postmodern signals of indeterminacy and epistemological uncertainty.

For her part, Molly Gloss is not so bold as to claim to be the direct heir to Northwest Indian tribes, nor does she so proclaim her protagonist. Unlike the original inhabitants of Le Guin's Valley of the Na, the tribes of the Northwest coast were not all murdered nor their cultures effaced. There are Native American writers fully capable of speaking for the region's hardly vanished native peoples and of choosing which, if any, traditional narratives to broadcast to the larger community. Thus, instead of drawing directly on indigenous myths, Gloss constructs another fictional memorate: a story *about* the stories of Sasquatch. The gentle beast-people with whom Charlotte lives are not the sacred creatures of native lore. Nor are they Indians, not even figurative Indians—their connection with native peoples is metonymic rather than metaphoric: neighbors, not stand-ins. They stand for a lost relationship, an occluded belief about the world, rather than for the actual peoples whose stories encoded and upheld those beliefs. They may not even exist: the Others too clearly represent Charlotte's longing for that which she knows her own people have destroyed. Charlotte may have made them up, as she herself recognizes:

> since coming out of the wild woods she has been able to do certain things
> she hadn't been able to do before: to hear and apprehend the voices of other
> creatures, especially birds, speaking in their own languages. Of course, very
> soon she would understand that this was a sign of starvation and madness—
> perhaps she already knew it. But in the weeks and months ahead she would
> hold on to the notion that it was also a gift. (239)

Though there may not be any Sasquatches even within the fictional world, there is still Charlotte, and if she cannot fully believe in the story she has lived through, she has the power to make it true by telling it with all the force of her new storytelling voice. Whereas William Buckley gains his storyteller's ability by being inducted into tribal culture, Drummond must assemble hers from scraps of memory and textual fragments, though both also find continuity between the myths of their adopted homes and their own cultural heritage. Among the texts interposed among the diary entries are passages from Kwakiutl legends and anthropological records, but also from Genesis and

Beowulf and the *Epic of Gilgamesh*: surviving traces of the myths underlying Western civilization. And, to remind us that this is all a fiction, a patchwork, an offshoot of Vernean fantasy, there are passages from Drummond's *Tatoosh of the See-AhTiks; or, A Girl's Adventures Among Mountain Giants*.

The final voice we hear in the novel comes from a story from Drummond's new collection. Called "Tatoosh," it differs considerably from the earlier adventure tale. Its narrative voice is collective, a "we" that includes the tribe of Sasquatches and all the other sources from which Gloss has assembled her metamyth. The Tatoosh it tells of is, literally, unearthly: "we could see his form still fluttering in the air—it was the form which is taken by human people and certain bears and by ourselves, though those stucallah'wah people said this person wasn't human, wasn't bear, wasn't one of us" (252).

Tatoosh, whom the narrators call "Bearded Man," is an unnaturally pale and hairy creature that invades their realm, acting as if there were no one already present, digging and burning and fouling the waters. He is a giant, a monster:

> word reached us that the Bearded Man had been killing people over on the yoncalla prairie [. . .]. Blood and death are a familiar thing, but there was something in the air and in the red mud footprints at that place, something unfamiliar even to the old ones among us, something malignant and unappeasable. (254)

This metalegend awards the storyteller's prerogatives to Bigfoot and makes the invading European American (like Le Guin's backward-headed Little Man) into the mysterious other, the giant Tatoosh. His is a dark magic, and this is a tragic myth, but Gloss allows us some hope at the very end:

> In the Moon When Tight Buds Unfurl, Wolverine found a lost child belonging to the Bearded Man and brought this child to us. We have been keeping it safe. (255)

Having suffered through two children's deaths (one human and one Sasquatch), we have earned this one rescue. One child, at least, survives to live in the world of myth. Like Murrangurk's murdered nephew, she has been taken into the Dream.

This final embedded story is the most explicitly fantastic part of the book, and yet it is the culmination of all the carefully documented realism that almost makes us forget the entire premise is fantastic. In Garner's novel—perhaps because it is based on a true story—the fantastic is allowed to emerge more openly. *Strandloper* is packed full of impossible coincidences and visions. In the Murrangurk section, especially, the Dreamtime of Aboriginal myth is just a turn of the head away from daylight reality. In Gloss's novel, which is compounded of legends and pulp fictions, everything is soberly documented and pinned down by convincing detail. Both Gloss and Garner suggest that fantasy operates most effectively when it exploits the resources of realistic fiction—and thus of written history—but puts them in service of myth. The myths, however, must be swallowed whole, with all their pain and obligation, as well as their talking beasts and wonderful transformations. And lovers of fantasy must acknowledge that our connection to myth is indirect, second-hand, the product of deliberate reconstruction. Both novels suggest that the task of reconstructing myth is difficult, perhaps endless. Both end with a call to further imagining. "Here," as Garner's final lines sum up, "is the start of the Dream,/and how the sweet sorrow is sung" (200).

V. Metafantasy

None of the examples in this chapter is what the average reader thinks of as fantasy. None tell of wizards; only *Silk Road* has dragons, and those are hardly of the sort one slays to rescue a damsel or save a kingdom. None of the books discussed is part of a series or set in a faux-medieval world. There are no evil lords, no elves, no magical jewels, no lost heirs: none of the fantasy clichés that Diana Wynne Jones lovingly skewers in *The Tough Guide to Fantasy-Land*. Yet these stories are not so far removed from the rest of the fantasy genre. Even some of the more derivative, sprawling, best-selling, role-playing-game-approximating products of that genre are surprisingly nuanced in their approach to myth, and the best of conventional fantasy turns out not to be very conventional at all. Fantasy series and stand-alone novels by Patricia McKillip, Charles de Lint, C. J. Cherryh, Steven Erikson, Sarah Monette, Lois McMaster Bujold, Robin Hobb, and Steven R. Donaldson, for instance, reveal their authors' extensive knowledge of anthropology, comparative mythology, classical literature, history, and folklore. Their stories do not usually break the generic rules—heroes stay heroic, if troubled; prophecies are fulfilled in unexpected ways; quests are completed, though at great cost. However, they often make the very structures of fantastic storytelling do metafictional work: calling attention to authorial decisions, linking different levels of reality, calling on readers to fill in gaps and extend the stories past endings.

A number of typically postmodern devices have their analogues among fantasy's conventions. Many fantasies, for instance, establish two or more competing realities, divided by some sort of barrier or wall, as in Neil Gaiman's *Stardust* (1998) or Garth Nix's *Sabriel* trilogy (1995–2003). Such barriers function not only as challenges to the characters but also as signals to the reader: they represent generic, as well as geographical, boundaries, dividing realist narrative from fantastic and thereby highlighting the conventional nature of each. Another fantasy commonplace is the lost spell or forgotten rune on which the stability of the realm depends. Such spells are examples of *mise en abyme*: miniature versions of the whole story embedded within the larger narrative. They cannot simply be recovered from a ruined tower or cave in the wilderness, where the quest seems to lead; rather, they must be remade, re-forged like the Blade That Was Broken in *The Lord of the Rings*. The original act of creation must be recapitulated and meaning thus reimposed on the world. Examples include the forgotten songs of shaping in McKillip's *The Bards of Bone Plain* (2010) and the broken "Bond-Rune, the sign of dominion, the sign of peace" (122) that is found and remade by the wizard Ged in Le Guin's *The Farthest Shore* (1973). These spells are as metafictional as any self-reflexive twist in a Borges story, but they also work within the conventions of fairy tale and romance. They are narrative maps, object lessons in story creation and meaning making. They illustrate Tolkien's idea that fantasy world building is a form of subcreation through which we come to a fuller understanding of the primary world and its principles. Postmodern but also archaic, they are as old as allegory or fable.

Other fantasy symbols can similarly be read—should be read—as narrative signposts, instructions in the art of reading creatively. Any form of magical vision, from Coyote's eye to the farseeing palantirs of Tolkien's Middle-earth, indicates the acquisition of knowledge and thus should be looked at carefully to see how the viewer's perspective affects what can be known. Voices and languages have a similar metafictional significance: anyone who speaks in a voice of command or through the mouth of another temporarily takes on the role of storyteller and demiurge. Magic itself always carries a metafictional charge. Thus, when a story offers rival models of magic, as in Laurie J. Marks's *Fire Logic* (2002), in which air, water, earth, and fire "logics" reflect different *Weltanschauungen*—both fundamental personality types and ways of being in the world—each type of magic is clearly limited and perspectival. In *The Other Wind* (2001), the culmination of Le Guin's Earthsea cycle, the wizardry through which readers have thus far viewed the world and its meaning is likewise revealed as only one way of seeing: hidden in the heretical lore of the island of Paln and the cults of the Kargad Empire is a wisdom not available to the wizards of Roke, and even their collectively human perspective must be supplemented by a dragon's-eye view.

Any character who changes form, such as Arthur under Merlin's tutelage in T. H. White's *The Sword in the Stone* (1938), takes on new knowledge with that form, crossing barriers of age, class, sex, or species. Every narrator possesses magical traits: invisibility, omniscience, travel at the speed of thought. Every happy ending is a prophecy fulfilled. The most conventionalized of narrative forms can also be the most epistemologically sophisticated: fairy tales have never hidden their construction and thus have never tried to fool the listener into mistaking poiesis, or making, for mimesis, the simple imitation of reality.

Fantasy naturalizes metafiction, makes it part of the scenery and the plot. If, as I have suggested, the fantasy genre offers a narrative bridge between direct experience and mythic patterning, then fantasy is doing what memorates have always done. The stories people tell about their own brushes with the supernatural and glimpses of the numinous are no less than folk metafictions. They comment on the content and form of traditional legends, and they remind listeners that the truths they are hearing are channeled through fallible, fearful beings like themselves. The eye that observes, the voice that tells, the history that is remembered: all belong to the storyteller, and in the process of oral transmission every audience member is taught how to move from the role of passive listener to that of active performer. Along with that creative power comes responsibility: each generation of narrators strives to reproduce the story as it was given to them and to tell it with the appropriate rituals and proper respect.

That is the situated knowledge of myth. What science is still struggling to come to terms with, myth has always comprehended: that to know something is to be known by it. Near the end of her essay, Haraway points out some unexpected benefits of relinquishing the illusion of disinterested objectivity:

> Acknowledging the agency of the world in knowledge makes room for some unsettling possibilities, including a sense of the world's independent sense of humor. [. . .] The Coyote or Trickster, embodied in American Southwest Indian accounts, suggests our situation when we give up mastery but keep searching for fidelity, knowing all the while we will be hoodwinked. I think these are useful myths for scientists who might be our allies. Feminist objectivity makes room for surprises and ironies at the heart of all knowledge production; we are not in charge of the world. We just live here and try to strike up non-innocent conversations by means of our prosthetic devices, including our visualization technologies. No wonder science fiction has been such a rich writing practice in recent feminist theory. I like to see feminist theory as a reinvented coyote discourse obligated to its enabling sources in many kinds of heterogeneous accounts of the world. (199)

Haraway mentions with approval one explicitly epistemological genre of fiction, the one with "science" in its name, but her remarks apply equally aptly to another such genre, which could well be called "myth fiction." Mythopoeic fantasy is another "coyote discourse." As such, it does not deal in assurances and wish fulfillments so much as in cognitive disruptions and cosmic jokes. Fantasy heroes, at least in self-aware fantasies, never come away unscathed, nor do readers. Rethinking the common notion of fantasy as escape, we can see the ordinary world as the frying pan out of which we escape and mythic awareness as the fire we fall into, a painful and renewing flame like the bed of burning roses in George MacDonald's *The Princess and the Goblin*.

VI. Back to the Beginning

Le Guin's 2008 novel *Lavinia* comes back to some of the same issues of knowledge, vision, and responsibility that she explored in "Buffalo Gals" and *Always*

Coming Home, but in dialogue with one of the foundational mythic texts of Western literature, Vergil's *Aeneid*. When the philosophers and poets with which this book opened began thinking seriously about myth, Vergil's was one of the core texts they had in mind. He played a major part in the process of transforming oral narrative into literature, going beyond retelling old stories in poetic or dramatic form and actually inventing, with significant help from Homer, a new story of national origin. Le Guin retells the tale of Aeneas but focuses on the last stage of his adventures, his arrival at what was to become Rome, and she focalizes the story through the barely imagined figure of Lavinia, the princess of Latium who becomes Aeneas's queen. The novel is faithful to Vergil's version of events, although, as the afterword explains:

> My desire was to follow Vergil and not to improve or reprove him. But Lavinia herself sometimes insisted that the poet was mistaken—about the color of her hair, for instance. And being a novelist and wordy, I enlarged upon and interpreted and filled in many corners of his spare, splendid story. But I left out a good deal, too. The palaces and tiaras, the hecatomb sacrifices, the Augustan magnificence he gave to his setting, I reduced to more plausible poverty. The Homeric use of quarrelsome deities to motivate, illuminate, and interfere with human choices and emotions doesn't work well in a novel, so the Greco-Roman gods, an intrinsic element of the poem, are no part of my story. (275)

Thus Le Guin's conversation with Vergil includes her use of both historical information and novelistic convention to counter his claims about the people and events. However, this is not one of those misguided attempts to strip the magic from some ancient story, like movies about the Trojan War or King Arthur that remake those landmarks of fantasy into merely human drama. In *Lavinia*, the Homeric gods are gone, but the numinous remains; the book is as much about myth and its meanings as it is about power and politics.

In fact, the numinous is explicitly invoked—or rather, taking the word back to its origin, the *numen*. Le Guin's use of this term closely corresponds with that of Rudolf Otto, who first adapted the Latin term for divine will or presence to designate a particular state of mind and being. Otto's "numinous" deliberately strips the concept of its moral and theological associations in order to be able to give a name to

> this feeling which, emerging in the mind of primeval man, forms the starting-point for the entire religious development in history. "Daemons" and "gods" alike spring from this root, and all the products of "mythological apperception' or 'fantasy' are nothing but different modes in which it has been objectified. And all ostensible explanations of the origin of religion in terms of animism or magic or folk-psychology are doomed from the outset to wander astray and miss the real goal of their inquiry, unless they recognize

this fact of our nature—primary, unique, underivable from anything else—to be the basic factor and the basic impulse underlying the entire process of religious evolution. (*Idea* 14–15)

Otto's formulation has become an important part of folkloristic analysis. Lauri Honko, citing Otto, suggests that such numens underlie supernatural legends, as well as memorates (16). They may be products of physiological processes or inexplicable external events or a combination of the two. In each case, an individual attempts to make sense of the numinous experience by transforming it into story, and those personal experience stories are then retold and reshaped to form the community's repertoire of explanatory narratives. Le Guin follows the chain of transmission backward from literature to legend to numen: she takes myth back to basics, in the awestruck contemplation of the wholly other. Here is Le Guin's—or rather Lavinia's—description of the encounter with the numinous:

> The sacred place was in a grassy glade deep in the forest, marked out in a rough square with a rock wall no higher than my knee. Within that enclosure the sense of the numen, the presence and power of the sacred, was strong and strange. (*Lavinia* 27)

The novel similarly takes other myth words back to their original meanings. Lavinia explains that her people are pagans because they live in the *pagus*: "the pattern of the farmer's fields, outlined by the paths between the fields" (26). Her response to the sacred is *pious*, not because she conforms to some religious regimen but because she tries to be "responsible, faithful, open to duty, open to awe" (22). In the sacred place, one of the numens Lavinia encounters (along with remnants of ancient sacrifices and a glimpse of an ancestral spirit guide in woodpecker shape) is the dying *poeta* whose account of Aeneas is both our only record of and the source of great misunderstanding about her life. Lavinia does not know the word, which has not yet come into her language from Greek: "'I am a poet, Lavinia.' I liked the sound of the word, but he saw I did not know it. 'A vates,' he said. I knew that word of course: foreteller, soothsayer" (43). And *numen* is again defined, with etymological precision, in terms of in an even more fundamental experience:

> The nod of a head is such a small thing, it can mean so little, yet it is the gesture of assent that allows, that makes to be. The nod is the gesture of power, the yes. The numen, the presence of the sacred, is called by its name. (86)

Le Guin does not redefine *myth*, but the entire story calls us back to the origin of myth in the extraordinary and inexplicable aspects of ordinary life. Though the Homeric gods are missing, their Italic counterparts are ubiquitous, not in humanized form but as felt presences. Lavinia quizzes the poet on his depiction:

"What do you mean, Juno got into them?"

"She hated Aeneas. She was always against him." He saw that I was puzzled.

I pondered this. A woman has her Juno, just as a man has his Genius; they are names for the sacred power, the divine spark we each of us have in us. My Juno can't "get into" me, it is already my deepest self. The poet was speaking of Juno as if it were a person, a woman, with likes and dislikes: a jealous woman.

The world is sacred, of course, it is full of gods, numina, great powers and presences. We give some of them names—Mars of the fields and the war, Vesta the fire, Ceres the grain, Mother Tellus the earth, the Penates of the storehouse. The rivers, the springs. And in the storm cloud and the light is the great power called the father god. But they aren't people. They don't love and hate, they aren't for or against. They accept the worship due them, which augments their power, through which we live. (64–65).

This way of seeing the gods is both contemporary and historical—or, more properly, archaeological in that Le Guin is separating layers of myth long viewed as a single body of tradition, like the images of angels discussed in chapter 6. She explains:

One thing I was trying to deal with was the fact that native Roman religion had little or no myth, as far as we can tell. What myths the Romans had were human—founding myths like Romulus and Remus, or history-become-legend, like the Tarquins or Horatius at the bridge. Their divinities were without stories. They were presences, belonging to a certain place (grove, hearth, field). They had no history, no stories.

I find this interesting and impressive. So I tried hard to make it clear that the "Italian counterparts" of the Greek pantheon originally were nothing of the kind. But they were so understood by the Greeks, who co-opted them, and taught the Romans to understand them so. (e-mail to author)

Like Jane Harrison, Le Guin sees the origins of myth in the pragmatic rituals of the household, rather than in cosmic struggles or anthropomorphic fables. Also like Harrison, she sees in this preliterate state of mythology something worth returning to:

Most people would say these non-person, mythless deities are more "primitive." That always becomes a value judgment, so I prefer to say that they were gods but not "gods" as we understand "gods." I feel that to understand and accept that is to escape, however briefly, from a fixed, limited, conventional understanding of the divine, almost inescapably enforced upon us by all the great religions and their myths (except possibly Buddhism). (e-mail to author)

Lavinia's explanations of her beliefs are thus metahistorical as well as metafictional (like all of her conversations with Vergil) and metamythic. They invite readers to reexamine the gods, heroes, transformations, and revelations that have come down to us from vanished oral cultures via literary retellings and to think about they ways we are formed by those *mythoi* and how we use them to make sense of our lives, to justify behavior, to probe the unknown, to delight ourselves with wonders. *Lavinia* shows us the archaic within the modern and the modernity of the archaic, with the fantastic serving as a bridge between eras. Lavinia's dialogues with her poet, framing the epic the way memorates frame legends, validate his account even as they question its assumptions. They situate the myth within that which Lavinia knows with her entire being: duty, pain, love, mystery, and the hard work of living in the wake of a hero. The metafictional and the fantastic work together to bring the story into the present. In Le Guin's interpretation of Vergil, the story is reinvented, as it must be in every generation, using the newest knowledge of the past and employing contemporary perspectives: feminist, scientific, literary, and personal.

Coyote makes no appearance in *Lavinia*; or, rather, she comes disguised as Grandfather Picus, the woodpecker whose touch gives Lavinia access to the mysteries of the sacred wood. Yet the novel illustrates Haraway's coyote discourse: irreverent and sacred, limited and multivocal, as grounded in the past as careful research and powerful imagination can make it but at the same time thoroughly modern. The legendary queen chats with the Roman poet using a voice supplied by the twenty-first-century writer: in this three-way conversation we have a parable about the possibilities of mythopoeic fantasy. *Lavinia* is pagan, pious, and poetic: pagan in being grounded in real things such as pagus and forest, passion and loss; pious in being dutiful and yet open to all possibilities of inspiration and interpretation; poetic not only in the beauty of language and elegance of construction but also in its vatic truth telling.

All the fantasies discussed in this chapter share those qualities: reverently pagan, skeptically pious, stealthily poetic. They treat myth as something real and powerful, not to be trifled with but neither to be taken straight. In the long-standing negotiation over proper meanings and uses of myth, these are some of the most sophisticated and emotionally satisfying arguments. Steering a course between orthodoxy and trivialization, Larsen, Garner, Gloss, and Le Guin demonstrate how powerful fantasy can be as an art form and as an argument about tradition, belief, and impossible truth. They take metafictionality to a new level of urgency and immediacy: every narrative disruption and authorial wink is necessary to the enterprise of finding a new way into myth without claiming ownership of myth. Their version of fantasy situates mythic knowledge in such a way that we can neither take it literally nor dismiss it. It insists that we pay for that knowledge with our whole beings and accept the burden of history along with the pleasures of entertainment. In return, it offers an eye made of pitch to complement that of flesh. With both eyes in conjunction, we get a view that is murky and distorted but also deep and sometimes golden.

{ NOTES }

Introduction

1. This term, which encapsulates both the predictability and the non-nourishing quality of much commercial fantasy (think of spray "cheese" in a can), was coined by Joseph Major and William December Starr in an online discussion group, rec.arts.sf.written, in a series of messages dated October 17, 1999.

2. I have collected a number of these dismissals over the years, from early reviews of *The Lord of the Rings* to recent attempts to explain away the popularity of Harry Potter. A typical example is an editorial in *The New York Times Book Review* in which Rachel Donadio bemoans the displacement of literary fiction by nonfiction. "How can you say that," she has the reader ask rhetorically, "when the latest installment in the Harry Potter series sold more than four million copies at the bookstore box office in its first weekend alone?" But this seeming counterexample is a mere "installment," not a real book, and its victory is a mere box office record. Donadio falls back on the word "escape" to describe what fantasy does, as opposed to "illuminating today's world." She regrets the disappearance of "experimental fiction" but does not notice the narrative experiments that are constantly being conducted under the cloak of the fantastic.

Chapter 1

1. The interaction between the concepts of myth and fantasy parallels the equally complex interplay between notions of fantasy, or fancy, and the imagination in Romantic philosophy and literary theory. Though that interplay is outside the scope of this study, I recommend that the interested reader consult Stephen Prickett's illuminating discussion in the first chapter of his *Victorian Fantasy* (1979).

Chapter 5

1. For fuller discussions of science fantasy as a genre, see the Taxonomic Interlude in this volume, as well as Wolfe, 107, and Attebery, "Science Fantasy."

Chapter 6

1. These polling data from the 2007 Baylor Religion Survey are subject to considerable interpretation. I have combined the responses of "probably" and "absolutely" to get a total of 81.4% who believe in angels. For God, the categories are "I have no doubt that God exists" at 63.4%, "I believe in God but with some doubts" at 11.7%, and "I sometimes believe in God" at 1.9%, for a total of 77%. The next category is "I believe in a higher power or cosmic force," at 11.5%. This figure seems to represent belief in something other than

a personal deity, but some respondents might view themselves as belonging with the more traditional believers. On the other hand, these people might also, if given a more nuanced choice, identify their belief in angels as something more abstract or metaphoric—"spiritual guides" or "benevolent powers"—than the humanized figures of Hallmarkian and Thomistic literature.

2. Margaret Bennett (1991) offers a selection of fairy legend material from the Scottish Highlands. Bill Ellis (2003) discusses memorates and legends about alien abductions. Elaine Lawless (1988) explores narratives about encounters with the Holy Ghost, and William A. Wilson (1976) the Three Nephites. Substantial treatments of the connection between religious legend and memorate include Lauri Honko (1964) and Linda Dégh and Andrew Vázsonyi (1974).

3. *The Renegade* was the first of a number of novels from Harlequin's Intrigue line of romances incorporating angels into the romantic suspense formula. Rival publisher Silhouette followed up with its own Desire line of more erotic angel fantasies. Other angel romances have appeared under the Warner Forever imprint and Flare's Teen Angel series for young adults. As romance fiction has become increasingly specialized, there is even a line of time-travel Western angel paranormal romances (!) called Angel's Touch from Dorchester's Love Spell imprint. The owner of my local used bookstore has carefully sorted all these out and marked them on the spine with an A for Angel; they are what she describes as "high demand" items and can only be purchased with the return of another high-demand volume. Many more recent angel romances are published in electronic format; these include gay or lesbian romances such as James Buchanan's *Redemption* (2007).

4. The same theme of desire for an angel that can only be fulfilled with that angel's incarnation as a human shows up in the Hong Kong film *Lavender*, or *Fan yi cho* (2000), a Hollywood-style *film blanc* with a number of twists that clearly signal its New Age cosmology. Along with Western-derived guardian angels, the plot revolves around Eastern-style reincarnation and purely Californian aromatherapy.

5. Philippe Hamon's term *megatext* is invoked within science fiction criticism to indicate that genre's particular relationship to, and dependence on, a reader's knowledge of science as well as generic convention. Here, the comparable body of narrative motifs and assumptions derives from oral tradition and scripture.

Literalist Interlude: Burning Harry Potter

1. When asked, as she was in 2000 at the Toronto International Festival of Authors, whether her books promote Satanism, Rowling's typical response is, "No, you are a lunatic." (Eichler)

Chapter 7

1. Though I am quoting from the fuller treatment in Bechtel's dissertation, the idea of syncretic fantasy was first proposed in Bechtel's 2008 article "The Word for World Is Story: Syncretic Fantasy as Healing Ritual in Thomas King's *Green Grass, Running Water*."

2. For a fuller treatment of these and earlier Australian SF writers, see my article "Aboriginality in Science Fiction" (2005), from which parts of this chapter are adapted.

Chapter 8

1. Le Guin first heard the Coyote eye-juggling story from her father, in a version she suggests might have been Yurok (e-mail to author).

2. A comparable concept is Clifford Geertz's "local knowledge," which Le Guin says "had quite a lot of resonance for me" (e-mail to author).

3. According to Le Guin, "I must regret that my passion carried me beyond the facts. There's enough left of the Wappo language that a small vocabulary or dictionary of it exists" (e-mail to author).

{ WORKS CITED }

Introduction

Baxandall, Michael. *Patterns of Intention: On the Historical Explanation of Pictures*. New Haven and London: Yale UP, 1985. 58–59. Print.

Carpenter, Humphrey. *Tolkien: A Biography*. Boston: Houghton, 1977. Print.

Donadio, Rachel. "Truth Is Stronger Than Fiction." *The New York Times Book Review*. Aug. 7, 2005. Web. 1 9 2005.

Tolkien, J. R. R. "On Fairy-stories." *Tree and Leaf*. London: Allen, 1964; Reprinted in *The Tolkien Reader*. New York: Ballantine, 1966. Print.

Tompkins, Jane. *Sensational Designs: The Cultural Work of American Fiction 1790–1860*. New York and Oxford: Oxford UP, 1985. Print.

Chapter 1

Blake, William. *Milton a Poem*, Copy A. London, 1811. *The William Blake Archive*. The British Museum. Web. Feb. 16, 2011.

Bulfinch, Thomas. *The Age of Fable: or Beauties of Mythology*. Boston: Tilton, 1855. Project Gutenberg. Web. Feb. 16, 2011.

Clute, John. "Taproot Texts." *The Encyclopedia of Fantasy*. Ed. John Clute and John Grant. New York: St. Martins, 1997. 921. Print.

Dixon, Robert. Writing the Colonial Adventure: Gender, Race, and Nation in Anglo-Australian Popular Fiction, 1875–1914. New York: Cambridge UP, 1995. Print.

Docherty, John. "The Sources of Phantastes." *North Wind* 9 (1990): 38–53. Web. Feb. 16, 2011.

Dorson, Richard. "The Eclipse of Solar Mythology." *Myth: A Symposium*. Ed. Thomas A. Sebeok. 1955. Bloomington and London: Indiana UP, 1958. 25–63. Print.

Evers, Larry, and Barre Toelken. "Collaboration in the Translation and Interpretation of Native American Oral Traditions." *Native American Oral Traditions: Collaboration and Interpretation*. Ed. Larry Evers and Barre Toelken. Logan: Utah State UP, 2001. 1–14. Print.

"Fan Fiction and Academia, Part 2: Literary Theory, Kings, and Milton." *Sapience Speaks: Ramblings of an English Graduate Student*. April 6, 2009. Web. February 10, 2011.

Grimm, Jacob. Preface to the Second Edition (1844). *Teutonic Mythology*. By Grimm. Trans. James Steven Stallybrass. Vol. 3. 1883. New York: Dover, 1966. v–lv. Print.

Hawthorne, Nathaniel. *A Wonder Book and Tanglewood Tales*. Vol. VII of *The Centenary Edition of the Works of Nathaniel Hawthorne*. Ed. William Charvat *et al*. Columbus: The Ohio State UP, 1972. Print.

Lamb, Mary Ellen. "Engendering the Narrative Act: Old Wives' Tales in *The Winter's Tale*, *Macbeth*, and *The Tempest*." *Criticism* 40.4 (Fall 1998): 529–53. *Literature Online*. Web. Feb. 16, 2011.

Lévi-Strauss, Claude. "The Structural Study of Myth." *Myth: A Symposium*. Ed. Thomas A Sebeok. 1955. Bloomington and London: Indiana UP, 1958. 81–106. Print.

Longfellow, Henry Wadsworth. *The Song of Hiawatha*. Boston: Ticknor, 1855. *Google Books*. Web.

MacDonald, George. "The Fantastic Imagination." *The Gifts of the Child Christ: Fairy Tales and Stories for the Childlike*. Ed. Glenn Edward Sadler. Vol. 1. Grand Rapids, MI: Eerdmans, 1973, 23–28. Print.

Manlove, Colin. "Did William Morris Start MacDonald Writing Fantasy?" *North Wind* 24 (2005): 61–73. Web. Feb. 16, 2011.

Mathews, Richard. *Fantasy: The Liberation of Imagination*. New York: Twayne, 1997. Twain's Studies in Lit.Themes and Genres No. 16. Print.

Mendlesohn, Farah, and Edward James. *A Short History of Fantasy*. London: Middlesex UP, 2009. Print.

Prickett, Stephen. *Victorian Fantasy*. Bloomington: Indiana UP, 1979. Print.

Schoolcraft, Henry *Algic Researches, Comprising Inquiries Respecting the Mental Characteristics of the North American Indians*. New York: Harper, 1839. *Google Books*. First Series: Indian Tales and Legends. 2 vols. Web. Feb. 16, 2011.

Segal, Robert A. *Myth: A Very Short Introduction*. Oxford: Oxford UP, 2004. Print.

Shippey, Tom. "Imagined Cathedrals: Retelling Myth in the Twentieth Century." *Myth in North-west Europe*. Ed. Stephen Glosecki. Tempe, AZ: MRTS, 2007. 307–332. Print.

Stalleybrass, James Steven. Translator's Preface. *Teutonic Mythology*. By Jacob Grimm. Trans. James Steven Stalleybrass. Vol. 2. 1883. New York: Dover, 1966. v–viii. Print.

Thompson, Stith. "Myth and Folktales." *Myth: A Symposium*. Ed. Thomas A Sebeok. 1955. Bloomington and London: Indiana UP, 1958. 169–180. Print.

Toelken, Barre. *The Anguish of Snails: Native American Folklore in the West*. Logan: Utah State UP, 2003. Folklife of the West Series 2. Print.

——. "Beauty Behind Me, Beauty Before." *Journal of American Folklore* 117 (Fall 2004): 441–445. Web. Address to American Folklore Society. Feb. 2, 2011.

——. *The Dynamics of Folklore*. Boston: Houghton, 1979. Print.

Von Hendy, Andrew. *The Modern Construction of Myth*. Bloomington and Indianapolis: Indiana UP, 2002. Print.

Walker, Kath. *Stradbroke Dreamtime*. Sydney, Austral.: Angus, 1972. Print.

Wawn, Andrew. "Philology and Fantasy before Tolkien." Internet archive. Archived from original on Mar. 7, 2005. Web. Feb. 16, 2011.

Williamson, George Samuel. *The Longing for Myth in Germany: Culture, Religion, and Politics, 1790–1878*. Diss. Yale University, 1996. Ann Arbor: UMI Dissertation Services.2002. Print.

Taxonomic Interlude: A Note on Genres

Attebery, Brian. *Strategies of Fantasy*. Bloomington: Indiana UP, 1992. Print.

Bascom, William. "The Forms of Folklore: Prose Narratives." *Journal of American Folklore* 78 (1965): 3–20. *JSTOR*. Web. Jun. 29, 2012.

Crook, Irene. Unpublished MS and collection, Idaho State U., 1986.

Dégh, Linda. *Legend and Belief: Dialectics of a Folklore Genre*. Bloomington and Indianapolis: Indiana UP, 2001. Print.

Ellis, Bill. *Aliens, Ghosts, and Cults: Legends We Live.* Jackson: UP of Mississippi, 2003. Print.

Honko, Lauri. "Memorates and the Study of Folk Beliefs." *Journal of the Folklore Institute.* 1.1–2 (1964): 5–19. *JSTOR.* Web. 29 Jun. 2012.

Oring, Elliott. "How Legends Are True," *Idaho Yesterdays,* Spring 2008, expanded version. Web. Feb. 27, 2009.

Thompson, Stith. "Myth and Folktales." *Myth: A Symposium.* Ed. Thomas A Sebeok 1955. Bloomington and London: Indiana UP, 1958. 169–180. Print.

Toelken, Barre. *The Dynamics of Folklore.* Boston: Houghton, 1979. Print.

Tolkien, J. R. R. "On Fairy-stories." *Tree and Leaf.* London: Allen, 1964. Rpt. in *The Tolkien Reader.* New York: Ballantine, 1966. Print.

von Sydow, Carl Wilhelm. *Selected Papers on Folklore.* Copenhagen: Rosenkilde and Bagger, 1948. Rpt. New York: Arno, 1977. Print.

Chapter 2

Boyde, M. "The Poet and the Ghosts Are Walking the Streets: Hope Mirrlees: Life and poetry." *Hecate: An Interdisciplinary Journal of Women's Liberation* 35.1–2 (2009): 29–41. *Research Online.* Web. Mar. 20, 2011.

Carpentier, Martha C. *Ritual, Myth, and the Modernist Text: The Influence of Jane Ellen Harrison on Joyce, Eliot, and Woolf.* Amsterdam: Gordon and Breach, 1998. Print. Library of Anthropology Ser. 12.

Eliot, T. S. "Gerontion." *Collected Poems 1909–1962.* New York: Harcourt, 1971. Print. 29–31.

———. Introduction. *All Hallows Eve.* By Charles Williams. New York: Pellegrini and Cudahy, 1948 Rpt. Vancouver, BC: Regent, 2003. ix–xviii. Print.

———. "Ulysses, Order and Myth." *Selected Prose of T. S. Eliot.* Ed. Frank Kermode. New York: Harcourt, 1975. 175–178. Print.

———. "The Waste Land." *Collected Poems 1909–1962.* New York: Harcourt, 1971. 51–76. Print.

Glyer, Diana Pavlac. *The Company They Keep: C. S. Lewis and J. R. R. Tolkien as Writers in Community.* Kent, OH: The Kent State UP, 2007. Print.

Gauntlett, Edward. "Charles Williams and Magic." *Newsletter of the Charles Williams Society* 25 (2008). Rpt. online by The Charles Williams Society. 2010. Web.

Harrison, Jane Ellen. *Ancient Art and Ritual.* London: Williams and Norgate, 1913. Rev. ed. 1918. London and New York: Oxford University Press, 1951. Print.

———. *Prolegomena to the Study of Greek Religion.* Cambridge: Cambridge UP, 1903. Print.

———. *Themis: A Study of the Social Origins of Greek Religion.* Cambridge: Cambridge UP, 1912. Print.

Hemingway, Ernest. *A Moveable Feast.* New York: Scribner's, 1964. Print.

Jameson, Fredric. Postmodernism: or, The Cultural Logic of Late Capitalism. Durham: Duke UP, 1991. Print.

Julius, Anthony. *T. S. Eliot, Anti-Semitism, and Literary Form.* Cambridge: Cambridge UP, 1995. Print.

Lindop, Grevel. "Charles Williams and His Contemporaries." *Charles Williams and His Contemporaries.* Ed. Suzanne Bray and Richard Sturch. Newcastle: Cambridge Scholars, 2009. 2–17. Print.

Mirrlees, Hope. *Lud-in-the-Mist*. 1926. New York: Ballantine, 1970. Print.

———. *Paris: A Poem*. Richmond: Hogarth, 1919. *Hope Mirrlees on the Web*. Web. Mar. 2, 2011.

Moorman, Charles. Arthurian Triptych: Mythic Materials in Charles Williams, C. S. Lewis, and T. S. Eliot. Berkeley and Los Angeles: U of California P, 1960. Print.

Mortimer, Patchen. "Tolkien and Modernism." *Tolkien Studies* 2 (2005): 113–129. *Project Muse*. Web. Mar. 20, 2011.

Oziewicz, Marek. One Earth, One People: The Mythopoeic Fantasy Series of Ursula K. Le Guin, Lloyd Alexander, Madeleine L'Engle and Orson Scott Card. Jefferson, NC: McFarland, 2008. Print. Critical Explorations in Science Fiction and Fantasy 6.

Perloff, Majorie. *The Poetics of Indeterminacy: Rimbaud to Cage*. Princeton UP, 1981. Print.

Phillips, K. J. "Jane Harrison and Modernism." *Journal of Modern Literature* 17.4 (Spring 1991). 465–476. Web. Mar. 20, 2011.

Pound, Ezra. *Make It New: Essays*. London: Faber, 1934. Print.

Roessel, David. "'Mr. Eugenides, the Smyrna Merchant,' and Post-War Politics in 'The Waste Land.' *Journal of Modern Literature* 16.1 (Summer, 1989). 171–176. *JSTOR*. Web. Feb. 23, 2011.

Shippey, Tom. *J. R. R. Tolkien: Author of the Century*. Boston: Houghton, 2000. Print.

Swanwick, Michael. *Hope-in-the-Mist: The Extraordinary Career and Mysterious Life of Hope Mirrlees*. Montclair, NJ: Temporary Culture/Henry Wessells, 2009. Print.

Tolkien, J. R. R. *Letters of J. R. R. Tolkien*. Ed. Humphrey Carpenter with Christopher Tolkien. Boston: Houghton, 1981. Print.

Williams, Charles. *All Hallows Eve*. London: Faber, 1945. Vancouver, BC: Regent, 2003. Print.

———. *War in Heaven*. London: Faber, 1930. Grand Rapids, MI: Eerdmans, 1967. Print.

Williams, Raymond. *Marxism and Literature*. Oxford and New York: Oxford UP, 1977. Print.

Woolf, Virginia. *Mr. Bennett and Mrs. Brown*. London: Hogarth, 1924. Print.

Chapter 3

Bilbro, Jeffrey. "Phantastical Regress: The Return of Desire and Deed in *Phantastes* and *The Pilgrim's Regress*." *Mythlore* 28.3–4 (Spring/Summer 2010): 21–37. Web. May 6, 2012.

Broome, F. Hal. "The Scientific Basis of MacDonald's Dream-Frame." *The Gold Thread: Essays on George MacDonald*. Ed. William Raeper. Edinburgh: Edinburgh UP, 1990. 87–108. Print.

Carpenter, Humphry. The Inklings: C. S. Lewis, J. R. R. Tolkien, Charles Williams, and Their Friends. London: Allen & Unwin, 1978. Print.

———. *Tolkien: A Biography*. Boston: Houghton, 1977. Print.

Durie, Catherine. "George MacDonald and C. S. Lewis." *The Gold Thread: Essays on George MacDonald*. Ed. William Raeper. Edinburgh: Edinburgh UP, 1990. 163–185. Print.

Fetterly, Judith. The Resisting Reader: A Feminist Approach to American Fiction. Bloomington: Indiana UP, 1978. Print.

Gaarden, Bonnie. "'The Golden Key': A Double Reading." *Mythlore* 24.3/4 (Winter/Spring 2006): 35–52. Web. May 6, 2012.

Gray, William. "Pullman, Lewis, MacDonald, and the Anxiety of Influence." *Mythlore* 25.3/4 (Spring/Summer 2007): 117–132. Web. May 6, 2012.

Johnson, Joseph. George MacDonald: A Biographical and Critical Appreciation. London: Pitman, 1906. Web. May 6, 2012.

Lewis, C. S. "The Anthropological Approach." *Selected Literary Essays by C. S. Lewis*. Ed. Walter Hooper. Cambridge: Cambridge UP, 1969. 301–311. Print.

——. *The Great Divorce*. 1946. New York: HarperCollins, 2001. Print.

——. *Collected Letters*. 3 vols. Ed. Walter Hooper. London: HarperCollins, 2004–2006. Print.

——. Preface. *George MacDonald: An Anthology*. Ed. C. S. Lewis. New York: Macmillan, 1947. Print.

——. "Sometimes Fairy Stories May Say Best What's to Be Said." *On Stories: and Other Essays on Literature*. Ed. Walter Hooper. New York and London: Harcourt, 1966. 45–48. Print.

——. *Surprised by Joy: The Shape of My Early Life*. Orlando, FL and London: Harcourt, 1955. Print.

——. *Till We Have Faces: A Myth Retold*. New York and London: Harcourt, 1956. Print.

Lindskoog, Kathryn. "Mark Twain and George MacDonald: The Salty and the Sweet." *Mark Twain Journal* 30.2 (Fall 1992): 26–32. Web. May 6, 2012.

MacDonald, George. "The Fantastic Imagination." *The Gifts of the Child Christ: Fairy Tales and Stories for the Childlike*. Ed. Glenn Edward Sadler. Vol. 1. Grand Rapids, MI: Eerdmans, 1973. 23–28. Print.

——. *George MacDonald: An Anthology*. Ed. C. S. Lewis. New York: Macmillan, 1947. Print.

——. *Lilith*. 1895. Grand Rapids, MI: Eerdmans, 1981. Print.

——. *The Princess and Curdie*. Philadelphia: McCay, n.d. Print.

——. *The Princess and the Goblin*. London: Dent, 1949. Print.

——. *Robert Falconer*. 1868. Whitethorn, CA: Johannesen, 1995. Print.

Manlove, C. N. *Modern Fantasy: Five Studies*. Cambridge: Cambridge UP, 1975. Print.

McGillis, Roderick. "'A Fairy Tale Is Just a Fairy Tale': George MacDonald and the Queering of Fairy." *Marvels & Tales: Journal of Fairy Tale Studies* 17.1 (2003): 86–99. *Project Muse*. Web. May 6, 2012.

Miller, Laura. The Magician's Book: A Skeptic's Adventures in Narnia. New York: Little, 2008. Print.

Myers, Ellen. "Creation in the Writings of George MacDonald." *Creation Social Science and Humanities Society Quarterly Journal* 8.1 (n.d.): 1–6. Web. Feb. 16, 2005.

Reis, Richard H. *George MacDonald*. New York: Twayne, 1972. Print. Shippey, Tom. "Imagined Cathedrals: Retelling Myth in the Twentieth Century." *Myth in Early Northwest Europe*. Ed. Stephen Glosecki. Tempe, AZ: Arizona Center for Medieval and Renaissance Studies, in association with Brepols, 2007. 307–332. Print.

Wolfe, Gary K. *David Lindsay*. Mercer Island, WA: Starmont, 1982. Starmont Readers Guides to Contemporary Science Fiction and Fantasy Authors 9.

Wolff, Robert Lee. The Golden Key: A Study of the Fiction of George MacDonald. New Haven, CT: Yale UP, 1961. Print.

Chapter 4

Bradley, Marion Zimmer. "Responsibilities and Temptations of Women Science Fiction Writers." *Women Worldwalkers: New Dimensions of Science Fiction and Fantasy*. Ed. Jane B. Weedman. Lubbock, TX: Texas Tech P, 1985. 25–41. Print.

Campbell, Joseph. *The Hero with a Thousand Faces.* 3rd ed. Novato, CA: New World, 2008. Print. Bollingen Series XVII.

Cawelti, John. Adventure, Mystery, and Romance: Formula Stories as Art and Popular Culture. Chicago: U of Chicago P, 1976. Print.

———. *The Six-Gun Mystique.* Bowling Green, OH: Bowling Green U Popular P, 1970. Print.

Cohn, Dorrit. Transparent Minds: Narrative Modes for Presenting Consciousness in Fiction. Princeton, NJ: Princeton UP, 1978. Print.

Crook, Irene. Unpublished MS and collection. Idaho State U. 1986.

Fowler, Karen Joy. *Sarah Canary.* New York: Holt, 1991. Print.

Fredericks, Casey. The Future of Eternity: Mythologies of Science Fiction and Fantasy. Bloomington: Indiana UP, 1982. Print.

Garner, Alan. *Elidor.* London: Collins, 1965. Print.

———. *The Moon of Gomrath.* London: Collins, 1963. Print.

———. *The Owl Service.* London: Collins, 1967. Print.

———. *The Weirdstone of Brisingamen.* London: Collins, 1960. Print.

Hufford, David J. "Beings without Bodies: An Experience-Centered Theory of the Belief in Spirits." *Out of the Ordinary: Folklore and the Supernatural.* Ed. Barbara Walker. Logan: Utah State UP, 1995. 11–45. Print.

Jones, Diana Wynne. *Dark Lord of Derkholm.* New York: Harper, 1998. Print.

———. *The Tough Guide to Fantasy-Land.* Rev. and updated ed. New York: Penguin, 2006. Print.

———. "Two Kinds of Writing?" The Medusa: The Journal of the PJF 1 (1990): 1–4. Rpt. Chrestomanci Castle: The Diana Wynne Jones Homepage. Web. June 28, 2012.

Langford, David. "Bibliography Blues." *SFX* 120 (Aug. 2004). Web. June 28, 2012.

Laubenthal, Sanders Anne. *Excalibur.* New York: Ballantine, 1973. Print.

Lawless, Elaine. "'The Night I Got the Holy Ghost…': Holy Ghost Narratives and the Pentecostal Conversion Process." *Western Folklore* 47 (Jan 1988): 1–19. Web. Mar 2, 2012.

Lewis, C. S. *An Experiment in Criticism.* Cambridge: Cambridge UP, 1961. Print.

Lowe, Nick. "The Well Tempered Plot Device" *Ansible* 46 (July 1986). Web. June 28, 2012.

Moorman, Charles. *Arthurian Triptych: Mythic Materials in Charles Williams, C. S. Lewis, and T. S. Eliot.* Berkeley and Los Angeles: U of California P, 1960. Print. Perspectives in Criticism 5.

Oring, Elliott. "How Legends Are True," *Idaho Yesterdays* (Spring 2008), expanded version. Web. Feb. 27, 2009.

Paxon, Diana. *Brisingamen.* New York: Berkley, 1984. Print.

Rieder, John. *Colonialism and the Emergence of Science Fiction.* Middletown, CT: Wesleyan UP, 2008. Print.

Sullivan, C. W., III. *Welsh Celtic Myth in Modern Fantasy.* New York: Greenwood, 1989. Print. Contributions to the Study of Science Fiction and Fantasy 35.

Tatar, Maria. *The Hard Facts of the Grimms' Fairy Tales.* Princeton, NJ: Princeton UP, 1987. Print.

Tolkien, J. R. R. "On Fairy-stories." *Tree and Leaf.* London: Allen, 1964; Rpt. in *The Tolkien Reader.* New York: Ballantine, 1966. Print.

Travers, P. L. *Mary Poppins.* 1934. Rev. ed. 1962. New York: Harcourt, 1962. Print.

Von Sydow, Carl Wilhelm. *Selected Papers on Folklore.* 1948. New York: Arno, 1977. Print.

Chapter 5

Alexie, Sherman. "How to Write the Great American Indian Novel," *The Summer of Black Widows*. Brooklyn, NY: Hanging Loose, 1996. 94–95. Print.

Attebery, Brian. "Science Fantasy." *Twentieth Century American Science Fiction Writers. Dictionary of Literary Biography*. Ed. David Cowart and Thomas L. Wymer. Vol. 8, Part 2. Detroit: Gale, 1981. 236–242. Print.

Bradford, Clare. "The Making of an Elder: Patricia Wrightson and Aboriginality." *Children's Literature Matters*. Ed. Robin Pope. Burwood, Victoria: Australian Children's Literature Association for Research, 2001. 1–11. Print.

———. Reading Race: Aboriginality in Australian Children's Literature. Melbourne: Melbourne UP, 2001. Print.

Brown, Michael F. *Who Owns Native Culture?* Cambridge, MA: Harvard UP, 2003. Print.

Brust, Steven, and Megan Lindholm. *The Gypsy*. New York: Tor, 1992. Print.

Campbell, Joseph. *The Hero with a Thousand Faces*. Third ed. Novato, CA: New World, 2008. Print. Bollingen Series XVII. Clarke, Arthur C. *Profiles of the Future: An Enquiry into the Limits of the Possible*. Rev. ed. 1973. New York: Popular, 1977. 39, n. 1. Print.

Eco, Umberto. The Role of the Reader: Explorations in the Semiotics of Texts. Bloomington: Indiana UP, 1979. Print.

Evers, Larry, and Barre Toelken. "Introduction: Collaboration in the Translation and Interpretation of Native American Oral Traditions." *Native American Oral Traditions: Collaboration and Interpretation*. Ed. Larry Evers and Barre Toelken. Logan: Utah State UP, 2001. 1–14. Print.

Foley, John Miles. "Foreword." *Native American Oral Traditions: Collaboration and Interpretation*. Ed. Larry Evers and Barre Toelken. Logan: Utah State UP, 2001. vii–xvi. Print.

Grossman, Michèle, and Denise Cuthbert. "Forgetting Redfern: Aboriginality in the New Age." *Meanjin* 57.4 (1998): 770–788. Print.

Lees, Stella. "Classics: Then and Now." *FWY* (Winter 2002). 1–6. Web. Feb. 25, 2004.

Lewis, C. S. *Till We Have Faces: A Myth Retold*. San Diego and New York: Harcourt, 1956. Print.

Molina, Felipe S., and Larry Evers. "'Like this it stays in your hands': Collaboration and Ethnopoetics." *Native American Oral Traditions: Collaboration and Interpretation*. Ed. Larry Evers and Barre Toelken. Logan: Utah State UP, 2001. 15–57. Print.

Murray, John. "Inheriting the Land? Some Literary and Ethical Issues in the Use of Indigenous Material by an Australian Children's Writer, 1960–1990." *Literature and Theology* 10 (1996): 252–260. Print.

Petaja, Emil. *Saga of Lost Earths and the Star Mill*. New York: Daw, 1966. Print.

———. *The Stolen Sun and Tramontane*. New York: Daw, 1967. Print.

Purtill, Richard. *Enchantment at Delphi*. San Diego: Harcourt, 1986. Print.

———. *The Golden Gryphon Feather*. New York: Daw, 1979. Print.

———. *Lord of the Elves and Eldils: Fantasy and Philosophy in C. S. Lewis and J. R. R. Tolkien*. Grand Rapids, MI: Zondervan, 1974. Print.

———. *The Mirror of Helen*. New York: Daw, 1983. Print.

———. *The Stolen Goddess*. New York: Daw, 1980. Print.

Swann, Thomas Burnett. *Green Phoenix*. New York: Daw, 1972. Print.

———. *How Are the Mighty Fallen*. New York: Daw, 1974. Print.

Tolkien, J. R. R. *Letters of J. R. R. Tolkien.* Ed. Humphrey Carpenter with Christopher Tolkien. Boston: Houghton, 1981. Print.

Wilson, Darryl Babe, and Susan Brandenstein Park. "Wu-ches-erik (Loon Woman) and Ori-Aswe (Wildcat)." *Native American Oral Traditions: Collaboration and Interpretation.* Ed. Larry Evers and Barre Toelken. Logan: Utah State UP, 2001. 157–175. Print.

Wolfe, Gary K. Critical Terms for Science Fiction and Fantasy: A Glossary and Guide to Scholarship. Westport, CT: Greenwood, 1986. Print.

Wrightson, Patricia. *Balyet.* New York: McElderry, 1989. Print.

——. *The Dark Bright Water.* London: Hutchinson, 1979. Print.

——. "Hero and Everyman." *Magpies* 1 (March 1993): 5–8. Print.

——. *The Ice Is Coming.* London: Hutchinson, 1977. Print.

——. *Journey Behind the Wind.* (Original title *Behind the Wind*). New York: Atheneum, 1981. Print.

——. *Shadows of Time.* Sydney, Australia: Random, 1994. Print.

——. "When Cultures Meet." Introduction. *The Wrightson List.* By Peter and Patricia Wrightson. Milsons Point, NSW, Australia: Random, 1998. ix–xxxv. Print.

Yep, Laurence. "Dragons I Have Known and Loved." *Journal of the Fantastic in the Arts* 21:3 (2010): 386–393. Print.

Zelazny, Roger. *Creatures of Light and Darkness.* Garden City, NY: Doubleday, 1969. Print.

——. *The Dream Master.* New York: Ace, 1966. Print.

——. *Eye of Cat.* New York: Pocket, 1982. Print.

——. *This Immortal.* New York: Ace, 1966. Print.

——. *Lord of Light.* Garden City, NY: Doubleday, 1967. Print.

Chapter 6

* *Adventures of Mark Twain.* Dir. Will Vinton. Will Vinton Studios, 1985. Film.

Aquinas, St. Thomas. *Summa Theologica.* Trans. Fathers of the English Dominican Province. New York: Benziger, 1947. Vol. 1. Print. 3 vols.

Ballard, Mignon F. *Angel at Troublesome Creek.* New York: St. Martin's, 1999. Print.

"Belief in Angels." The Association of Religion Data Archives: Quick Stats. Web. Jan. 4, 2010.

"Belief in God." The Association of Religion Data Archives: Quick Stats. Web. Jan. 4, 2010.

Bennett, Margaret. "Balquhidder Revisited: Fairylore in the Scottish Highlands, 1690–1990." *The Good People: New Fairylore Essays.* Ed. Peter Narváez. 1991. Lexington: UP of Kentucky, 1997. 94–115. Print.

Berger, Peter L. A Rumor of Angels: Modern Society and the Rediscovery of the Supernatural. Garden City, NY: Doubleday, 1970. Print.

Clark, Lynn Schofield. From Angels to Aliens: Teenagers, the Media, and the Supernatural. New York: Oxford UP, 2003. Print.

Crowley, John. *Ægypt.* (Retitled *The Solitudes*). New York: Bantam, 1987. Print.

——. *The Deep.* New York: Berkley, 1975. Print.

——. *Engine Summer.* New York: Bantam, 1979. Print.

——. *The Translator.* New York: HarperCollins, 2002. Print.

Dégh, Linda, and Andrew Vázsonyi. "The Memorate and the Proto-Memorate." *Journal of American Folklore* 87:345 (July-Sep. 1974): 225–239. Print.

Doyle, Tom. "Competing Fictions: The Uses of Christian Apocalyptic Imagery in Contemporary Popular Fictional Works. Part One: Premillennialist Apocalyptic Fictions." *Journal of Millennial Studies* 1:1 (2001). Web. May 26, 2010.

———. "Competing Fictions: The Uses of Christian Apocalyptic Imagery in Contemporary Popular Fictional Works. Part Two: Anti-Apocalyptic Fictions." *Journal of Millennial Studies* 1:1 (2001). Web. May 26, 2010.

Elgin, Suzette Haden. "Magic Granny Says Don't Meddle." *The Magazine of Fantasy and Science Fiction* 67:2 (August 1984). 84–91. Print.

Ellis, Bill. *Aliens, Ghosts, and Cults: Legends We Live.* Jackson: UP of Mississippi, 2003. Print.

Gardella, Peter. *American Angels: Useful Spirits in the Material World.* Lawrence: UP of Kansas, 2007. Print.

Greenblatt, Stephen. *Shakespearean Negotiations: The Circulation of Social Energy in Renaissance England.* Berkeley and Los Angeles: U of California P, 1988. Print. The New Historicism: Studies in Cultural Poetics 4.

Honko, Lauri. "Memorates and the Study of Folk Beliefs." *Journal of the Folklore Institute* 1:1/2 (1964): 5–19. Web. Feb. 4, 2009.

Hume, Kathryn. Fantasy and Mimesis: Responses to Reality in Western Literature. New York and London: Methuen, 1984. Print.

Lawless, Elaine. "The Night I Got the Holy Ghost…": Holy Ghost Narratives and the Pentecostal Conversion Process." *Western Folklore* 47:1 (Jan. 1988): 1–19. Web. Feb. 4, 2009.

Le Guin, Ursula K. "Legends for a New Land." *Mythlore* 15:2 (Winter 1988): 4–10. Print.

———. *Rocannon's World.* New York: Ace, 1966. Print.

L'Engle, Madeleine. *An Acceptable Time.* New York: Farrar, 1989. Print.

———. *Many Waters.* New York: Farrar, 1986. Print.

———. *A Swiftly Tilting Planet.* New York: Farrar, 1978. Print.

———. *A Wind in the Door.* New York: Farrar, 1973. Print.

———. *A Wrinkle in Time.* New York: Farrar, 1962. Print.

Long, Lisa A. "'The Corporeity of Heaven': Rehabilitating the Civil War Body in *The Gates Ajar.*" *American Literature* 69:4 (Dec. 1997): 781–811. Web. Feb. 4, 2009.

MacAvoy, R. A. *Damiano.* New York: Bantam, 1984. Print.

———. *Damiano's Lute.* New York: Bantam, 1984. Print.

———. *Raphael.* New York: Bantam, 1984. Print.

* *Michael.* Dir. Nora Ephron. New Line, 1996. Film.

Morrow, James. *Towing Jehovah.* New York: Harcourt, 1994. Print.

One Magic Christmas. Dir. Philip Borsos. Disney, 1985. Film.

Phelps, Elizabeth Stuart. *The Gates Ajar.* Boston: Osgood, 1878. Web. May 10, 2010.

Pope, Hugh. "Angel." *Catholic Encyclopedia.* Ed. Charles G. Herbermann et al. Special ed. New York: Encyclopedia Press, 1907–1913. Vol. 1. Aac–As. 476–481. Print. 15 vols.

Rice, Anne. "The Angels Among Us." *Parade* (20 December 2009). 8–9. Print.

Shippey, T. A. *The Road to Middle-Earth.* Boston: Houghton, 1983. Print.

Singh, Nalini. *Angel's Blood.* New York: Berkley, 2009. Print.

Springer, Nancy. *Metal Angel.* New York: Roc, 1994. Print.

St. Armand, Barton Levi. "Paradise Deferred: The Image of Heaven in the Work of Emily Dickinson and Elizabeth Stuart Phelps." *American Quarterly* 29:1 (Spring 1977): 55–78. Web. Feb. 4, 2009.

St. George, Margaret. *The Renegade*. New York: Harlequin, 1996. Print.

Tepper, Sheri S. *A Plague of Angels*. New York: Bantam, 1993. Print.

"Themes: Angels–Archangels–Guardian Angels–Dark Angels." *Sci-Fan: Science Fiction and Fantasy Books by Theme*. Web. Jan. 4, 2013.

Twain, Mark [Samuel Clemens]. "Extract from Captain Stormfield's Visit to Heaven." *The Oxford Mark Twain*. New York: Oxford UP, 1996. Print.

Utley, Francis Lee. "The Bible of the Folk." *California Folklore Quarterly* 4:1 (Jan. 1945), 1–17. Web. Apr. 10, 2010.

Valenti, Peter. "The Film *Blanc*: Suggestions for a Variety of Fantasy, 1940–45." *Journal of Popular Film* 6:4 (1978): 294–304. Rpt. *Film Blanc: The Cinema of Feel-Good Fantasies*. Web. Apr. 12, 2010.

Willard, Nancy. *Things Invisible to See*. 1985. New York: Bantam, 1986. Print.

Wilson, William A. "The Paradox of Mormon Folklore." *Essays in the American West, 1974–75*. Ed. Thomas G. Alexander. Provo: Brigham Young UP, 1976. Rpt. in *Idaho Folklife: From Homesteads to Headstones*. Ed. Louie Attebery et al. Salt Lake City: U of Utah P, 1985. 58–67. Print.

Literalist Interlude: Burning Harry Potter

Bakker, R. Scott. "The Skeptical Fantasist: In Defense of an Oxymoron." *Heliotrope* (Aug. 2006). 32–38. Web.

Eichler, Leah. "Promotion: J. K. Rowling Does Toronto." *News Shorts. Publisher's Weekly*. Web. Mar. 3, 2012. Rpt. of "J. K. Rowling Does Toronto." *Publisher's Weekly* (Oct. 30, 2000). 20.

Graves, Kersey. *The World's Sixteen Crucified Saviors*. 1873. Secular Web. Web. Feb. 17, 2012.

Kjos, Berit. "Shadowmancer! A Christian book for 'children' and teens?" (February 2005). *Kjos Ministries*. Web. Feb. 23, 2012.

———. "The Spirit behind the Lion King." *Kjos Ministries*. Web. Feb. 12, 2012.

Le Guin, Ursula K. *A Wizard of Earthsea*. Berkeley: Parnassus, 1968. Print.

MacDonald, George. "The Fantastic Imagination." *The Gifts of the Child Christ: Fairy Tales and Stories for the Childlike*. Ed. Glenn Edward Sadler. Grand Rapids, MI: Eerdmans, 1973. Vol. 1. 23–28. Print. 2 vols.

Montenegro, Maria. "Shadowmancer: A Tangled Tale." *Christian Answers for the New Age* (April/May 2004). Web. Feb. 23, 2012.

O'Brien, Michael D. *A Landscape with Dragons: The Battle for Your Child's Mind*. San Francisco: Ignatius, 1998. Print.

Pullman, Philip. "The Darkside of Narnia." *Observer* (Oct. 1, 1998). Rpt. in *The Cumberland River Lamp Post*. Web. Feb. 20, 2012.

Santee, Casey. "Pastors Concerned by Message in Trilogy: Group Says Books Promote Atheism." *Idaho State Journal* (November 27, 2007). A 1+. Print.

Taylor, G. P. Interview by Dick Staub. "DS INTERVIEW: G. P. Taylor, Shadowmancer." *Culture Watch* (June 17, 2004). Web. Feb. 22, 2012.

Taylor, G. P. *Shadowmancer*. London: Faber, 2003. Print.

Thomas, Ann. "Occult: Shadowmancer and Wormwood" (Mar. 30, 2005). *Reachout Trust*. Web. Feb. 23, 2012.

Chapter 7

Attebery, Brian. "Aboriginality in Science Fiction." *Science Fiction Studies* 32 (2005): 385–404. Print.

Bechtel, Greg. Message to author. June 20, 2012. E-mail.

——. "The Word for World Is Story: Syncretic Fantasy as Healing Ritual in Thomas King's *Green Grass, Running Water*." *Journal of the Fantastic in the Arts* 19.2 (2008): 204–223. Print.

——. "The Word for World Is Story: Towards a Cognitive Theory of (Canadian) Syncretic Fantasy." Diss. U. of Alberta, 2011. Print.

Chambers, Claire. "Postcolonial Science Fiction: Amitav Ghosh's *The Calcutta Chromosome*." *Journal of Commonwealth Literature* 38 (2003): 57–72. Print.

Chandler, A. Bertram. "The Mountain Movers." *Galaxy* (Mar. 1971). Rpt. in *Centaurus: The Best of Australian Science Fiction*. Ed. David G. Hartwell and Damien Broderick. New York: Tor, 1999. 63–81. Print.

Chandra, Vikram. *Red Earth and Pouring Rain*. New York: Little, 1995. Print.

Dowling, Terry. "Dancing with Scheherezade." *Parabolas of Science Fiction*. Ed. Brian Attebery and Veronica Hollinger. Middleboro, CT: Wesleyan UP, 2013. 24–35. Print.

——. *Rynemonn*. Sydney, Australia: Coeur de Lion, 2007. Print.

——. *Rynoserros*. Aphelion, 1990; Parramatta, NSW: MirrorDanse, 2003. Print.

Gelder, Ken, and Jane M. Jacobs. *Uncanny Australia: Sacredness and Identity in a Postcolonial Nation*. Melbourne: Melbourne UP, 1998. Print.

Ghosh, Amitav. The Calcutta Chromosome: A Novel of Fevers, Delirium & Discovery. New York: Avon, 1995. Print.

Granville, Austyn. *The Fallen Race*. New York: Neely, 1892. Print.

Heiss, Anita. "Writing about Indigenous Australia: Some Issues to Consider and Protocols to Follow: A Discussion Paper." *Southerly* 62:2 (2002): 197–205. Print.

Hopkinson, Nalo. *Brown Girl in the Ring*. New York: Warner/Aspect, 1998. Print.

——. "Essay: Code Sliding." Dec. 6, 2006. *NaloHopkinson.com*. Web. Feb. 26, 2012.

——, ed. *Mojo: Conjure Stories*. New York: Warner, 2003. Print.

——, ed. Whispers from the Cotton Tree Root: Caribbean Fabulist Fiction. Montpelier, VT: Invisible Cities, 2000. Print.

Hulley, Charles E. *The Fire Crystal*. Sydney, Australia: Mystic, 1994. Print.

Love, Rosaleen. "Trickster." *Mortal Fire: Best Australian SF*. Ed. Terry Dowling and Van Ikin. Rydalsmere, NSW: Hodder, 1993. 157–162. Print.

Mezlekia, Nega. *The God Who Begat a Jackal*. New York: Picador, 2002. Print.

Muecke, Stephen. *Textual Spaces: Aboriginality and Cultural Studies*. Kensington: New South Wales UP, 1992.

Narogin, Mudrooroo. Writing from the Fringe: A Study of Modern Aboriginal Literature. Melbourne, Australia: Hyland, 1990. Print.

Okorafor, Nnedi. "Between Cultures." Interview. *Locus* (December 2007): 76–78.

——. *Who Fears Death*. New York: Daw, 2010. Print.

Pratt, Mary Louise. "Arts of the Contact Zone." *Profession 91*. New York: MLA, 1991. 333–340. Web.

Scott, Bill. *Boori*. Melbourne and Oxford: Oxford UP, 1978. Print.

Silko, Leslie Marmon. *Ceremony*. 1977. New York: Penguin, 1986. Print.

Stone, Graham. Review of *Envisaged Worlds*, ed. Paul Collins. *Science Fiction News* 53 (1978): 7–12. Print.

Strasser, Dirk. Editorial. *Aurealis: Australian Fantasy and Science Fiction* 4 (1991): 4. Print.

Walker, Kath. *Stradbroke Dreamtime*. Sydney, Australia: Angus, 1972. Print.

Watson, Sam. "I Say This to You." *Meanjin* 53.4 (Summer 1994): 589–596. Print.

———. *The Kadaitcha Sung*. Ringwood, Victoria, Australia: Penguin, 1990. Print.

Weller, Archie. "Indigenous Mythology." *The MUP Encyclopaedia of Australian Science Fiction and Fantasy*. Ed. Paul Collins. Melbourne: Melbourne UP, 1998. 95–97. Print.

———. *Land of the Golden Clouds*. St. Leonards, NSW, Australia: Allen, 1998. Print.

Chapter 8

Attebery, Brian. *Strategies of Fantasy*. Bloomington: Indiana UP, 1992. Print.

Garner, Alan. *Strandloper*. London: Harvill, 1996. Print.

———. "The Voice in the Shadow." *The Voice That Thunders: Essays and Lectures*. London: Harvill, 1997. 146–177. Print.

———. "The Voice That Thunders." *The Voice That Thunders: Essays and Lectures*. London: Harvill, 1997. 223–241. Print.

Gloss, Molly. *Wild Life: A Novel*. New York: Simon, 2000. Print.

Haraway, Donna. "Situated Knowledges: The Science Question in Feminism and the Privilege of Partial Perspective." *Simians, Cyborgs, and Women: The Reinvention of Nature*. New York: Routledge, 1991. 183–201. Print.

Hardman, M. J. "Thank You, Ursula." *80! Memories and Reflections on Ursula K. Le Guin*. Ed. Karen Joy Fowler and Debbie Notkin. Seattle, WA: Aqueduct, 2010. 48–56. Print.

Honko, Lauri. "Memorates and the Study of Folk Beliefs." *Journal of the Folklore Institute* 1.1–2 (1964): 5–19. Web. Dec. 12, 2007.

Jones, Suzi, and Jarold Ramsay, eds. *The Stories We Tell: An Anthology of Oregon Folk Literature*. Corvallis: Oregon State UP, 1994. Print. The Oregon Literature Series, Vol. 5.

Larsen, Jeanne. *Silk Road: A Novel of Eighth-Century China*. New York: Holt, 1989. Print.

———. "The Tale of Jian Lu-Sen: Metafiction and other Border Crossings." *Paradoxa: Studies in World Literary Genres* 4.10 (1998): 305–320. Print.

Le Guin, Ursula K. *Always Coming Home*. New York: Harper, 1985. Print.

———. "Buffalo Gals, Won't You Come Out Tonight." *Buffalo Gals and Other Animal Presences*. New York: Plume, 1987. 17–51. Print.

———. Message to the author. June 21, 2012. E-mail.

———. *The Farthest Shore*. New York: Atheneum, 1973. Print.

———. *Lavinia*. New York: Harcourt, 2008. Print.

———. "Legends for a New Land." *Mythlore* 56 (Winter 1988): 4–10. Print.

———. "A Non-Euclidean View of California As a Cold Place to Be." *Dancing at the Edge of the World: Thoughts on Words, Women, Places*. New York: Grove, 1989. 80–100. Print.

McHale, Brian. "What Was Postmodernism?" Dec. 20, 2007. *Electronic Book Review*. Web. May 26, 2012.

Mendlesohn, Farah. *Rhetorics of Fantasy*. Middletown, CT: Wesleyan UP, 2008. Print.

Otto, Rudolf. The Idea of the Holy: An Inquiry into the Non-Rational Factor in the Idea of the Divine and Its Relation to the Rational. Trans. John W. Harvey. 1923. New York: Galaxy, 1958. Print.

Toelken, Barre. *The Dynamics of Folklore*. Rev. and expanded ed. Logan: Utah State UP, 1996. Print.

Wedge, J. H. "Narrative of William Buckley." 1836; rpt. in The Life and Adventures of William Buckley: Thirty-Two Years a Wanderer Amongst the Aborigines of the Unexplored Country Round Port Philip by John Morgan. 1852; rpt. Canberra: Australian National UP, 1980. 165–171. Print.

{ INDEX }